Antoinette Sibley
Reflections of a Ballerina

Antoinette Sibley

Reflections of a Ballerina

Barbara Newman

HUTCHINSON

London Melbourne Auckland Johannesburg

1746

© Barbara Newman 1986

First published in 1986 by Century Hutchinson Ltd

Brookmount House, 62-65 Chandos Place, London WC2N 4NW

Century Hutchinson Publishing Group (Australia) Pty Ltd
16-22 Church Street, Hawthorn, Melbourne, Victoria 3122

Century Hutchinson (NZ) Ltd
32-34 View Road, PO Box 40-086, Glenfield, Auckland, 10

Century Hutchinson Group (SA) Pty Ltd
PO Box 337, Bergvlei 2012, South Africa

Set in Linotron Baskerville by Input Typesetting Limited, London

Printed and bound in Great Britain by
Redwood Burn Limited, Trowbridge, Wiltshire

ISBN 0 09 164000 8

ILLUSTRATIONS

Displaying the CBE at the gates of Buckingham Palace, November 1973. Photo: Dennis Barnard

Rehearsing *Manon*, Derek Rencher in foreground. Photo: Reg Wilson

Manon with Anthony Dowell as des Grieux. Courtesy The Dancing Times

Manon with David Wall as Lescaut. Photo: Leslie E. Spatt

Opening night of *Manon*. Kenneth MacMillan is beside the Queen Mother. Photo: Donald Southern

Modelling for charity, May 1977. Photo: Daily Express

A Month in the Country with Mikhail Baryshnikov. Photo: Graham Brandon. By courtesy of the Trustees of the Theatre Museum, Victoria and Albert Museum

With her husband, Panton Corbett. Courtesy A. Sibley

With Sheila Bloom. Courtesy A. Sibley

Eloise and Isambard Corbett. Courtesy A. Sibley

Every effort has been made to identify the photographers whose work is reproduced in this book and to obtain their permission for its publication.

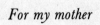

For my mother

INTRODUCTION

My mother has always said, 'If you want to know, ask.' I wanted to know how a ballerina is created—who inspires her, what influences shape her, where her motivation comes from—so I took my questions to a ballerina and asked her to search her own experience for the answers, and she was kind enough to do so.

At my request, Antoinette Sibley followed her memory back through the years to trace the events of her life and glorious career. The facts as she views them today, lit by her maturity and clarified for her by the passage of time, form the heart of this affectionate study of an exceptional dancer. By sharing their private insights and professional assessments with me, the people closest to her illuminate her achievements still further. I am deeply indebted to them all, and grateful for the privilege they have granted me of painting a portrait of artistry in the words of the artist herself and of those who know the woman and her work most intimately.

I have made no attempt to discover Antoinette Sibley's favourite colour or where she buys her children's clothes or whether she can cook, because those are not the things that interest me about her. I'm also not interested in comparing her to any other dancer, in challenging your opinions or in telling you which of her performances you should have liked best or admired most—that's up to you.

The string of questions to which I wanted answers led me into a labyrinth of method and motive, reason and emotion. Exploring the life of one ballerina I caught glimpses of the elusive process by which every ballerina transforms artifice and rigidly disciplined movement into natural passion and pure grace. Perhaps, in these pages, you will glimpse it too.

For their patience and generous assistance, I owe a further debt of gratitude to Janet Judd, Royal Ballet Press Office; Francesca Franchi, Royal Ballet Archives; Audrey Harman, Royal Ballet School Archives, and Iris Law, Royal Ballet Administration; to Sarah Woodcock, Sue Merrett, Graham Brandon and Patricia Lousada; to Joan Brandt, Roger Houghton and Paul Sidey; and especially to Andrew Hewson and Elizabeth Cropper.

B.N.

London
April 1986

xii

At the end, in a golden shower of light, the ballerina stands alone. Blossoms rain down on her from the dark, satin ribbons snapping as they fall. White-wigged pages in crimson velvet approach her, kneel solemnly at her feet, emptying their arms of baskets and bouquets, and back away, bowing. A cloud of applause fills the cavernous space before her, and a cacophony of hoarse, deep-toned cheers strike and chime against each other like bells. As she lifts her arms to embrace the acclaim the tiny ballerina lifts her face and lights the theatre with a smile that blazes to the last seat of the last row. Sinking slowly into a deep curving curtsey, she accepts the riotous homage with a ritual of gratitude that does not end until the heavy curtains finally extinguish her smile and hide her body for the last time.

Some nights, people stand in place and stamp their feet in a slow, insistent rhythm like the crowd at a football match, willing Antoinette Sibley to reappear so they can roar their adoration even louder. Sometimes they pound the backs of their seats or the dusty velvet that encircles each balcony to let her know they are still there, waiting eagerly for another glimpse of her, another chance to thank her for the indefineable magic of her dancing.

Behind the curtain, Antoinette Sibley shifts from one foot to the other. Face slick and mascara smudged with sweat, thighs quivering with tension released, she waits obediently for the stage manager's instructions. A reigning ballerina of the Royal Ballet for more than twenty years, she will not leave the stage without his permission. If he says 'That's all,' she will turn directly towards her dressing room, handing her

I

flowers absently to the dresser, calling to a friend, reaching up to loosen her headdress. If he says 'Go,' she will dart before the curtain, slipping her wide smile smoothly in place, and bow again—to her partner, to the public, to her passionate fans, whose faces by then will be pressed together at her feet, as close to her as they can get.

Only when she fails to reappear is the performance finally over. Chattering with excitement the audience drifts up the aisles, trailing laughter and silken scarves over their shoulders. Backstage, under the work lights, a tired woman steps from the shimmering aura of the ballerina and heads for the comfort of a hot shower and a late dinner. As heavy-footed stagehands lug her canvas palace into the shadows, a trio of her courtiers—already anonymous in their blue jeans and sneakers—slips through the growing crowd at the stage door and cross the street to the tube. The day will end for them as it always does, with the tedious ride home and exhaustion.

For Antoinette Sibley the long day lasts a little bit longer. The devoted fans want autographs and snapshots; pressing flowers into her flower-laden arms they want her to smile, to look at them, to wait for them to look yet again at her. A nod, a soft word of thanks will link them, for a fleeting second, to her greatness. If she is privileged to command such devotion, then she is also obligated to acknowledge it graciously. Exhaustion and dinner must wait while the courtly exchange is danced out. 'We love you. Thank you,' say the faces that fall back reluctantly as she moves towards her car. 'Thank you for loving me,' says her sweetest smile. And then the car glides carefully forward and the crowd drifts away and the street suddenly seems quite dark—in fact, it is raining.

Antoinette Sibley announced her retirement from the ballet on 4 May 1979. In November of 1984 she said to me, 'Eight weeks with this dreadful thing on my chest and I've only just got off the antibiotics. And of course my little Henry's had it too. And then we didn't know if Anthony would be on or not. We only got *Thaïs* on at the last minute and the first performance was only a sketch because we didn't know if his back would hold out and we were changing all the lifts, just making them up, literally, the day before. And then only the two rehearsals of *Varii*—we didn't know if he could do that, so of course I didn't know *who* I'd be dancing with. Now I have

2

these *Raymonda*s to get on, and I've not been able to go out of this house except to dance, I've been so weak. Well, it's just been the most horrible, horrible gruelling time. I can't even remember a time like this, ever.'

Two weeks later she said, 'Wednesday I'm taking ten of them to a matinée because I didn't give Eloise a proper birthday, and Thursday my husband's arranged a dinner because I haven't given him any time at all, and Friday we're off to the country.'

Away from the theatre, Antoinette Sibley is just a woman with a family and a career, and like every woman in that position she is constantly running out of time. Her husband, Panton Corbett, is a banker with a passion for tennis. Her children—Eloise, born 1975, and Isambard Henry, born 1980 —are simply children; they need attention, new shoes, pocket money, solace and occasional threats just like any other children. Between and around her professional obligations—daily class, rehearsals, fittings, performances—Antoinette moves from Henry's eye doctor to Eloise's Girl Guide ceremonies, from Harrods to the garage to a seat at Wimbledon.

Engraved invitations stand six deep on her marble mantelpiece. Friends come to lunch, workmen come to paint the house and hang new curtains, school holidays come round with unfailing regularity. Her husband's hectic schedule takes him from the City to Hong Kong to shooting weekends in Norfolk. One day he returns home with a friend, the next day with mumps.

After years of snatching precious time to break in new nannies, who then decide to move on just when they're most needed, she has now dispensed with them entirely and manages both her elegant house in Belgravia and her country home in Oxfordshire by herself. She guards her private life jealously, eating breakfast with the family before it scatters and returning for tea with the children every afternoon her rehearsal schedule permits. She refuses to let her work separate her from her husband for more than two weeks. Apart from being a great ballerina with an international reputation, Antoinette Sibley is remarkably like anyone else.

3

One

'I am convinced that we shape no event as forcibly as events shape us.' *Ninette de Valois*

Once upon a time a long time ago a delicate princess was born in a shining castle deep in the heart of a green and pleasant kingdom. Up and down the countryside peasants and noblemen alike celebrated the birth with parades, feasts and fireworks, and their rejoicing lasted through the changing of the seasons and indeed for many years.

It's tempting to think of Antoinette Sibley as a royal princess, marked from birth to wear a glorious crown of achievement, fated to become the first home-bred English ballerina, guided by benevolent fairies and groomed by wise magicians to lead England's Royal Ballet through fabled years of triumph. If you ever saw her dance you could easily believe that dancing was her destiny, that the fusion of line, movement and music lay in her very bones, that seamless grace and radiant charm were her natural inheritance.

Pretty conceits perhaps, but all fairy tales, and if you believe them you convert an individual into a cliché and dismiss a lifetime of effort in a misguided attempt at appreciation. Antoinette Sibley was not born great: she achieved her greatness and much of it was thrust upon her. Chance helped create her title and fortune helped carve her crown, shaping a bit of luck here and an accident there so fortuitously that she seemed to become a ballerina by magic. Of course the magic was an illusion. Antoinette Sibley became a ballerina after days and days and years of hard work. There is no other way to do it. From childhood to retirement you must force your body into the studio and through its paces—exacting, unnatural, exhausting paces—on six days out of every seven. You must accept constant criticism with thanks, accept praise with humility, accept a regimen that dictates what you can eat, when you can rest, how much you can play. You must accept—or ignore—pain and disappointment, and resign yourself to never-ending fatigue. And when you think you will go mad trying to perfect what you know can never be perfected, you must continue trying.

An old adage says, 'If you miss one day's class your body knows it, two days and your teacher knows it, three days and the audience knows it.' A real-life princess would have minions or servants to do the work for her—in former times the Empress of Japan never even had to walk for herself but was always carried. A fairy princess would attain her throne effortlessly; most likely a handsome prince would win it for her and hand it over with his heart. But a dancer must do it all herself, for her entire life, and that's precisely what Antoinette Sibley did.

She was not born in a shining castle. She was born, on 27 February 1939, in a nursing home in Bromley, and her first home was a few towns away, in Petts Wood, a leafy corner of Kent about twelve miles from London. 'I can remember the sitting room went out into the garden through French windows,' she says, 'and the garden was mainly silver birch trees, hundreds of them, and brambles. You walked out onto a little path and from the path there was a sheer drop onto the brambles. I love those trees; my father always compared me with them, so I always associate them with myself. Not that I love myself, but they're very very thin, delicate-looking things, but as strong as anything. They bend with the wind and swing back and bend again—they don't break.'

Curled in the corner of her white sofa, newly washed hair floating around her scrubbed face, Antoinette appears as frail as the trees she describes, but she is just as supple and resilient. Though illness and injury have dogged her entire life, bending her again and again, daring her to swing back, she is now in her mid-forties and still dancing.

'Three weeks after she was born,' recalls her mother, 'she had gastro-enteritis, but a lot of babies get that. We were fortunate in having a good doctor and she pulled through that

5

all right. And then she did have an accident at the fire, the first time she ever crawled. She was a thumb child, she used to put her thumb in her mouth, that was her comfort, and she had a habit of clutching the satin edge of her blanket and feeling it at the same time. On this occasion she spotted her blanket airing. It was some distance from the fire—we had an open, coal fire in a big, red-brick inglenook fireplace—but it was on a big sheet of stiff brown paper, and as she pulled one corner towards her, the other corner, possibly five feet away, turned around and went into the fire. She wouldn't have noticed. I heard her cough and I opened the hatch between the two rooms—I was getting her lunch ready in the kitchen—and saw smoke everywhere. It really was very frightening.

'But she was a bonny child, full of vim and vitality, extremely sure-footed and agile. She never went through a clumsy phase as a lot of children do, when they bump against this and they don't see that on the floor. You could rely on her much more than I could rely on myself: if anything had to be trodden on, she would miss it. I wouldn't. And her equilibrium, her balance, was always very good. She used to rush up the sides of hillocks and dells like a little chamois. When we were at Criccieth, and she was only five then, my husband would lift her up to the top of those towers they had, forts, about eight feet tall, and she'd walk round the edge and jump down as lightly as anything.

'Now he was a person who was very light on his feet. Had there been male dancers in his sort of society, he might well have made a good dancer. His movements are quick, he can anticipate and his balance is so good. He was always a good athlete, a long jumper, a good runner at school, captain of cricket, you name it. He was very good at football until his knee cracked up with cartilage trouble, and he then switched to tennis. He used to play for Essex. He played with people like G. P. Hughes, Pat Hughes, who was one of the best tennis players that England ever had.

'And Ted liked to walk. He's getting too old for it now but we walked a lot, did the Passes in Switzerland and things like that, and he also did the London to Brighton Walk. By the time the war was over and things started going again, he really was immersed in business. He didn't keep up much of

6

his sport, but he's always encouraged the girls. If we went for a walk in the country, there'd always be a point at which he'd say, "I'll race you to the next tree." '

Asked about her parents, Antoinette responds, without a hint of hesitation, 'The main thing is that they have been such hard workers. They have always worked—very hard, over the top actually, stretched to the limit—and working's been part of our process in growing up.' Her father, Edward George Sibley, was born in 1902 and was a member of the London Stock Exchange from 1937 to 1951. With his wife, Winifred, eleven years his junior, he later formed a film company called International Arts Productions. Antoinette remembers one of their efforts with great affection. A second-feature film which her parents wrote and produced, *Swiss Honeymoon* ran for five weeks at the London Pavilion in 1947. It then toured the British film circuit and later appeared several times on BBC television. 'It was my first film,' Antoinette boasts proudly, 'and I had one line. All I had to say was "I'm going home tomorrow," but I had to *keep* saying it.' The Sibleys eventually established a chain of forty-four bakery and catering shops and opened both a shopfitting concern and a commercial garage as sidelines to their catering business.

'My father's done everything. He often says that maybe if he had put more of his eggs in one basket, it would have been better. Sometimes you lay yourself thin, spread yourself too much. My parents went through a bad time when lots of people did, right after the war. They lost all they had because nobody could afford cakes or restaurants or any luxuries like that. Everyone was just trying to survive. For five years they ran only the Bromley shop, which had been the original shop of the whole enterprise, managing it themselves.'

But in certain ways Winifred Sibley was lucky. She may not have set out to produce films or manage restaurants, but neither was she helpless in the face of her shifting, often confusing circumstances. Her early professional training had given her two invaluable tools to carry into the future, discipline and diligence, both of which she wielded with skill and patience. Mrs Sibley had started out to be a dancer.

'There were lots of dancing schools around,' she explains, 'but when I started you couldn't concentrate on ballet. You took ballet, it was a nice thing to do and it was very good

training, but you had to have tap, musical comedy, Greek . . .
I had it all. I went to Lea Espinosa, who had a studio in
Piccadilly Circus, for ballet and I also went to Max Rivers
for tap and musical comedy and to Santos Casani, who had
a ballroom school. They were all in London because they
specialized.

'But you must remember that there was very little you
could do if you wanted to dance professionally because there
was nowhere you could join. There weren't very many actual
ballet companies, virtually none. A few formed for a short
period to do ballet club performances, but mostly it was
visiting companies like Diaghilev, Pavlova, and I was too
young for both of those.

'I was with Lea for a few years; she didn't have her own
company but she used to supply girls to various companies.
And at one point she was asked if she could supply dancers
for a new company which was being formed by [Alicia]
Markova and [Anton] Dolin—this was about '35—and she
said, "Would you like to go along?" Well, I couldn't because
it was on tour. That's all they could do; they couldn't rely on
a London theatre, so it would have meant going on tour a
lot. And I was teaching the children, the juniors, at
Espinosa's, and running a small school at Petts Wood. I used
to rent a room at the local inn for evening ballroom classes,
and I also rented a studio in Orpington, which was the next
stop along the line, where I taught children as well.'

Given a mother who was a dancer and teacher and a father
who was a dedicated amateur athlete, how could Antoinette
help rushing into a life of dancing or competition or both?
Wouldn't she have gone straight from her hands and knees
to the tips of her toes? Not at all. Although she clearly remembers the barres in the front room of the house in Petts Wood,
and the lilt of the Gold and Silver Waltz on the old record
player that accompanied the ballroom classes, Antoinette
never once took a dancing class from her mother. She has no
recollection at all of her very first ballet classes. In fact, she
declares she never gave a single thought to ballet until she
was far from home and confronting it by happenstance.

Petts Wood was home until she was six, and then the family
moved further into Kent to The Mount, a large Edwardian
house with ten acres of garden on Westerham Hill. The house

offered splendid, sweeping views to the village of Westerham a mile away and beyond it to the estates on the far side of the Darent Valley, one of which, Chartwell, was Winston Churchill's country home from 1922 until his death in 1965. But having such an illustrious figure for a near neighbour made no impression at all on Antoinette. Her earliest memories, understandably, are of her family and friends, and the pranks and pets and fun that make childhood, in retrospect, seem a perpetual summer.

'One thing I remember from Petts Wood is that my mother used to keep chocolate drops in a glass dish on the sitting room table. I loved chocolate—I still do—and I can remember stuffing them in my mouth and then hearing her come, not having time to put them back, and putting them down my pants. And rushing out after she spoke to me, because there was a loo somewhere out the back, and seeing what a disaster I'd made and how was I going to explain all this.

'My first boyfriend lived next door. He was called Michael Hucks and he had two sisters: Judith, who was my age and a great friend of mine, and her baby sister, Diana. I just adored him—I mean, nothing less than absolute adoration—and I tried to be a tomboy so he would think I was nice. I remember desperately climbing trees and jumping over fences, anything that would impress him. I thought that if I was more like a boy, he might think I was good news. He was much older than us, and I don't think really looked at us at all. But I used to keep bank for him in Monopoly—that was in the school holidays. I knew them up to when I was twelve or thirteen, and that's as close as I ever got to him, keeping bank.

'The other thing that's very vivid about Petts Wood is that when I went in to the Hucks's one day for tea, they all stood around the table saying their prayers—you know, "Please God, thank you for food," whatever they say. Well, I'd never seen this. My parents were agnostic, and I wasn't brought up to know very much about religion. Then we all sat down to eat the meal, and they all stood up afterwards to do it again. And I thought, "Aha. Now I know how it's done," and I went "Bla bla-bla bla-bla." I thought I'd join in. They were absolutely furious with me because it was being blasphemous. But as far as I was concerned, I didn't know what they were doing, it sounded like a mumble-jumble, and I thought "Well, as I missed out the first time, I'd better try to pull my weight the second."'

'I was a terribly naughty child, all throughout, and I suggested to Judith one day that we play hairdressers and I cut her hair all off short. She had very long hair, almost down to the waist, and I cut it into a wonderful fringe so it'd look a bit more like mine. Well, her father, who was at war, was coming back for the first time in years. He'd never seen the baby in his life, and they were having this big photo taken so he could take it wherever he went in the war. Her hair wasn't cut beautifully, you can imagine—it was all over the place, simply appalling. My mother wasn't spoken to for ages because of that.'

'She *was* naughty,' Winifred Sibley laughs, 'she must have been, but she used to look angelic when she was caught, and I couldn't always believe she was until I was faced with it occasionally. She was just a funny little thing, not really a rascal, but in fact I think she used to boss them around a little bit. The Hucks family were very good friends; they would all dress up together, and they didn't do it just for their own amusement: they liked an audience. And when her little sister came, Antoinette used to run performances and charge a penny for the performance and another penny for the programme.'

'Later, when we had a wonderful big house right at the top of Westerham Hill,' Antoinette goes on, 'I do remember getting these two girls—*not* the boyfriend, of course—dressing them up in little white costumes and making them dance for this ballet on the lawn, with me being the lead. This was after I started formal training, and I thought I was absolutely wonderful at it all; of course they'd never done a step in their lives.

'I had a bicycle in Westerham—it's the only one I can remember so I guess it was the first. And I had a goat called Netta after me, Netta instead of Antoinette, and I had the most beautiful cat called Fluffles, a tabby cat with an M over her eyes. And I used to dress up the frogs; I'd catch them and cut out old sheets and dress them in little white aprons. They're probably roaming around now in their awful grey outfits. I loved animals, I used to talk to them. I was really closer to them, in a funny way, than to grownups.

'And my sister Georgina was born there, the day after my own birthday, when I was nine. I always felt as if she was my own child. I could immediately cuddle her, and I could dress her up as well. Dolls weren't my cup of tea—I always had teddy bears—but she was my doll and I absolutely adored her. I was an only child until I got my sister, and I was lonely. I didn't know anybody who was just by themselves. Everybody always had brothers and sisters, and I didn't. And when I went to stay with them their mother was always at home: my mother always seemed to be working. Of course I longed for brothers and sisters, and I always wanted one older than me, which was impossible.

'When my sister was born I was called to the headmistress's study at Tring. Of course I was petrified because as I was such a naughty child I was often called there, and I thought "Oh God, what have I done now?" And she said, "I've got some very good news. Your father's on the phone"—you see, he was waiting to speak to me. And he said, "You've got the most wonderful baby sister. She's got brown eyes and she's very beautiful." I was so thrilled, but at the same time my first instinct was of absolute jealousy because the one person in my life who had always idolized me was my father. I suddenly thought, "I'm not with them. She's with them and I'm here." That was the first knife of jealousy going in. But the moment I saw her it was all lost because she was so beautiful, like a little gypsy, with curly hair and olive skin. Imagine being born with olive skin! It's too absurdly wonderful. I'm as white as a sheet. And I don't remember any more pulls in that jealous direction at all, so obviously my father was marvellous about it when I did get home.'

Antoinette tilts her head, as if listening. Speaking of her father, she suddenly hears her childhood. 'My father used to rock me, singing, "Antoinette, *gentille* Antoinette," on and on, to the tune of *Alouette*. This was *my* song, always my song, and I must have been quite young still for him to cradle me like that. And he loved opera. He took me to see my first opera, *La Bohème*, at Covent Garden. We sat in the stalls circle, over the brass section, and half the time we were drowned out of our minds by the brass. So the first impression I remember of the Opera House is the theatre itself, and the happiness and excitement and grandeur and sadness, all intermingled, that were in the opera, which is still my passion. I was eleven. I must have been in the Opera House before because I went to see *The Fairy Queen*, with [Moira] Shearer and [Margot] Fonteyn, Beryl Grey and Michael Somes, everybody was in it. I don't remember it, not a thing about it, but I do remember the opera, where we were sitting more than anything else, and just being very moved by it all and how I loved it.

'My parents both loved music and there was always a lot of music going in our house. Until very recently I thought everybody lived like this. How do you know that every house hasn't got the wireless tuned in to Wagner? But my husband's father doesn't like music; maybe he said he became tone-deaf, but music has never been part of his life. And of course I find that really hard to understand—I just thought everybody loved it.

'My father's family had those wonderful musical evenings. It was one of those large Victorian families, all girls except him, all ravishingly pretty, five or six sisters with wonderful red hair, and they all played an instrument or sang. I didn't know them at all . . . well, it's wrong to say not at all but I never heard them play an instrument. All this music was when they were young.

'But certainly my Grandma and Grandpa on my mother's side both played the piano—that I do remember. I knew them very well and I absolutely adored them. They lived in Ilford, in Essex, and it was my treat when I used to go and stay with them. They had a copper bath they'd put in front of the fire for me, and my grandfather had one of those shaving leathers, the strap, and a real cut-throat razor. They would always have sing-songs around the piano, "Run Rabbit, Run Rabbit, Run, Run, Run," all that sort of thing, real get-togethers.

'It always reminds me of my grandmother's when I pick the red currants and the black currants from our garden in the country, because I always did the picking at her house. And my grandfather was great fun. He was a Scot and I think I get my love of whisky from him; it's my favourite tipple and it was his. He'd been in the battle of the Somme but he had managed to come through it, and in no way was he a depressed or chippy man. He wasn't a nervous, worrying person at all, just always happy—a quite different character from me—and I always remember Grandma as being happy as well.

'And I don't mean this in a derogatory way, of course, but they were like ordinary people for me and I didn't know many ordinary people. I was always at boarding school so I didn't really know family life as such, and my parents were always so busy and working so hard. But my grandparents were all the day at home, in a homey family atmosphere, wonderfully ordinary, and it made a great impression on me.'

When Antoinette was born in 1939 the world was striding towards a future it could only partially perceive, and redefining 'ordinary' as it went along. Nylon was introduced in 1939, as were pre-cooked frozen food, transatlantic flight for commercial passengers and the potato chip. *Gone with the Wind* and *The Wizard of Oz* lit the silver screen; *Finnegans Wake* and *The Grapes of Wrath* were hot off the press. On the site of a former city dump in Flushing Meadow, New York, the massive Trylon and Perisphere towered over the 1939 World's Fair, awesome symbols of the modern age and its unprecedented wonders. The future was becoming the present in that sprawling fantasyland christened the World of Tomorrow, and 45,000,000 spectators would finally flock to the Fair to see it for themselves.

In England the future arrived on 3 September 1939 when war was declared. Within days blackout curtains shrouded every window and makeshift air-raid shelters stood shakily in many gardens; barrage balloons hung in the sky, as one onlooker observed, 'like ephemeral coconuts'. Food was rationed from January 1940 and clothing from June 1941, by which time you couldn't buy tobacco, bitter beer or razor-blades in any of the shops, and no one had a scrap of paper to wrap up what you could still buy.

The Blitz began in September 1940 and lasted until the following May, pinning London under nightly attack for two solid months and eventually leaving more than three and a half million houses either damaged or destroyed. Schools closed as children were evacuated to the relative safety of the countryside; factories closed as workers were called up; even Regent Street was briefly closed to traffic while the rubble in Piccadilly was cleared away. As the war stretched on, travelling became increasingly difficult since petrol was strictly rationed and railway services severely curtailed. Anyone could purchase powdered or dried food, imported from America in vast quantities, but there wasn't a loaf of white bread, a fresh lemon or a bottle of wine to be found anywhere. People ate nettle purée and cultivated vegetable patches in Hyde Park. Atop the Wellington Arch at Hyde Park Corner, an air-raid siren nestled in constant readiness between the wheels of Quadriga, the winged chariot of peace.

Time has transformed many of the survivors into heroes and the details of their daily struggles into statistics. But when Winifred Sibley sat in her daughter's cool, green drawing room in London more than forty years later, speaking of the war's invasion of her family's private life, her low, calm voice betrayed neither pride nor pain, but simply the sense of having done what needed doing, what anyone would have done.

'I was teaching dancing, but within months of the time she was born the teaching dried up because the war started. Dancing schools closed down, "for the duration" as they put it, and the children were sent away out of the bombing area. That was really the beginning of the boarding schools for dancers; until that time I don't think any of them had academic lessons—they just had dancing lessons.

'The little school that Antoinette went to as a baby evacuated miles out into "the safe part of the country", and it was Maidenhead! That's the kind of ideas people had, that as long as you were out of London, you were all right. I used to take her up to London for one baby's class a week, she must have been about two, and while she was there I would probably take a refresher course, upstairs in another studio. They did a little *tendu* and another little *tendu* and put their arms up. It was just the idea of moving to music and having other children with you. Well, this school, the Cone school, joined forces with the Olive Ripman school, which was primarily ballroom, and took this little place in Maidenhead. It didn't last for long because that very soon got almost as dangerous as anywhere else, and they came back again.

'But before that, when war first broke out, we had decided that the safest thing to do was to try to get over to my sister who was living in Canada. I had a very close cousin in Liverpool, so we went up and stayed with her for a while,

14

trying to get a berth on a boat to Canada. Very difficult: everybody was trying to get away. People who didn't have any ties here decided they might just as well go away and save their own skins—they weren't particularly keen to do any war work—but that was just a minority. Most of them were people trying to get their children out of the country.

'So we waited for months and months and we simply couldn't get anything at all. Every once in a while there would be a lull and we would come back to London for a month or two, and then we'd go back again and have another go. It was rather hard going. By this time my husband was trying to do about fourteen different jobs; he was working with the St John's Ambulance and he was also trying to run companies and a business, and every now and again he'd try and dash up to Liverpool to spend a weekend with us. I'd left him alone, but there were so many wives and children who were also doing the same as we were doing that there were odd husbands all over the place, and they'd often get together. If there was an air-raid they'd get in the cupboard under the stairs or get inside the shelter for a bit. The war dragged on for a long time and a lot of different things happened—it was almost different lives you were living.

'But we never got to Canada—we never did get a berth. So I thought, "I wonder if it's possible to get her to a little nursery school, a boarding school. And as she's so young, I will go with her and see if I can live there with them. I'll help, I'll do anything." Every profession was short of staff. Whatever you did, you were called up; they were even drafting people of a certain age, who weren't married and had no children, into the factories, because every bit of help was needed. So I chose a school from a *Nursery World*, and when we got there—it was in Buxton Spa—I'd never seen such a snowy place. Antoinette wouldn't remember this; she was only a year.

'A woman who had been a nurse ran this ... what nowadays we would call a geriatric home, in a very big old house. She'd decided that with the war and people needing to find a home for their young children, she'd take in children as well. When I got there I found that she'd got quite a number of small children, and the person who was running the baby side of it was a delightful woman who had two children of her own, one of them a matter of months, and was very pregnant. I couldn't really imagine how she could cope with all these people. Well, I had arranged to stay for two weeks and I did; I worked quite hard, helping as I said I would, and then I had no compunction about taking Antoinette away. I couldn't have left her there in those conditions. With the best will in the world they couldn't possibly look after those children.

'Of course I was always in touch with Ted on the telephone, and he agreed that I should look for some sort of apartment there, away from the school, and I did. And we quite enjoyed it, but I thought, "This is a life but not a life." You tried to make the best of what you could, but on the other hand you felt you were wasting a lot of time. So we went down to London again.

'And then one of our neighbours said, "Oh, we've got a cousin with an old manor house near Banbury." It had got to the stage where people who were comfortably settled in the country were being asked in no uncertain terms by the government to take people in, and they hurried to get people they knew rather than be landed with people they didn't know. You can't really blame them, but they didn't realize they were living in a sort of heavenly world that was almost an ivory tower. It was all fine for them, possibly with a home farm and unlimited butter and eggs, but they were ignorant of how other people were having to live. It was quite unreal.

'So we went there for a little while. It wasn't all that big, but it was a very interesting old manor house. They had to have the water pumped up every day, but they had a gardener to pump it up! You see, they didn't have to do their own chores. The cows were milked, and the milk was put in a big basin in the cellar, on a great slate slab that kept things cold. But then, against that, it was hard work. Even for the lady of the house, it was still quite hard work.

'So Antoinette's first few years were dotted about a bit, but when she was that small I was always with her. It wasn't until she was perhaps three, three and a half, that she finally went to the boys' school outside Shrewsbury. I think it was called St Christopher's; it was a boys' prep school that had been based in Chislehurst, which was close to Petts Wood. They had evacuated but they had room for more children and

16

they were taking boys *and* girls—the headmaster also had children of his own. He was all right and the wife was very nice, but Antoinette hadn't been used to having a very aggressive male around. This chap would shout across the fields at the boys with a terribly gruff voice, and the fact that he didn't shout at her made no difference; he was sort of a giant that she was fearful of. It was a bit intimidating for a little girl too because it was Victorian Gothic, in red brick—it had been a stately home.

'I stayed in a farmworker's house in the village for about a fortnight so I could see her every day, and I used to bath her before she went to bed, gradually get her used to the environment. Then I came down to London and I went back about a month later to spend another weekend and it rather frightened me. When I went to see her of course I was all open arms, dying to meet her. She was all dolled up with a clean dress and bows in her hair, which she'd never had at home, looking so spruce, and she took one look at me, turned round and tore madly across the fields as if she never wanted to see her again. It took me quite a while before I could make contact with her again. I think I had caused her hurt by leaving her and she didn't want to be hurt like that again, so she'd rather not pick up that relationship. It's understandable.

'But she didn't stay there very long because she obviously wasn't happy there. I met Miss Cone, quite by chance, in London one day and she said, "We're starting a school in Leicestershire, but unfortunately we're only taking them at seven," which Antoinette wasn't quite. The next time I saw Miss Cone, not very long after that, she said, "We're so pleased. The parents of one of the children of the school have a farm in Criccieth and they've offered us the farm for the duration. It won't hold very many children, but at least we can take the young ones as well." So that's where Antoinette went and she was very happy there.

'Then after the war the school in Wales went back to its farm family and the Cone-Ripman school moved to Tring, which was a very big country house before the war, owned by the Rothschild family. All the big firms evacuated London and invariably took the wives and families with them, and the Rothschild bank did too. They moved out to their family home, one of their many family homes, at Tring Park. When the war was over and they all started trooping back to London—they brought the bank back and all the employees and their families—the original Rothschild people who had lived in that house didn't want to go back there again. It had to be altered again to fit it for domestic rather than office use, and they couldn't get the sort of servants they used to get because nobody wanted to go back into service. A lot of these stately homes changed altogether; they could no longer go back to what they were in the earlier years of the century. So the Cones were able to get a lease of the premises and turn it into a school—that's how it happened.

'It was an enormous place and a very big undertaking for them. I will say this for the three Miss Cones: they were good business women as well as good teachers. They managed to get all sorts of financial advice and, no doubt, help. But of course they'd been a very well-known school anyway for many years, so I'm sure they weren't short of a penny or two. They also had good legal advice, and they turned it into a trust, the Arts Educational Trust, and that helped them with putting more of the profits into running the place and buying the equipment they wanted.'

In September 1945 the *Dancing Times* reported that 'the very close working arrangements which have existed during the war years between the Cone and the Ripman Schools have now been firmly cemented by the formation of a company to be known as "Cone-Ripman Schools Ltd." Classes will be continued as usual both at the Ripman School, 120, Baker Street, and at the Cone Schools, 43, Upper Grosvenor Street. In addition, there will be the Cone-Ripman College (residential) occupying Tring Park, Tring.' The very first term at Tring began on 25 September, with 100 children in residence. Antoinette's account of how she came to be one of them differs from her mother's: it is less a tale of causes than of effects.

'Going away to boarding school was a really big shock to me. The first one I went to was a place near Shrewsbury, a boys' school, and the only thing I remember was the headmaster. He adored me but I just couldn't stand him because he screamed and shouted at the boys and smacked them, and he always called me Topsy. I took that as the biggest insult, because somehow to leave my home, to leave my parents and then be called a name that was not my name was as if I had nothing to hang onto. I remember watching him being horrible to a little boy, and then seeing his complete change of personality, like Jekyll and Hyde, as he spoke to me—he was all sugar with me. Children are so clever. No one gives them credit, but they understand about human nature quicker than anybody. They know immediately if they like somebody, why they like them, if that person can be relied on. They're very quick in assessing personalities. Usually you're protected by your parents, but in this particular instance I wasn't because of the war.

'I was mortified at being separated from my parents, and I built up this armour around myself to try to cope with it. My mother said that when she first came to visit me, I wouldn't take any notice of her at all; I just ran away from her as fast as I could go. I couldn't bear the contact again; having been so hurt I didn't want to open myself up again. This was the first time I'd ever needed this armour. The wound had been so horrific for me, and I couldn't allow myself to open up and be warm to her because I knew she would be going away again and I wouldn't be able to cope.

'Being a rather sensitive child, I had to cope with it so many times. It happened to hundreds of people during the war, I'm not the only one. But as far as I was concerned, I just didn't like where I was. Even now, to this very day, I can't ever have a suitcase in my room overnight—I get so nervous. If I go away I have to pack it the day I'm going. My God, I've travelled the world for years and years, I've been on five-month tours of America, so it's not as if I'm not used to travelling. But that suitcase means going away from home and stupidly I still don't like it. It's absolutely ridiculous.

'I remember nothing about that school except for this awful headmaster, but I do remember the next boarding school, which was not much later. It was a much smaller affair and we were in the most wonderful farmhouse, in Criccieth in Wales. True, I wasn't happy—being away from home I was miserable—but this was the best place I ever went to away from home in that it was a farm. If the geese were out there, the teachers couldn't come to school! You know how frightening geese are, and they'd keep the teachers away. We used to go across the tiny beach to swim, but we had to wait for the trains to go through because the railway went across the beach. We were there at the end of the war, for D-Day. All the children in England went up to the mountains and lighted bonfires so you could see them all over the country. There weren't many children in our school, but we went up Snowdon, the highest one of all, to light ours.

'I did understand why we were doing it because when I was at Petts Wood I had the first really frightening experience of my life. We probably had a shelter in our house, but this time we went a few houses up the road and down into a shelter in somebody else's house. And while the bombs were going overhead—the silence and the sheer fright of it all—I asked my mother to get me an orange juice. Everybody said, "No, you wait till it's over," but I insisted—you know how you can get round your mother. And my darling mother, angel that she is, went to get me an orange juice, and as she left, the bomb fell. And my mother didn't return immediately. Well, the fear, the guilt of making her go! Of course she did return, she didn't get killed, but the houses were bombed at the end of the road, just past our house.

'So of course I knew the joy when the war was over, because I did know what it was about. Everything was blackout, you weren't allowed to show any light, and we had clothing coupons but no clothes. No fresh food—I was brought up on tinned food. I didn't know what eggs were about; even though I was in a farmyard, we always used to have tinned eggs. In fact I couldn't bear eggs at first because they were so greasy compared with the dried stuff we had in tins, which was like scrambled eggs. We didn't have much meat and I hated spam, hated tongue, all the things you got in tins. Almost no fruit, but there were lots of apples around and gooseberries, which I used to eat 'til I was sick every year. Literally. We'd go and pick them for the school, and although I knew they were going to be out for weeks, plenty of them, I couldn't control myself and go back another day. I wouldn't, and I was sick every time.

'Then when the war was over we went to the big Cone-Ripman school—it's now called Arts Educational—in Herefordshire. It was the most amazingly beautiful house, and it gave me my taste for magnificent architecture and houses. It was absolutely like a palace, a little like Buckingham Palace but on a smaller scale. It had the most wonderful staircase and rooms with silk damask on the walls, green and red and I think gold. And the grounds were amazing: beautiful gardens and herbaceous borders, and then just the fields for running and doing nature trails. And the most incredible ballroom; we were all put there when we had chickenpox, so we wouldn't mix. I remember it was Christmas and we couldn't join in the Christmas party.

'And we had massive studios, like the new ones at the Opera House, on that scale, with wonderful floors, all wood, and we always had a piano. The classrooms I don't remember so well; I think they were around the back where the stables would have been. Those weren't the beautiful rooms. The dormitories certainly were, and we did our ballet lessons in those beautiful rooms.

'But what is important to say is that I didn't just do ballet at this school. I did tap, I did musical comedy, singing, Greek dancing, ballroom dancing, acting . . . I had a complete theatrical training, from the age of six.

'I think I probably had my first dancing lessons there. Tap was my preference, and I was really a rather good tap dancer. I used to do a whole routine to "Buttons and Bows", singing it as we were tapping it. We had the most wonderful tap teacher; I can't remember her name but she looked like Kay Kendall: very thin, very tall, very long nails, very sophisticated. We'd have a pianist, but to tap out a rhythm, she'd tap it with her long, long red nails on the piano, and I always thought this was amazing. I don't think I'd ever seen red fingernails before, and she was probably the first sophisticated woman I'd ever seen. Bright red talons, like they wear in America now, and bright red lipstick. Very un-schooly. She made a big impression on me.

'Ballet I remember finding very hard, right then and there, and I wasn't mad about it because it was such hard work. I was quite sensible at that age and I did realize you needed such concentration and you had to be perfect in everything, and I didn't particularly like dancing to be perfect. I just liked to move. I had a marvellous ballet teacher, luckily for me, Miss Mackie. She was very quiet, not strict but it had to be right; you couldn't sickle your foot or roll because this would be bad for you. I think of her as rather the ideal teacher

21

at that time, but I found it very tiring and I didn't like it very much.

'What I loved was the tap dancing and I loved acting. We did this exercise, imagining yourself going down a long tunnel and what would happen if you met somebody. It wouldn't be frightening, maybe it would be somebody playing a joke on you or maybe it would just be your sister. You had to imagine these situations and how you would respond to them, and then re-enact every person, so you were already making characters for yourself. I loved doing things like that, using my imagination in that way. That was fun, whereas the ballet wasn't fun.

'I was there from age six 'til ten, and I was really desperately naughty. I suppose being lonely and away from home, I wanted people to like me, and the way to be liked with children is to be the naughty leader. They like you because you're the wicked one, the fun one. You get them into scrapes and think of all these escapades, and then take all the blame. At school I was that naughty leader, always, I suppose because I longed to be loved. I must have been impossible, but it was only in fun. For instance, I figured a good way to get extra pocket money was if I kept the pot under my bed and if anybody wanted to go on it they'd have to pay me a penny. Sure it worked, until they complained to my mother and she stopped me doing it.

'I can also remember that in one of the dormitories I was the only one on a top bunk—there was only one bunk. Well, that's fine, except that when we had our midnight feasts I'd be the only one caught. They'd all jump into bed and I'd still be clambering up the bloody old bunk, so I naturally got the blame. I was constantly in trouble, but I wasn't always awful. I used to go around each bed with my best friend, Sally Judd—she then became Sally Gilpin, she married John Gilpin—singing lullabies to send them to sleep, I at the head and she at the tail. So we weren't so awful; although I did get the money for the pot, at least I did do some nice things.

'I was always a very frightened person—I suppose because I'd been away from home since the age of three—and I didn't trust anybody other than my parents. I had no reason to trust anybody. I absolutely loathed the Sister at the school, and she hated me. When I wash my hair, handfuls come out and always have, all my life, and she told me I was going to be bald by the time I was twenty-one. I do remember divulging either that to my parents or how awful she was to me, and my mother told her off in front of me and she completely refuted it. She put her arm around me and said "Oh, you *know* how much we love you." Right there in front of us I saw another side of her, all smarming and sickly and sweet, and I knew this was the two faces.

'Oh, I had friends. I obviously told Sally Gilpin things and another friend was Wendy Crye, but I don't think I told anybody all my real worries and fears, because it's grownups you go to with those. My parents used to come up at half-term to see me, and I was home at the holidays, but even when I went home I wouldn't open up. It must have been a horror for my parents; they could never get anything out of me. I was petrified that if I didn't show my best face they might reject me. I thought if they saw me in a bad light, maybe they wouldn't like me. They only saw me for such a short time and they only really knew me from the letters that I failed to write. So I wasn't even true in those short whiles.

'You see, I also wasn't interested in words. In school I always loved French and maths, but English was dreadful. I hated writing essays and I hadn't the imagination or the time with language. With acting and dancing, yes, but with words, no. Funnily enough, I loved reading, but mainly books about hospitals because I also longed to be a nurse. I was sent to the London Clinic to have my tonsils out just after the war, and that's obviously where I got my taste for this nursing bit.

'You couldn't get anybody into any hospitals in England then because everything was so crowded with the soldiers, so I had to hang about and hang about. Of course I didn't complain to anyone about my dreadful sore throats until it was too late, and then they discovered that I'd got this TB gland as a result. I was really ill with that for years and years; my neck used to swell up about five or six inches, really big, like another little head. I remember going for treatment from Sadler's Wells, at ten; they had to keep piercing it to get the stuff out. What I felt like with this thing on my neck! It was ghastly—the pain of it all and the horror, absolutely appalling. And my mother's sure it wouldn't have happened if she had known about the tonsils being so bad.

23

'But this is the trouble with boarding school—that's why I hated it so much. I didn't tell anybody anything. I certainly never told my parents because when I got home I only wanted them to love me. You couldn't tell the teachers anything, you couldn't tell the girls because they would laugh. So I never really opened up till I got my best friend, Sheila Bloom, when I was about seventeen.

'Oh, I mended from all these things; I was very energetic and athletic and I didn't really think much about them. But this wretched gland did bother me a lot, and I was also sent away to a sanatorium because I was a carrier of diptheria. In fact, I think it was when I had diptheria that they told me I was going to be bald at twenty-one, and until I got to twenty-one and still had some hair on my head, I thought it was going to happen. So with this thing on my neck and being bald, I thought, "Oh boy, I'm going to be terrific!" '

Of course no one yet knew what Antoinette was going to be. Whatever her parents may have hoped, or guessed, they never actually saw her at work in the studio. Joyce Mackie might have glimpsed a certain potential, but with her death in 1978 her first-hand observations died too. And according to the present secretary at Tring, all the files and records of those immediately post-war years have long since disappeared and with them, all the curriculum outlines and timetables. So it's as hard to discover what went into the future ballerina's early training as it is to find an objective, adult assessment of what she got out of it.

But Sally Judd insists today that she knew even then what lay in store for Antoinette—and that Antoinette did too. Digging into her memory for her cherished mental snapshots of childhood, Sally Judd also found amazingly vivid images of Tring, far more precise in their details than any the school could provide or Antoinette remember.

'The day was divided in half, half lessons and half dancing classes. There was only one educational classroom in the building and it was quickly moved to the Clock House, the stable buildings. Dancing classes happened in the main house, in rooms which became named. The Assembly Hall, a big brown room with a balcony running across it, was where we had assembly and prayers every morning at 9:00. The Ballet Room was white. Then there was the Red Room with the

Staff Room next door. The Ballroom was the only room named after what the Rothschilds had used it for. There was a sanitorium on the left of the main hall, with Victorian wallpaper, mâd vines that wound up it and psychedelic flowers, most unrestful. The San. was where you went normally if you were sick, but if it was overflowing, like with epidemics of flu or chicken pox, they put beds in the dancing rooms. Then off the Assembly Room was the Drama Room, which was very small. We did our classes there.

'We were both tiny juniors, absolutely minute, when we started; I was just seven and Antoinette became seven the following February. We did everything: Greek, tap, character, which was called National in those days. Musical Comedy, which went up on the board as Mus. Com., was really early Ginger Rogers, bending and stretching, and part of Mus. Com. was Acro., Acrobatics. A green rubber mat was unrolled for that, on which we would do somersaults and cartwheels and try to get down into splits. We were also taught choir and group singing, and we both fancied ourselves very musical.

'An awful lot of clothes were required for all of this. For Greek you wore a flowing crêpe tunic, any colour you wanted, tied at the waist with a dressing gown cord, and bare feet. Because the floors were all Lord Rothschild's original wood floors, the splinters were incredible. We were constantly having bits of wood dug out of our bums and knees.

'Then there was a perky little skirt for tap, and a black tunic for ballet with white socks. No tights—just bare legs; nothing was available then and it was a long time before Danskin arrived in this country. I always think of standing at the barre, looking at the blue mottled legs and the goose-flesh of the girl in front of me. The whole house was freezing—you'd go to bed fully dressed, with more clothes on than when you got up. Then for National you had a black skirt with multi-coloured ribbons on the bottom that went on over the ballet tunic, and character shoes. My National skirt was made out of blackout material and bits of ribbon my mother found in the bottom of her sewing basket. People were very resourceful then.

'There was tap maybe twice a week, and we usually had ballet every day. Miss Mackie preferred to teach the Cecchetti method, but we took RAD exams one term and Cecchetti the next. It was obligatory to do both; you didn't have a choice. It was very confusing for a child; all the arm positions were numbered differently in the two methods and all the positions of the feet had different names and numbers as well.

'Tap was wonderful for what it taught you about rhythm. In the first tap class I expected to tap, but instead we sat down on the floor and clapped all the way through the class. First you were told to clap counts 1, 3, 5 and 8. Well, that's easy. Then you had to clap counts 2, 4 and 6—easy again. Then they said, "Clap counts 1-3-5-8 and then 2-4-6 and then alternate them," and they got more and more complicated. I can still do it now because the rhythm was so engrained.

'There were pianists for all the classes and one used to come into the room with a knitting bag, a cup of tea and a cigarette. And she could do all those things at once: play the piano, knit, smoke the fag and drink the tea. She'd wedge the knitting needles up under her arms while she was playing, and then the minute she finished the last chord she'd just pick her hands up off the keyboard and grab the needles and go on with that.

'Greek was based on mythology, movements like friezes. We had to imitate throwing a javelin, killing a deer, lighting the Olympic flame. And we did actual stories; the teacher would make up a dance describing Pandora's box, like a long *enchaînement*. There were exams in Greek, but not in National, which were the German, Dutch, Russian, Polish, Hungarian dances, dances from different parts of France and England, three or four a term. One was expected to know them all.

'And for ballroom we had to wear gilt sandals. Antoinette came one term before me, from Criccieth, with the boys, but the school rapidly decided the boys must go, with the result that we had to learn ballroom with each other: "You be man." "No, I'll be man this week." It was wonderful.

'The other, non-dancing classes were such fun. All children love words and sounds and puns, so it was fun learning tongue-twisters and producing sounds for voice production. Mime and acting were two distinct things. Mime consisted of learning to be very clear about everyday things. If you were demonstrating someone sewing, with nothing there at all, you'd take up the needle carefully, hold it up to the light to find the eye, thread it, draw the thread out and knot it, so

26

anyone could tell at once what you were doing. And if it wasn't clear, the teacher would say, "That has no truth in it. You didn't convince me at all." So it was very specific and precise.

'Antoinette and I were a very scrawny pair. I had matchstick arms and legs and a huge belly—I had been nearly starved during the war—and she was very thin and weedy-looking. Food came in a regular pattern: grey mince on Monday with tinned peas that came out like bullets; stew on Tuesday that was more gristle and fat than anything else. Sliced white bread with margarine for tea. A half pat of butter for each person for breakfast, and cornflakes and toast. Supper was always tomatoes on toast or baked beans on toast. They did what they could, I suppose, and we were allowed to bring things from home for tea, if we were lucky enough to have some honey or jam or Marmite.

'I never felt anything *but* homesick. I cried and cried. The feeling of desolation on Sunday night has never left me. There's nothing to occupy you, no lessons, no dancing, nothing—just church and lunch and a house meeting. We didn't travel at all; when you went back to school you wouldn't see your parents till half-term six weeks later. We called it prison. We weren't allowed to phone, but we had to write to our parents on Saturday morning, and the letters came out stilted and horrible. One was very much alone there. You had to do it yourself, had to work out how to organize all these clothes, your whole life.

'Sister Benson was a dragon. She was a trained nurse, very big with an enormous bust and a booming voice, and all the matrons who looked after one, like Miss Grub, seemed incredibly fierce as well. You were supposed to get into bed and go to sleep at lights out, which was 8:30, but it was still broad daylight then in the summer. We were locked in and we couldn't go to the loo. That's when we charged for the pot. It wasn't always a proper pot—sometimes it was two jam jars. The object was to get them full so somebody could go out with them and see what was happening. So nobody used to go to the loo before bed, and they'd all be desperate to go by the time lights went out. Antoinette and I twigged right away that we could make a fast buck if we confiscated the pot and charged them all so they wouldn't pee on the floor. Weren't we ghastly? There was a thrill in being really horrible.

'When Antoinette was taken away and sent to the Royal Ballet school I became the worst rebel. I decided to flood the school to get myself expelled so I could follow her. I put all the plugs in the basins and the baths on the top floor where our dormitories were, and turned all the taps on. I caused an enormous amount of damage but they still wouldn't chuck me out.

'There was a broom cupboard on the top floor where we used to lock ourselves in to plot. She told me the facts of life there: she told me babies came up the loo, and I didn't sit down on a loo till I was about thirteen—I just sort of squatted over it, with trembling thighs. We used to play pranks together. We'd bounce on the beds until the springs collapsed and we'd have midnight feasts, and we were always turning ourselves into swans. We'd pinch sanitary towels from the senior girls—thick, cotton, wadded things with a loop at each end that was supposed to go into a belt—and we'd hook them over our heads from one ear to the other. The deadly seriousness of Antoinette's face as she looped this thing over her head!

'There must have been ballet books in the library that we looked at, or else where did we get the idea to become swans? We were certainly brought up to go into ballet companies, and we dreamed about what we would do and what we would dance and how our lives would be, and of course that included marriage. Antoinette said she would marry Michael Somes—she must have been about eight or nine. And I had to come up with a reply—this conversation was also in the broom cupboard—to match her. There was really no other dancer in England at that time but Robert Helpmann, who I knew would be much too old for me ever to marry. But just the week before John Gilpin had visited the school; he was a young beautiful dancer who the headmistress had told us was on his way to wonderful things. So I managed to remember his name and I said, "That's all right. You can have Michael Somes because I'm going to marry John Gilpin."

'Antoinette lived in Westerham on the hill and we often spent time together during the holidays. We used to dance all the time, to 78 records. At children's parties, eventually everyone would stop dancing and look at her. It was perfectly natural for her to dance; she enjoyed it. There was nothing aggressive or showing off about it. She was always the centre of attention, but just because she always loved dancing. It wasn't done in a pushy way.

'But at school the dancing was deadly serious and it was competitive, even then. Antoinette and I had it all worked out between us to be ballerinas. I had some doubts about myself because of my physique, but I didn't want to let on and I wanted to try to keep up with her. She was absolutely determined, and I could see even then that she was going to be one.'

Mrs Sibley picks up the story on a different day: 'When we read that [Ninette] de Valois was taking the place at Barons Court and starting a full school, with academic work as well as dancing, and she would take them from the age of nine, we wrote for an audition. We were followers of the Vic-Wells Ballet, and I had had an odd class at Sadler's Wells, so that move made a lot of sense to us. I said, "Don't you think it's a shame to take her away? She's quite happy where she is." And Ted said, "Yes, but if this is the right direction, the sooner the better. They take them from nine and she'll soon be nine. And she'll make other friends there." Ted always insisted that if she's going to do anything at all, you can't do better than give her the best. Not only will she get the best tuition but also the best artistic background, and the competition will be of better quality. I think it did work out that way actually.

'I don't think I had really thought very deeply about a career for her. Because I'd done so much dancing myself I might have thought automatically that she would find fun in doing it. And Ted's a very logical, analytical sort of person, and weighing her up it did seem obvious to him that with that physique and lightness and delicacy, it was probably worth pursuing if she took a fancy to it.

'I don't think it ever occurred to me that she would be a singer, simply because there'd never been anybody in my family who could sing. It might have occurred to Ted, but for singing you don't have to start so young. If you're going to be a good dancer you have to start reasonably young, and it happened that she did more dancing when she was very

29

young because she had to be found a safe spot and this was a happy safe spot, doing something she loved. It was just very fortunate. We'd get reports from Tring every term, but we rather took them for granted. You'd get things like "Must try harder with her spelling" or "Must try harder with turning her foot out," but we didn't really take them very seriously. But I think Ted realized that if she turned out to have a liking for it, she could be quite good at the dancing.'

By that time, Antoinette had not only spent several years absorbing the fundamentals of classical ballet, but she had also appeared for the first time before an audience larger than her family, when the staff at Tring staged little entertainments in the garden for Parents Day. 'I vaguely remember something about the Seven Dwarfs, but I don't know which one I was.' ('She was Bashful,' laughs Mrs Sibley.) 'I think it was for students at the end of term; I don't remember mothers and fathers being there. I certainly never did any dancing like at a school theatre.

'My first ever performance, before I landed on the Opera House stage, was at the end of a pier. I'd gone with my mother, it was in the summer, and I did a tap dance and won a prize, I got her some face powder in a pretty glass dish.' As proud mothers often can, Mrs Sibley recalls the details: 'We had joined forces with friends and taken a house for the holiday in Bognor Regis, I think it was 1948. When the theatre company ran a talent contest for the children, Antoinette danced a solo based on her acrobatic ability linked with musical steps, and her natural delicacy came over as a dance performance far removed from the usual circus-type acrobatic routine. She was presented with a powder container which she passed to me, and I still have it.'

When the Royal Ballet school first loomed as a possibility, Antoinette had grown into a bright and lively nine-year-old with a mind of her own. She made a large part of the decision to leave Tring herself, though not the part you might expect. A romantic would guess that perhaps she'd caught a whiff of greasepaint in the seabreeze blowing across that pier, or sensed that the cheerful sound of applause held precious hints of love and approval. But in fact, as she was indeed 'quite sensible at that age', she had a perfectly sensible reason for her decision.

'I definitely danced because my parents put me in a dancing school. I probably wouldn't have thought of it off my own bat, but I don't know because I didn't have to—that was their decision. They put me in a theatrical school, and then having done that they saw how I developed and what I was good at. And although ballet was certainly nothing that I wanted to do—I mean, at nine years old I wasn't ambition-struck and I certainly didn't want to be a ballerina—my reports must have been rather good. When it was mooted to me to come to the Royal Ballet school I leaped at it, for no other reason than getting to London. I was nearer my parents in London than I was at this bloody boarding school, and at least I could then get home at weekends.

'I realized I must be quite good at ballet because I would pass the exams and my teacher would congratulate me. We did dancing exams the same as school exams; you spend the whole year doing the work and at the end you just take the exam in it. It's no big deal—I mean, it's a big deal if you pass or fail, but I wasn't that much enamoured of the ballet anyway, so it wasn't life or death. I didn't think, "Oh, I'll never be able to dance again if I fail," because I didn't think of ballet in those terms. I hadn't seen a ballet performed. I wasn't like Fred [Ashton] who saw Anna Pavlova, or I wasn't like Anna Pavlova who had seen *The Sleeping Beauty*. I didn't have any love of it like that. It was purely a means to an end: if I was good enough and I could get to the Royal Ballet school, then I'd live in London. Ballet was a ticket to London.'

Two

'Every dancer has a teacher as well as a mother. If a girl is born with straight legs it is to her mother's credit. If they are still straight when she is eighteen, it is to her teacher's.'

G. B. L. *Wilson*

A child entered the Royal Ballet school in the summer term of 1949, and a dancer came out six years later. The difference between them is that a child asks for help until he can help himself and then he stands alone and makes his own decisions. A dancer asks for help every day of his life; the stronger he becomes the more of it he needs and wants. He makes very few decisions by himself and he is obedient forever. When you devote yourself to the study of classical ballet, you learn more than a series of steps and positions named in French. You learn dignity, discipline and tradition. You also learn that you will never know as much as your teacher, never master your subject, never leave the classroom. You will never be allowed to relax your vigilance over your body. And as long as you are inside the studio you will do as you are told. Always. All ways. You are not permitted to refuse.

But teachers and attitudes vary, and what kind of a dancer you become depends largely on what kind of training you receive. While the ballet vocabulary is the same all over the world—academically precise in theory, anatomically logical in execution—dancers are not automatons and their bodies are not identical. Every dancer is different, and in some dancers the difference is the first thing you see.

Ninette de Valois, the founder of the Royal Ballet and its school, declares that 'from the very beginning Antoinette was

32

a child of enormous talent. And it wasn't only a question of her talent: it was a question of her general makeup, her limbs, her body. The main thing is to have the right body. And she had the attitude of a little extrovert, which is what we like, and she was musical, which was very useful. Oh, we all knew she was going to the top. It was quite obvious.'

Ailne Phillips, who was the school principal and then de Valois' own assistant, maintains that 'we knew there was something there. You can tell if there's an exceptional talent roaming around, waiting to be caught. There's a quality, an awareness, that they can give even when they're being auditioned—that's necessary above everything else. And musicality—very very important.'

Winifred Edwards, Antoinette's first teacher at the school and her life-long friend, puts it this way: 'One very quickly realized she was special. Right from the beginning she was a dancer. There was that harmony. She did not have a perfect body for ballet—not the way Jennifer Penney has a perfect body, or Nana Gollner—but she had talent, which is a gift from God. Amongst all those funny little junior girls, there was that intense face, that purity of line. She was "marked".'

Antoinette's first response to the school, on the wet winter morning of her audition, was to walk right by it. She wasn't lost or confused; she knew perfectly well what she was doing. 'I never said anything to my mother. I didn't say "I'm not going in." I just kept walking, right past the door. And she went, "You've gone past." And I said, "I know." I'm always very nervous before a performance and I always was with exams. Hysterically nervous. So I guess it was just nerves; I thought, "I'd rather not have to go through the terror of all this."

'I was even a nervous child, and I used to eat wool. But it had to be crinkly wool, I mean, not all blankets would do. Overcoats were very good, my bear was rather good, and my school uniform was absolutely threadbare—you ask my mother. It always has to be crinkly wool; after you pick it out you feel it before you either eat it or chuck it away. I used to absolutely love it. I suppose it was a nervous habit, but it lasted for ages.

'At the audition I don't remember being nervous while we were dancing and I don't remember what we did, but it

33

wasn't very much. We all wore white and I had a number pinned to my tunic. Ursula Moreton was one of the people who was there and I think Ailne Phillips, and definitely Miss Edwards was taking the class for the audition. But I don't think they examined us so much on what we'd learned, what our ability was at that moment, but more on what our foreseeable ability would be. How we looked, how we presented things, not just what we could do.

'But what I remember more than that is that when I arrived at the school for my first day, the person standing at the foot of the steps, i.e. where I literally walked in, was Miss Edwards with her stick. They don't use them any more, but they all had a stick in those days. They'd tap the rhythm out on the floor like the old ballet masters, and help you with your turnout and point with it and tap you where you were wrong. And she looked just like what my impression had always been of a ballerina, her hair done in a little bun at the nape of the neck, very slight, beautiful face, minute, and little white shoes on. Of course as a child one always thinks people look old, and I thought she looked old then. And she said, "You're late," and I *was* late. I'm always late. I've been late for everything, always in my life, and I was true to form with this. Of course the one thing Miss Edwards is not is late for anything. Everything's perfect and punctual, and to her a ballerina is all these things as well. Neatness was one of the things and behaving well . . . oh, everything went towards it.'

De Valois herself would have agreed: everything went towards the shaping of a ballerina, and if the students could absorb their teachers' conduct and attitude along with their precise technical corrections, so much the better.

Leaving as little as possible to chance, Madam—as de Valois is always known—surrounded her future dancers with a staff whose dedication matched her own and whose professional knowledge derived, like hers, from their own experience. Like Madam, Ursula Moreton had studied with Enrico Cecchetti and danced with Diaghilev's Ballets Russes. She was also a pupil of the great mime artist Francesca Zanfratti, whose mime, according to de Valois' memoirs, 'was perfection itself. She taught my head teacher, Ursula Moreton, about 200 gestures, with every detail of footwork and transfer of weight.' Harijs Plucis had trained with Nich-

34

olas Legat and danced with Ida Rubinstein's company; Claude Newman had appeared with Michel Fokine's company and, with Ailne Phillips, in Madam's own Vic-Wells Ballet from its earliest performances in 1931.

Winifred Edwards had danced for four years with Anna Pavlova's company and then toured and taught in America with Theodore Kosloff. In 1922 in Hollywood, a thirteen-year-old named Agnes de Mille took her very first ballet lesson, a private one, from Miss Edwards, who was called Vera Fredova during her years with the Russian ballet. De Mille's autobiography enshrines her teacher as she was then, twenty-five years before Antoinette laid eyes on her: 'She was as slim as a sapling,' de Mille writes, 'and always wore white like a trained nurse. She parted her hair in the centre and drew it to the nape of her neck in glossy wings, Russian style. She was shod in low-heeled sandals. She taught standing erect as a guardsman, and beat time with a long pole.' Having retired from dancing in 1934 to come home to England and nurse her mother, Miss Edwards returned to it in 1946 in order to qualify as a teacher in de Valois' new school. 'I got away from the barre on my pointes on my fifty-second birthday,' she proudly proclaims today.

'Miss Edwards taught us discipline,' says Christine Beckley, who progressed through the school alongside Antoinette and is now a member of its staff. 'She ran our class as she had been brought up, and she was very strict. Everything had to be immaculate—our tunics, our shoes and tights and hair. We were never allowed makeup, except a little lipstick in the Upper Fifth [form]. We had a *great* education over our feet, and foot inspection every week for corns, ingrown toenails, properly cut toenails, and fingernail inspection as well. We were not allowed to bite our nails. Antoinette and I both did and we were severely disciplined with detention. It was a nun-like existence for children, only instead of doing it for God you were doing it for the ballet.'

Miss Edwards' dedication to ballet came to her as a matter of course, and often in the most unexpected guises. 'When the school first opened in 1947,' she relates, 'we were all on coupons and we all looked ghastly. Madam said she'd like to see the whole of the lower school in white, and I was all fired up with enthusiasm. I talked to the art mistress about designing a pattern, and between my friend Miss Curling and some of the mothers we cut them in six sizes.' You could identify each of the six forms by the colour of the belt and headband worn with the white tunic. 'It was cherry for Junior One, royal blue for Junior Two, mauve for Junior Three. Junior Four had the prettiest one, a pale lily-of-the-valley green which Anya Linden—Lady Sainsbury—modelled for Madam. Lower Five wore the same, and for Upper Five Madam said she wanted grey, so they wore smokey grey with very pretty lavender-blue belts and headbands. Those were very unpopular because the sweat showed. But by Easter term the first year a proper dance uniform was organized for all the dancers in the school.

'I taught them to prepare their shoes as Pavlova used to prepare hers, how to darn them and sew the ribbons on. And I ran the wardrobe, on my own money, for a long time, so they had no excuse for not darning their shoes as they could buy the ribbon and the thread *from me*. When they went to have pointe shoes fitted I gave them a note with some points about their feet to take to Mrs Freed, and they showed me the shoes they brought back before they soiled them. I saw them all in, Junior Four, on Friday afternoon to see if they had blisters, and at the beginning of every term I inspected every single foot—all the girls and the junior boys—for athlete's foot or verruca.'

Naturally the school made its own, more ordinary demands on the students. The rules read, in part, 'No jewellery or watches may be worn in school; no pupil may attend evening performances at theatres, cinemas, etc. from Monday to Friday inclusive during term; every girl must wear her hair neatly and suitably arranged; whenever the (green uniform) coat is worn, gloves must be worn.' The children were not only required to rest every day after lunch, but expressly instructed to lie on their backs and shut their eyes.

But any child might encounter similar regulations at any school. However, Miss Edwards remembers doling out potatoes at lunch to girls who refused them with shrugs and embarrassed giggles. 'I knew they didn't want to eat them because they were fattening, but I said to them, "We hope that you are going to become artists, in which case you will travel, when the company is on tour, and be guests at various tables. You've got to learn to eat what is handed to you. Manners make an artist. Nobody minds who your parents were or what your background is. The only thing that matters is yourself as an artist."

The Sadler's Wells school was not just any school, nor could it afford to be. Any school could educate children; any school could train dancers whose fortunes, as dancers, were only problematic. But as the fortunes of the Sadler's Wells Ballet continued to soar, so did the requirements of the school that fed it.

When the company left the Sadler's Well Theatre and took up residence in the Royal Opera House, early in 1946, it could boast of two rising stars in Margot Fonteyn and Robert Helpmann, a repertory of sixty-seven works, and a slavishly faithful audience. Encouraged by the obvious success of de Valois' enterprise, which had blossomed in fifteen years from a nuclear company of seven dancers, the Sadler's Wells Foundation decided to invest a large share of the ballet's wartime profits in new premises for its peacetime school. De Valois had always hoped to establish a school like the great dance academies of Imperial Russia, where students would receive an academic education along with their professional one. Once the abandoned Froebel Institute building at 45 Colet Gardens had been purchased, she could begin to fashion reality out of her long-cherished ambition. And reality for de Valois meant creating a school that would shape the nation's representative dancers.

The new Sadler's Wells school opened on 29 September 1947 with fifty-five students, all of them girls; twelve boys were enrolled the following year. Fees were set at fifty-five guineas a term for students aged ten to fifteen and twenty guineas for those over fifteen, and by 1951 forty of the school's 100 pupils were receiving some scholarship assistance. 'I had to prove myself,' Antoinette explains earnestly. 'I remember taking an education exam, nothing to do with the dancing, in a little local school in Westerham, not even in my own school, and I won a scholarship. I sat the exam at eleven, but I didn't need to use it until I was thirteen, at which point the school did give me the grant.'

For the first time, the school had its own home, separate and distinct from the company's workplace, where it could at last provide the younger students with a general education. They studied a standard curriculum of English language and literature, history, maths, French, geography, science, music and art, which prepared them to take a General Certificate of Education at sixteen. They also had a daily ballet class of just over an hour, taught early in the morning when they were considered most alert and receptive, and weekly classes in Dalcroze eurythmics, *plastique* and folk dancing. At sixteen, having passed through six forms, the student graduated into the upper school and became a student, first in the 'dancing Sixth' form and then in the Theatre Class. Lessons and dancing now swapped places. Academic studies occupied the first hour of the day while more concentrated vocational training claimed the balance with classes in pointework, *pas de deux*, character dancing, mime and repertory.

'The school was far more selective then than it is now,' Christine Beckley points out. 'There were fewer students and the drop-out was minimal. They didn't take much dead wood; Madam only took what she wanted and she had an incredible eye. It was like a private education. We were aware we had a very privileged life, and the teachers thought we were special *because* we were training to be dancers.'

'But there's nothing worse than an idiotic dancer or a silly, thoroughly uneducated dancer,' de Valois exclaims with a spirited toss of her head. 'And I think education teaches them discipline. Half the time, just having to learn to read and write you suddenly find something you're going to be interested in. Take myself: at the age of nine, the only day in the week that I looked forward to was Tuesday. And I looked forward to Tuesday because I had to write a composition—that was the beginning of me wanting to write. All that worried me was the subject: I did not like writing about stupid subjects. I was punished by my governess once because she gave me a subject I thoroughly disapproved of. It was called The Bad and Good Uses of Money, and I said "I've never heard of anything so silly" and I refused to write it. But my wanting to write only came out through ordinary education, reading other things, trying to put sentences together and finding I loved doing it. So I think education is terribly important.'

So did the children, but for a much more compelling reason. Antoinette set it out quite simply: 'In my day we weren't allowed into the company unless we had five subjects for our School Certificate, so schoolwork was frightfully important to us. True to form, I wasn't particularly good during the term. I like things always to be exciting and it was a bit boring, so I didn't work that hard. Whereas I was very good at exams; I'd swot all night and usually come out first or second.

'I was very lucky in my teachers and I realize how important that is. We had the most wonderful headmistress called Miss McCutcheon, a very womanly woman, so beautiful. Madame Clouston was the French teacher; she used to take me to Derry & Toms, on at least two occasions, to the roof gardens to tea. I got on frightfully well with her. I think she thought I must be French because of my name, and I was very good at French, always had quite a good accent. Around that time my parents had Swiss nannies for my sister and they were French-speaking. My father thought it would be a good idea if we tried to speak French on Sunday, during lunch, so we'd start off doing that but I don't think we got very far.

'Miss Zambra, the art teacher, was one of my favourites. I loved art and what I was frightfully good at was sculpting on brick. We used to sculpt the bricks that you use for building houses, and I made the most wonderful dragon for my parents. I was also good at painting, but not portraits or animals. I couldn't copy anything—it always had to be something from my imagination.

'I also adored our music teacher, Miss Perrett; she wore the prettiest lace blouses and petticoats. When she crossed her legs at the piano, we could all see the borders of these petticoats, three inches of lace, absolutely exquisite. I've never seen such lingerie, even today. It gives you an idea of femininity and an added interest in the subjects if teachers are like this.

'I was always very good at maths, but I couldn't do the sums the way the teacher taught me. She was wonderfully patient, Mrs Teague. She was another of my favourites and she understood me very well. I remember her one day getting down on the floor with me, with a blackboard, and trying to work out a way to do the sum, because I could get the result all right but I couldn't do it her way. I got there, always, in the end, but I could only do it my way. And bless her, she *let* me do them in my way and that was the clever thing, because if I'm made to conform it does something odd to me.

'Like, much later, when I thought I had to go to class every day—Margot did, everybody did—it felt like something was boiling over inside. Now when I can't go to class every day and I do my own class sometimes, I don't find this awful iron lung atmosphere. And she was very clever in not making me conform.' 'Antoinette could dominate a maths class,' Christine Beckley states flatly. 'She would say, "I'm sorry, I can't go on to the next thing because it doesn't make sense." She had to have a logical answer for everything.'

'I was very bad at English,' Antoinette continues, ticking the subjects off on her fingers, 'and very good at history—I love anything to do with history. I never learned dance notation; I probably should have done but I never could and I never have. I used to climb out of the window into the garden when they weren't looking to get out of that one. And I absolutely hated geography. I found it so disagreeable that I would do anything to be sent out. I'd either have my desk up and be eating chocolates or talking with somebody next to me, which was all forbidden, so they'd send me out of class. Or I would just never appear.

'I was always having detention. I was made a prefect, and when they announced me in prayers everyone laughed because I was known to be such a naughty girl. I was actually called in to Miss McCutcheon's office afterwards, and she said, "I expect you're wondering why you've been made a prefect," and I said I was sort of interested. She smiled, and she had a wonderfully lopsided Irish smile, and she said, "Because I thought it would be the only way that you could realize how hard it is keeping people in order." Of course I was a fantastic prefect because I knew every move. It's like using a thief to catch a thief; I used to be three jumps ahead of them.

'But they were just pranks—it was all a joke. I know the teachers liked me so I couldn't have been just ghastly, and I know I had a way with them because I liked them. But I had always not liked discipline, which is why I didn't like ballet in the first place. If it hadn't been to get to London to be nearer my parents, to this day I still wouldn't be doing it.

'There was no White Lodge in those days so you had to

board out with other people. I boarded in the Talgarth Road near West Kensington, with Mrs Harrison—I was ten. It still wasn't home, but I saw my parents every weekend and it was just wonderful being able to get home all the time, I mean, the difference between living and not living. My mother used to stay up late with me every Friday night, listening to all I had to tell her about the past week. It meant a lot to me, because I realized she herself had to work every weekend.

'There were two or three other girls there too who were all at the school with me, one of whom, Jennifer Till, became another good friend of mine. And what was so good was that she also lived at Brighton—my parents moved to Brighton around this time—so we could go on the train together at weekends. She was a delightful girl. We used to play Monopoly—Monopoly's run through my life—and she broke her two front teeth playing it. We'd rock with laughter, literally, over the table and she smashed into the board. Chris Beckley was another good friend at this stage and so was Sue Lloyd, who was in *Crossroads*. She was always very glamorous, even at that age, and frightfully ahead of her time—she taught me the facts of life. So with these friends and going home weekends, I was obviously getting a lot more settled and a lot more happy.

'I did miss a lot of school with this TB of the glands; I certainly was "quaking" off to hospital and having them drained and all that. But I have this little bounce-back quality—God gives you something in return—so once it's over, some absolute nightmare like that, it's completely out of my mind. When I'm talking back on it now, to me it's gone, it's finished.'

The frightened, lonely child Antoinette had been at boarding school disappeared in London. In her place grew an ordinary schoolgirl of boundless energy and high spirits, who loved swimming and rounders, and could devour half a loaf of bread at one sitting: 'Bread and butter and jam, bread and butter and jam, bread and butter and jam, slice after slice. That's all I ever used to eat.' Aside from a 'grumbling' appendix that was routinely removed, and a regime of periodic puncturing and radiotherapy for her neck gland which dragged on for more than two years, she was essentially healthy and glad of it. 'People were weeded out every single

41

year. We had to go for medical examinations, measured for height, for weight, to see if we were going to get too big or too small or have a curved back. And if the bones were not forming the right way, that was it: out! We were very much aware of this because people were crying at the end of every year. It was very hard.'

Of course it was hard. Madam firmly believed that 'the main thing is to have the right body', and, according to Miss Edwards, Madam also thought that 'If you're over 5' 2", you're a character dancer.' So what saved Antoinette from the heartbreaking disappointment of being rejected by the school wasn't her health alone. She was also lucky.

Having failed her time and time again, Antoinette's body is generally held to be her great misfortune. In 1964 an enervating bout of glandular fever plucked her off the stage and kept her off for five months. She lost another six months in 1966 when a split muscle sheath in her left knee had to be surgically repaired, and many people, including Antoinette herself, believed her career was over when the cartilage in that knee tore during the filming of *The Turning Point* in 1976. Perpetually exhausted, perpetually underweight despite the pints of Guinness she has consumed to build herself up, she is plagued by colds she cannot shake, and nervous tension attacks her with depression or acne or both.

But to concentrate on her physical weakness is to grab the wrong end of the stick. The important thing about her body was not how it didn't work, or even how it did, but that by chance it was exactly the body Madam considered ideal for a classical dancer.

In America, George Balanchine was fashioning ballerinas in the image of the new world he had so passionately adopted, and using them to explore space and define dance as no one had ever done. To make neo-classical ballets for the twentieth century, he needed sharp, streamlined instruments, so his ideal dancer's body came to comprise a small head, short compact torso, and legs longer than long.

In Russia, once the Revolution had chased the aristocrats of the ballet to the West, a new breed of ballerinas rose from the ruins of artistic privilege. The incomparable Galina Ulanova danced like a spirit—elusive and eternal as an icon, hinting at untold mysteries—but she looked like a peasant, with the plain, wide face and sinewy legs and trunk of a labourer on the land. Maya Plisetskaya, her junior, might have leaped to the stage straight from a poster heralding the manifold glories of the new Soviet state. Her long strong body and extravagantly supple limbs and back could easily mirror the vastness, temperamental variety and power of modern Russia.

But in England Madam was encouraging dancers to move correctly, act discreetly and serve the choreography of the moment with humility. For the most part, the acclaimed works she and Frederick Ashton had choreographed for the fledgling Sadler's Wells Ballet demanded clarity of execution and subtle strokes of characterization, so large, bold dancers were inappropriate to them and large, bold emotions excessive. In Margot Fonteyn Madam had found a natural talent in a perfectly proportioned instrument, a classical dancer in a small, neat body, knit tightly enough in the joints that facile flexibility would never tempt her to unseemly flamboyance. The bodies de Valois knew best, starting with her own, and the dancers she admired most, like Tamara Karsavina and Alicia Markova, shared these physical attributes. Moira Shearer and Pamela May who, along with Fonteyn, led the company when it first came to the Royal Opera House, were classical ballerinas in the same mould: small, light, sweetly disciplined and scrupulously accurate.

Physically, Antoinette started along the path to this ideal when she was born, but it took the Sadler's Wells school to lead her into inhabiting it professionally. At first, dancing seemed to follow straight on from her training at Tring, with a daily ballet class and regular classes in *plastique*, which Christine Beckley describes as 'all the shapes of friezes. It made you aware of shapes and *épaulement*, the relationship of arms and body,' and Dalcroze eurythmics. 'I thought that was a bit funny,' Antoinette recalls, 'but I liked it. I'd done Greek before, turned-in stuff, in bare feet, which is very close to it, so it wasn't alien to me in any way. And I honestly like moving to music—it's that simple.'

De Valois felt more strongly about that aspect of the junior curriculum than the juniors did themselves: 'I swear by Dalcroze eurythmics. I had them as a child and I think they're terribly important. The principles are the relationship of

43

movement to music, and they teach dancers to listen and to understand their music so they know all the time signatures they're dancing to. I would much rather see a child do Dalcroze eurythmics at the age of eight than stretch on the floor—they'll get much further.

'You see, musicality is like talent: it's there, inborn, like a jump. You can ruin it if you teach a child badly or you neglect the development of its listening and understanding of music. You can do it a lot of harm. And when it's not there, that is when things like Dalcroze eurythmics are so helpful, because it gives them a discipline towards music which makes up for them not being very aware of it on their own.'

'It's awfully good for rhythm and timing,' observes Ailne Phillips. 'They're made to do things slowly, double time, treble time . . . It's not exactly a dance; it's more or less a grouping of musical changes. It's very good for them, to get everything in the body and the mind working.'

Antoinette also played the recorder while she was in the school, and studied music with Miss Perrett, dutifully singing or conducting along with the other children. But since her musicality was intrinsic rather than acquired, she has very little to say today about any formal musical education she might have received. It's not that music doesn't interest her: simply that she had learned to love it long before she entered a classroom.

Dancing, however, was something different, something she grew to love as she grew and as her exposure to it grew. Although the junior forms were meant to move from teacher to teacher, year by year, Antoinette actually began with Miss Edwards, spent one year with Margaret Graham, returned to Miss Edwards in Form Four, moved on to Ursula Moreton in the Lower Fifth, and finished up with Miss Edwards in the Upper Fifth. She is therefore not exaggerating when she says, 'Miss Edwards was my main teacher right the way through, my lasting teacher from my audition right through to when I went off to have Eloise. At different times I had Miss Moreton, I had Margaret Graham, I had Claude Newman for RAD, and then I started with Ailne Phillips and Pamela May and de Valois herself. Then Harold Turner, Harijs Plucis, they all came in later as well. But Miss Edwards was my mainstay all the way along. She taught Madam's syllabus, but I also had to take RAD exams up to a certain point and we also had to learn Cecchetti. So it was confusing in that we had to learn every syllabus.'

'I wouldn't dream of saying Antoinette had worked a syllabus,' Madam protests. 'What I did was to take the highlights from all the teachers I'd been to—they've all got their lowlights, you know, even the best of them—take what would be strengthening for the work in class from the various schools. A syllabus is not quite the word; it was a form of strengthening them. All I really was doing was steadying up their interpretations of what they were learning from various other, rather more static, syllabuses in certain schools. Steadying it up and making a more general form of it all for them. I really had to . . . what is the word to use . . . steady the boat. That's the right word, not syllabus.'

'There was no real set syllabus,' Ailne Phillips concurs. 'Madam was very much against that. She always said, "It's not a method." It developed in the teacher's course for the summer school. She was teaching then, always, and there were demonstrations by pupils of each grade to show the teachers what Madam wanted and what she was talking about. She had an elementary group, intermediate and advanced, and for each level there was barre work, a centre work, *adage*, allegro, pointe work.

'It was just something she'd put together herself. Not so flamboyant as the Russians, not very technical . . . A lot of it was quick work, very neat and tidy and very precise. She left it to the teachers in each grade to pick who they thought was the best person to do it, and then they came along and demonstrated to her. But the point was, she wanted to correct them in front of all the teachers, so they weren't supposed to be so completely trained that there was nothing for her to find fault with. Well, that's obviously impossible, you never get anybody you can't find fault with.

'There was always a reason for everything she told you, why she wanted you to do it and what it would do to you if you did it and how you could do it, how you could use yourself to the best of your ability.'

Antoinette was aware of that goal, using yourself to the best of your ability, from her very first classes with Miss Edwards. 'She worked on what I needed all the way along and still do and won't ever have, and that's a full turnout. I'm not by nature a turned-out dancer, so this is what she doggedly worked at, to try to get me as turned out and . . . well, as perfect as she could. She wasn't in any way a frilly dancer, she was absolutely pure and classical, and this is who we saw every day, teaching us. And of course she demonstrated every step perfectly; she had perfect turnout, wonderful legs and feet, so we could see what she wanted.

'I had to work on my feet in that I don't have those wonderful insteps, like Pavlova or Lynn [Seymour]. Even if they don't point their feet they looked pointed anyway, but I have to point mine all the time. But I've got very strong feet—I've been very lucky in that respect. I always remember that after *The Dream* Antony Tudor compared my feet to Spessivtseva's, and so had Madame Nijinska. When she came over to put on *Les Biches*, I understudied the Blue Girl and I was also supposed to do the Grey Girls at some point, but I was ill. The only thing she saw me do was rehearse Fred's *Scènes de Ballet*, which she was carried away by, and she said it was Spessivtseva I reminded her of. "Like Spessivtseva," she said, "so pure in the classical dancing."

'We had the softest shoes, which is another reason my feet were so strong, and we had to darn every pair, oh my goodness, yes, that was Miss Edwards. We only had one pair to last like a month . . . it could have even been one pair a term; they were frightfully expensive and none of us had any money. And another thing is that when I went to live in Brighton, when I was eleven, I used to run on the pebble beach at the weekends, barefoot, to strengthen my feet. I thought I wouldn't then get so many blisters because, you see, that was when I had my first pair of pointe shoes ever. I remember sleeping with them under my pillow at night—I'd never seen anything so beautiful, so tiny and such lovely pink satin. And I also remember wondering how I was ever going to get my feet strong enough. Interesting, isn't it? I don't put myself into torturous situations happily and I never think of myself as ambitious, but I do remember running up and down those stones, killing myself, probably because of those pretty shoes.

'Obviously Miss Edwards worked on every single thing—there were hundreds of other things—and I had her more or less every day. Another weakness was beats; I never

46

could beat well. And I had a very funny experience with that. When I was very young I was rather good at beating, and Margaret Hill—she became Margaret Graham—wanted me to do an *entrechat quatre*—she was teaching us, in fact, how to do them. I tried and tried, and I just couldn't do it. What I was doing was an *entrechat six* all the time, and she got so furious with me that she told me to stop showing off. I wasn't showing off at all! I was absolutely mortified that somebody should think that, and I've never been able to do an *entrechat six* since. Never. In *Ballet Imperial*, one of my best ballets, the ballerina has to lead the entire company doing *entrechat six*, and I was lucky if I did one or two out of the eight or nine. I got a complete blockage about it in my mind.

'So I had a problem with beats, problem with turnout, couldn't get my legs way up . . . not that Miss Edwards really taught that. That wasn't one of the things she pushed down one's throat. And she, as every good teacher, tried to get the best out of what she's looking at, rubs the jewel up the way she can.

'But also, outside of that, she always has been very close and careful with me. She took a deep liking to both Lynn Seymour and myself: Lynn, having come away from home, from Canada, and being so shy and nervous, and me not living at home. She took us both under her wing and we used to go to her home; that's why Lynnie and I knew each other so well. And even as late as when I got married to Michael Somes . . . Just when I'd been married a few months I got this dreadful glandular fever. I tried still to be able to look after him, but I couldn't look after myself let alone anybody else. Miss Edwards was very kind and said I could move into her flat and she would look after me. Absolutely amazing! I must have been there for months, and I was in bed all the time. So this closeness really lasted me right the way through; I still took private lessons with her even when I had got into the company.

'I suppose I saw a lot of her because I think I was one of the better pupils in class, although she never seemed to praise me, as opposed, for instance, to Barbara Fewster. When Barbara Fewster came in to teach, she came up to me at the barre the very first thing and said, "That's wonderful. Absolutely lovely." That's the first time anybody had ever

47

said that to me, and I almost cried—I suppose I was about sixteen. Miss Edwards didn't praise one like that, but I knew she had faith in me in that she gave me so much attention and so many corrections.'

Miss Edwards smiles ruefully as she recalls Antoinette's temperament as well as her talent: 'She is very precise about herself and what she does and how she does it, sometimes perhaps too much so. I am very precise too. I had a great affection for the child, which of course was necessary. At the same time I didn't let her get away with charm—she can wheedle the soul out of anybody, that one. She was difficult to teach at times and she could get angry, but it was anger at herself at not being able to achieve what she could or should. Her defence was "I don't understand it. I can't do it," and there are different ways of approaching that. On the whole, I found the best way was to ignore it.'

De Valois didn't ignore it: she took it into account and planned for it: 'I was the one to decide who was coming in, and you had to look upon them as individuals and see that they got under the right teachers. This is always frightfully important because it is possible to ruin a good dancer under the wrong teacher or the wrong *répétiteur* or the wrong choreographer. Now for Antoinette it was very necessary to come under Miss Edwards. For discipline, for one thing; she wasn't a disciplined child. I have a very funny story about her. There was assembly in the big hall at Colet [Gardens] and I came down along the passage and saw this chubby little demon rushing around, singing away. So I said to her, "Antoinette, what are you doing? Why aren't you at assembly?" She looked at me gaily and went on singing, "I'm an atheist, an atheist." She was a little monkey, but extroverts nearly always are at that age—they can't help it. She was very obedient, and sharp and quick on learning. She didn't resent correction; she saw the value of it. But she wasn't disciplined and she was quite self-opinionated, and Miss Edwards was wonderful for her. And the child had for her, which was so right, a great affection, which helped.'

Important as it was, Miss Edwards' influence on Antoinette was only one of the many that worked on her through her six years at the school. 'Now Miss Moreton didn't take me for many classes. She taught us mime and I found that fasci-

48

nating, talking without talking. Again it was acting but without using words. I was between the ages of about ten and sixteen—my gosh, thirty years ago—and mime was essential then for all the classical ballets. It was very much a part of classical ballet life. She was wonderful at it, and it was so hard to do, much harder than dancing. We were used to running around; you've learned to dance since the age of three, whereas you haven't learned how to walk and make it look elegant and natural and how to stand still. Pamela May could always do it wonderfully and of course Ursula Moreton, so we couldn't have had a better teacher.

'And in fact I learned all my mime scenes, which is even better than that, first of all from Miss Moreton and from watching Pamela in the Queen roles and in the ballets, but then Karsavina herself taught me the *Giselle* mime scenes and *Swan Lake*. And now we're talking about a prima ballerina assoluta. Imagine seeing the way she did it! And she did everyone's role—von Rothbart, Odette, the Prince—and it was really watching a great actress, like seeing Greta Garbo as Camille or Sarah Bernhardt as Lady Macbeth. But this was later; I must have been about nineteen or twenty then.

'*Pas de deux* classes were the fun ones. We had Harold Turner, who we were all in love with, so we would wear pink fishnet tights, which were the rage, and the lowest tops we could get, and lipstick, which of course we weren't allowed. We waited all week for our *pas de deux* class. I don't know how old he could have been, but he was utterly charming, a real man, and he adored women so that came out. He flirted with us and we flirted with him. He was a man of the theatre, a star in his own right, and he had an amazing effect on us all—we were about sixteen or seventeen at the time.

'And he made us relax, he was just full of fun and humour. Like de Valois; she had a great sense of humour, always. It was just like living . . . to dance was just like living. It didn't have to be absolutely correct all the time; it was trying to do very difficult things, but she had such a way with her that you would try these things because in a way she didn't mind if you fell over. It was a free, enthusiastic attitude, and with him the same. I don't remember the classes, I just remember him.

'Oh, we were with the boys all the time. I used to have lots of boyfriends there. We ate meals with them and we were outside resting with them . . . We had rugs and a tarpaulin to rest on; in the summer we all had to lie out where now they park the cars—that was our garden—and in the winter we rested in the Baylis Hall, where there are big cupboards where we put our rolled-up mats. Instead of lying out on the mats, the boys and I would get in the cupboards and lie in there. We had great fun.

'And then we also had Harijs Plucis to take *pas de deux*, who was quite different. He wasn't somebody I could easily respond to, he wasn't a charmer. He was at that point the head *répétiteur* of the company, a great friend of Michael's and Margot's, and it was, alas, only just before he died that I ever really got to know him properly. I wasn't somebody he responded to because I *was* naughty, I wasn't seen to be a great worker, always working and almost "religious" about it all. He could see I was sending it up or being stupid or a bit frivolous. He was a tremendous friend of Miss Edwards, who was a bit like him too, but I think she could see I had another side to me. She'd known me since I was a tiny little girl and she knew there was a more serious side, but he obviously couldn't see that side at all. He didn't really have much faith in me until we went to Vienna quite soon before he died. I had to do *Bayadère, Symphonic Variations* and *Enigma Variations* all in one night, and then I think he appreciated what I had to give.

'Whereas de Valois . . . I always adored her. She has been one of the most important inspirations in my whole life. She was such an enthusiastic person, so vibrant—just to see her, I immediately feel a million dollars myself. She was like Rudolf [Nureyev] in that respect, a real live wire and full of praise. Whereas Miss Edwards was a perfectionist, quieter, more dogged in a way and strict, de Valois wasn't. She'd forget your name half the time—she never did know my name, always called me Sibyl, which Anthony [Dowell] still calls me.

'Madam was the kingpin, the head of the company, the head of the school, Madam was everything. And everyone was terrified of Madam. I was never terrified of Madam. I think she quite liked me because she always liked naughty people—Bobby Helpmann, Pirmin Trecu, people with spirit.

I got on very well with her right from the start. It just clicked. Ashton terrified the life out of me, but Madam, never.

'She used to hold a summer school every year, in the holidays, for all foreign visiting teachers, and I was in contact with her mostly through that. She literally took the classes herself; she had three girls showing the jumps and *batterie*, three girls doing the pirouettes, three girls doing the set class, in each grade, and I was usually chosen to do this. I was very worried one year about maybe missing it because I had a bad appendicitis, but I did do it in the end. I think I'd just got out of hospital, bleeding away, my usual sort of drama, but I made it as I usually do.

'It was terribly important to me because it brought me close to de Valois, who inspired me with her enthusiasm. Because I wasn't nervous of her, I danced better for her. And also, because she wasn't such a perfectionist, I didn't worry that I couldn't get my legs up or jump higher than everybody or beat better. She seemed to like me for what I could do, and I got the most amazing confidence because what she wanted was to see someone dance, dance in their own way. Well, if somebody thinks that I can do it I'll prove to them that I can, and with her I would do anything. If she told me to jump over the moon I'd *jump* over the moon.

'And because she was small physically—she was rather my shape, I would imagine, when she was a dancer—and she moved frightfully quickly, which I do, the steps she would give were for quick dancers, so of course I could get my teeth round them. And I liked her mathematical mind; I have that sort of mind, and I can get it round the very complicated footwork she was always giving us. Nowadays it's changing; the dancers have got the very long legs and are getting the legs up, but they don't have the amazing speed we had or the facility to cope with awkward directions. It's in the mind and it's the way we were taught, I suppose because we were smaller.

'Quite soon we started being allowed to go and watch performances. Miss Edwards took Lynn and me to see Margot do *Lac*, but most of the performances we all went to, because we were the juniors in the school, were at Sadler's Wells Theatre, the touring company under Peggy van Praagh—I remember standing at the back every Saturday. So all the people I grew up admiring were not Margot, Michael Somes, the Covent Garden lot, but Svetlana Beriosova—Svetlana was my idol—Elaine Fifield, David Blair, Pirmin Trecu. I saw practically all the ballets Kenneth [MacMillan] did when they first went on—*Solitaire, Danses Concertantes, Laiderette*—as opposed to Fred's, because that company didn't do as many of Fred's ballets, and of course I saw Johnny Cranko's early works and *Pineapple Poll*. So this was the fun for me, and this is what I knew about ballet.

'I loved what I saw, really loved it, but it was nothing to do with what I was doing every day. I didn't think, as I was doing my *battements tendus* and my *pliés*, "Oh gosh, if I do this very well then I shall be doing what they're doing on the stage."

'But when I get to be about fifteen or sixteen, I do realize that people think I'm good. I know people come and watch the classes, I hear them whispering about me, and anyway I'm used, I'm chosen by de Valois for her summer school. And by this stage I realized that the dancing had an end in view. Up till now it had just been ghastly horrible class. You know, some days things wouldn't work, other days they would. I liked to dance but it was so impossible and so tiring and I was just trying to get it right, which I found so boring. But now suddenly—and I don't particularly know why—I realized that an arabesque wasn't just what I was told: not to sickle my foot, get my leg up this high, have my fingers put in a special way. It could be a sad movement, an ecstatic movement, a cruel movement. It was only like a word, and it was up to you how you used that word. Once I realized that ballet wasn't just physical torture, that it actually was a language I could speak my own way, tell my own stories and thoughts and how I responded to the music, then I was happy. Then I loved to do it, because it wasn't just grinding and horrible. I realized that in fact everything I was doing in class was just a means of expression. I could do it with humour, or not, or however I felt, and I could do it differently every day. And once I found that freedom—and freedom's really the word—although I still had to get certain things right and I still couldn't see the end result, I was enjoying it more.

'For me class is very depressing, more depressing than for most people because I'm not a good classroom dancer. I'm horribly embarrassed by myself in class and always have been, right up to this day. When I get exhausted and can't cope with it, at least now I've got the intelligence to go and work by myself so I don't need to embarrass myself with looking at me any longer. I've always been very aware that some people have the perfect physique—very high insteps, long legs—for doing all these mind-boggling things, none of which I could do. And I could see perfectly well with my two brown eyes that I was not a turned-out person—after all, this is what's drummed into you all the time—and I couldn't jump and I couldn't beat. So though I heard all these people saying things about me then, I couldn't rationalize why they were saying I was so good.

'I'm intelligent, I know what I can do. I've always been able to turn very naturally, but not if you put me under pressure. If you try and make me do it properly, I can't do it. I can only do it my way, in a natural way. I'm a good balancer, I have a good line, but these things aren't necessarily the more showy things. I can't jump like they can, I can't beat like they can, I can't get my legs up. And I could see, not necessarily one person doing everything better, but always somebody better than me at any one thing. Like if I was doing the decathlon, I'd see somebody jumping higher, somebody throwing the ball further. So it's always been an effort and it's always been a fight.

'Now I understand that probably my best facility is that I'm good at interpreting music in movement. I know that's a natural facility because I can see other people not doing it. I can see them doing things more precisely or more perfectly than me, but they don't necessarily interpret it or make it their own. But I have to like the music. That's why when we get into this modern stuff it's not so much the being in bare feet or the movement I can't cope with: it's the music that really doesn't in any way turn me on. If I have to start counting it's hopeless for me. I can't count, I don't want to dance counting. I like to dance to the music that I sing.

'And I think one of my facilities, which doesn't come through when you see photographs of me, is probably that I move naturally. Most people cover their eyes when they see videos of themselves. I'm really pleased! Because for the first time I can see something good. Possibly I'm a natural mover because I can't turn out like they all can.

53

'My instinct is to compete—I'm a born competitor. I don't know where it stems from, probably my own inadequacies in class, which was more or less all I was doing at school. I've always been good at exams, always good under pressure like that. Maybe I thought I had to prove myself in exams, but nevertheless that's when I was at my best.'

And the rest of the time, although she couldn't see it herself, she wasn't so bad either. 'When I had Antoinette, Lynn, Beckley,' Miss Edwards comments, 'we changed lines every day and changed places at the barre too, so neither my eye nor their sense of habit would get too fixed. We also had 'official places' for when the VIPs showed up. I'd whisper to them out of the corner of my mouth, "Official places," and they'd know just where to go. Without their mothers, they'd sort themselves out quite easily. They wanted to show off the better ones; it was their choice.'

Christine Beckley patiently explains what seems obvious to her: 'The teachers knew she was special and that's why it turned out such a good year, because she set the standard and we aimed to match her. She may not have felt the competition because she was the best in the class and the dominant one. We all waited every year until she chose her friends—she was so powerful *because* she was so good. She didn't know she had that power, but she did.'

'I remember one summer school,' Miss Edwards says softly, 'when she must have been at the advanced level, and she demonstrated a very beautiful *enchaînement* that Madam had composed. She was alone and there was that lovely sort of silence when she'd finished, a moment of magic. And Madam looked up at the teachers and said, "So you see what I mean," and the teachers were almost in tears.'

But Madam, in her usual brisk way, wipes the rosy glow from the scene with a few sensible words and exposes the bare facts which are, inevitably, more revealing: 'The summer school was to help the teachers more than the dancers. The dancers had to illustrate it all and that's where they think it was so wonderful, when really they were working very hard and showing off. They all did it—the classical ones—of course, and they all had to be good because the teachers had to see it well illustrated. So I chose good students. I had Antoinette, definitely.

'She was motivated to learn and get on, no question of that. She was an ambitious girl . . . well, she had to be. All the good ones had ambition. If they're talented they want the whole thing.'

Three

'Actually from a statistical point of view there is far more chance of being run over at Hammersmith Broadway than of getting on to Covent Garden stage.' *Arnold Haskell*

'My first performance ever was on 2 January 1956. I was the second swan on in *Swan Lake*, and the performance was a celebration itself because Margot had that day been honoured with a DBE. I remember it vividly, and last 2 January marked the thirtieth year that I've danced on Covent Garden stage.

'I remember getting to the theatre around 4:00, and I was terribly nervous because I'd never been on any stage in my life before except this tap dance I did on the end of a pier, where I got my mother her powder. So it was quite an event for me to come onto that *vast* stage and feel so frightfully noticeable as the second swan on. You're not hidden behind people, there's only one person there and you really can be seen.

'The Students were right at the top of the theatre in those days, by the wardrobe, and Shirley Grahame said she'd come and make me up. I started myself to try to get something together, but I really couldn't get myself to look like anything and I couldn't do my hair in a classical style. In fact I wasn't happy with my classical style until I did *Sleeping Beauty pas de deux* with [Peter] Schaufuss a few years ago. My hair is frightfully hard to keep up; it's very fine and hairpins make no difference at all to it.

'I don't remember learning to do the hair styles at the school. We were taught about makeup, but when we were Students, and I had been a Student for so little time, just from September to Christmas after I'd taken my School Certificate. So when I came to my first performance, Shirley did everything for me: made me up, got me ready, did my hair, my makeup, everything, and I must have been ready about 5:30 or 6:00, just sitting there, absolutely terrified, waiting for 7:30 to come along.

'And the trouble with me with nerves is that I forget the steps. I don't so much fall over, which is even worse for other people, when they find they literally can't do the steps because of nerves. I can do the steps, I can usually do them better with nerves, but what I can't do is remember them. So of course this was frightening, knowing I was the second swan on and in such a visible position.

'But Shirley stood behind me, she was Number 3, and she reminded me of the steps as we went along. She told me when to move, where to breathe or not to breathe, and I made it through with her help. She was wonderful—she absolutely got me through it. You see, I was probably told two or three days before that I was going on and I obviously went on because somebody was off. But I can't remember rehearsing beforehand and I can't imagine the company giving us many rehearsals of these ballets. And I only had that one term to be a Student; we would have started repertory classes then, but we can't have learned that much. So when I came to do that swan, I didn't know much about it.'

Except she knew how to dance. She may not have known which step followed which in the second act of *Swan Lake*, but she knew what the steps were and she could execute them all. She had learned, in the course of six years study, to stand on straight legs and jump from quickly bent ones; to do quarter-turns and then complete turns and finally doubles or triples without getting dizzy or falling over; to curve her arms so the elbows never protruded. She had learned to finish movements without rushing them at quick tempos and to fill space and time at slower speeds with fully stretched positions. She had learned to land from a jump without making a sound, and to twist her body and rearrange her limbs in endlessly shifting patterns without making a face. She could turn a series of French phrases into a string of steps as fast as they could be named, and perform the steps in any direction and at any speed. And if her body felt a natural preference for moving to one side or the other, she had learned to conceal it.

Of course there was still more to learn. She had never had to act, project, memorize a role, develop a character, maintain her energy for longer than the duration of a class, or engage an audience's attention and interest. But she had mastered the science of dancing well enough to move on to the art of dancing. Once she had passed her School Certificate and completed her basic instruction without mishap, the school was quite safe in slipping her into the corps de ballet without fear of embarrassment, either to its reputation or to her, and quite prepared to sit back and wait to see what would become of her.

Many young students never get that far. Either they lose interest or grow too tall or too fat, or rebel against the corrections, or crumble under the criticism. Some work too hard and damage their bodies; some don't work hard enough to build any strength. Day after day, year after year, they stand at the barre doing *pliés* and *tendus* to warm and stretch the ankles, *ronds de jambe* for flexibility in the hips, *frappés* and *battus* as preparation for beats. Then in the centre of the room, unsupported, they do long adagio *enchaînements* for balance and placement, curlicues of different turns, small jumps—in place or travelling, with beats or without—and then larger jumps. The unyielding discipline of the science destroys some. The boredom of repetition ruins others. And even those who refuse to give up know that they will never get all of it right.

'We had no outlet for performing except for summer school,' comments Christine Beckley, 'but I had complete faith in my teachers and did what they told me to do. I don't think I ever doubted. I remember sitting at Covent Garden with Antoinette, watching Margot and Michael dancing in *Apparitions*. She was as aware as I that we were going to get up on that stage. We were so single-minded, and those who didn't have that fell by the wayside.'

'You got reports every term,' explains Winifred Sibley, 'but you didn't feel absolutely secure about it. You were very pleased when you heard that Madam wanted Antoinette to do some demonstrating in the summer—that was very nice. Antoinette would come home and say, "Isn't it exciting? Madam said to all the teachers, 'When you come and see her *next* year . . .' " But you don't run away with the idea that it's all cut and dried and certain.

'But when she was about fifteen the school actually interviewed the parents. In our day it was Arnold Haskell, who was head of the school, and also Miss McCutcheon and Ursula Moreton, who was then head of the dance side. The idea was to let us know what they felt seriously about her prospects and discuss generally if they thought she had a chance to get into this company or if they didn't. We were rather overwhelmed because they sat us down and they said, "This is one of the happiest interviews we've conducted because it always gives us such pleasure to be able to say what promise someone has."

She was promising, yes, but not precocious, and she was still formally a Student when she first stepped onstage with the Sadler's Wells Ballet. She had worked through the summer holidays in her parents' shop and restaurant in Bromley, as usual, and had returned in September to the school and her place at the barre, also as usual. Nothing had changed except that she now spent more time dancing than she'd ever done, and classes in mime, *pas de deux*, and repertory had replaced her academic studies.

'When we got to the Sixth Form class, that Ailne Phillips used to take, it was the most incredible people: Marcia Haydée, Lucette Aldous, Lynn, myself—the men were separate. A quite extraordinary roomful, if you think of them now. It was the most amazing luck. And the marvellous thing about Babs' classes was that they were *so* hard. When she set an *enchaînement* you knew there was no way you could do it. But in her relaxed, matter-of-fact way, she would start you off and, to our utter amazement, we found we *could* do it. And it gave us a great deal of confidence.'

'We were certainly working to get the best out of each pupil as a dancer,' says Miss Phillips. 'As they matured you found out who was good and who was bad and who would make it and who wouldn't . . . more or less. You have to have great faith in them, in a way; a lot of them are so shy, so nervous and they get so worked up, they can't really show you their best at all sometimes.

'The Sixth Form was like a class of perfection. They had their technique up to a certain point, and after that they had to expand and work on any weakness they had. Antoinette's an elfin creature; she flits about like a butterfly all the time. I think her technical thing was not her feet so much, but that she had to get more stamina, she wasn't very strong.

'I always tried to give the class a certain amount of private tuition during the week. I'd take two together one day, two together another day, for different things they found difficult. Pointework for one, placing the body, or the things they were weak in or felt they wanted extra help in.

'I remember her in the school. As a small child she was an atheist, a little bit of a thing and so proud of it too, and she never went to prayers with the other children. She used to say, "There's no point trying to tell me someone's going to help me. I have to do it all myself." She hadn't very much faith in luck or opportunity or anything like that. She'd say, "*I've* got to do it all. *I* have to make the effort. Nobody else is going to do it. It's up to me," which sometimes is a little difficult if you're trying to teach her something.

'In my opinion, to get the best out of your pupil you've got to first of all have a little bit of knowledge of their character, how to approach them. Some need bullying, some need coaxing. Antoinette can be very obstinate; she gets an idea into her head and nothing in God's earth is going to move it. She wanted a tremendous amount of attention; she always wanted to be helped. But I don't think she thought of herself as the star of the class, not at all. She was . . . not the star, but at least she was someone of importance in the class.'

But neither that sense of importance nor the familiar school routine lasted long. Antoinette's Sixth Form remained intact only from September 1955 to Christmas, the three months that exactly coincided with the Sadler's Wells Ballet's fourth American tour. When the company returned to London in December, worn out by its travels and depleted by injury, Madam grabbed a handful of her senior students and shoved them unceremoniously into the least conspicuous gaps onstage. She probably didn't waste much time thinking about it. If you're running a classical ballet company and you've gone to the trouble of establishing a school to groom dancers for it, finding trained bodies to plug a few holes in the ranks is the least of your worries. If she had long-term plans or ambitions for those particular students, she wasn't letting on.

In any case, her abrupt decision had one clear and immediate effect, which was merely to change those students' lives, overnight and forever.

Antoinette appeared at Covent Garden in Act II of *Swan Lake* on 2 January and as a swan in Act II and a page in Act III in the 4 January performance. In *Coppélia* on 6 January, she was a child in Act I and danced with both the Midday Hours and the Evening Hours in Act III. On 7 January she was a page to Fairy Autumn in all three acts of Ashton's *Cinderella*. In the 20 January *Swan Lake* she danced with the corps swans in Act IV as well as Act II. By the end of January she had taken these various guises in sixteen performances out of the month's total of seventeen.

She had no contract with the company, no guarantee of one and, indeed, few expectations. But she speaks of her life before 2 January in terms of school: classmates, teachers and exams. And after that date there is nothing but the company: its dancers, its repertory, its standards and traditions. On that cold January evening, perhaps without even realizing it, she stepped off the top rung of one ladder and set her foot firmly on the bottom rung of the next. Her steady climb to the top of the school had brought her, promise and all, straight to the bottom of the company. She was not yet seventeen years old.

'It was a very humbling experience in a way. We were not used to the company being around us. I remember Moira Shearer walking through the school and us all gasping, seeing that beautiful woman. And Margot had been through to do class—I think she joined a couple of Pamela May's classes—and Gerd Larsen when she came back after her baby, and Violetta Elvin. But we were very shy of them and very respectful towards them. It really was the bowing of the heads and the backing away as they walked by—that's how we were all brought up. And although we'd seen them when they came through our school, it was not like they see us now, every single day in the canteen and things like that, because they also worked at the studios at Hammersmith, in the RCA film studios. So they didn't have as much to do with the school as we do now.

'I don't know what classes we still had to attend—we were betwixt and between. Because we were on so often we were doing rehearsals as if we were in the corps de ballet, but when we'd go to rehearsal we really did creep in a corner and shut up. There was no giggling—and this was a complete change for me—because we weren't, outside the rehearsal or inside, considered anything. In those days to be a teenager wasn't glamorous or wonderful in any way at all. We hadn't reached a fun age with gear things to do or wear; we just wore grownup clothes smaller. The Beatles hadn't yet emerged, so we hadn't found our own feet. Everything was drab and awful, and as teenagers we were considered the lowest of the low. We were really nothing.

'We started in January, and I did swans and things like that, pages and nymphs in *Sleeping Beauty*, we were fitted in a lot. I do remember being told that we were to be taken into the company and how thrilling that was, because none of us expected it. It didn't automatically follow that because you had worked with the company you were going in. You could go into the Opera Ballet or into the touring company; it wasn't necessarily into the first company.'

'Khrushchev and Bulganin came to a performance in April,' Christine Beckley recalls, 'and we asked Jack Hart if we could stay for the party. And he said, "Of course. As you're unofficial members of the company, of course." Which was the first we knew of it. We were officially in the company in July, and we earned seven pounds per week in the corps and no shoes came out of that. As Students we were paid by the act, but we never thought about it. We would have done it for no money at all.'

In July 1956, seven girls at the school were given corps de ballet contracts with the Sadler's Wells Ballet: they were Christine Alderton, Elizabeth Anderton, Christine Beckley, Jacqueline Daryl, Audrey Farris, Mavis Osborn and Antoinette Sibley. Antoinette's memory links her so closely to the company by then that what greeting cards casually call 'the first day of the rest of your life' had come and gone for her literally months before she signed the piece of paper that made it official. As to money, all she says is 'I always remember getting my first ever wage packet. It was from my father for helping in the shop in Bromley, but I don't know how much it was for. This is where my memory lets me down.'

Everyone in a classical ballet company dances all the time, day and night, except the anonymous girls in the corps de ballet who usually dance more. Everyone who signs a contract is automatically committed, for as long as he can endure it, to a bone-breaking, mind-numbing daily schedule that reads something like this: class 10:30-12:00; rehearsal 12:00-1:00; lunch 1:00-2:00; rehearsal 2:00-2:30; rehearsal 2:30-3:30; rehearsal 4:00-5:00; half-hour call for performance 7:00; performance 7:30-10:30.

Since Royal Ballet rehearsals are held in various studios at the school and the theatre, time must be allotted for travelling between Barons Court and Covent Garden, as well as for costume fittings, wig fittings, physiotherapy and massage, not to mention dentist appointments and private lives. Principals may only perform a single ballet in an evening, but the corps is often onstage in two or three, or in two or three acts of a long work where they are 'on' even when they're only dressing the stage and not dancing. They eat after a performance, bathe, wash their tights and sleep. That's all. Try spending an entire day, twelve hours or more, standing up, paying attention, moving silently, exactly and on command, and hiding all signs of effort and fatigue—oh yes, a ballet stage is not a tennis court—and see how you feel by nightfall. Or simply think about standing up all day: dancers can't work sitting down.

Antoinette didn't have time to think about it. Like Alice, hand in hand with the Red Queen, she was running as fast as she could just to stay in the same place. In February *Coppélia* disappeared from the schedule, *Swan Lake* and *Cinderella* remained, and she entered *Firebird* as one of Kostchei's twelve wives and Ashton's coronation ballet, *Homage to the Queen*, as an attendant to the Queen of the Earth. In March, when *Coppélia* came on again, she appeared only with the Midday Hours. She stayed in *Homage to the Queen*, *Firebird*, *Swan Lake* and *Cinderella* and added the Sons of Morning in de Valois' *Job* to her repertory. In May she rotated through *Swan Lake*, *Firebird*, and *Coppélia*, where she left Act III and went into Act II as a peasant girl. At the Edinburgh Festival in August she joined the crowd of Poor People in MacMillan's *Noctambules* and became a guest in Cranko's *The Lady and the Fool*. Remembering her in those crowds, Winifred Sibley smiles and says, 'She used to say, "Are you coming along to see it? I'm the fourth coming on, on the left, and I'm next to so-and-so," you know, all this description. And I thought,

"You don't imagine that I shan't recognize you?" You could spot her, of course, even at that time. When they were all doing the same thing, you could point out the different girls because they were all doing it slightly differently. But when they did completely different things individually, then you could see a resemblance to certain girls. Then they did look alike—it was surprising. Shirley Grahame often looked like Antoinette because she had the same colour hair; Shirley's tended to be rather more red, but under the stage lights you didn't notice that quite so much.'

The schedule changed again in the autumn. By September Antoinette was back with the Midday Hours in *Coppélia* and on with the corps in *Les Sylphides*, as a peasant girl (Act I) and swan (Act II) in *Swan Lake*, and as a child (Act I) and a Wili (Act II) in *Giselle*. By December she was listed as one of eight Maids of Honour in the Prologue of *The Sleeping Beauty* and with the 'Nymphs, Village Maidens, Peasants, Courtiers, Heralds'.

It was the first payoff for all the years of effort and repetition. Her muscles knew how to remember; endlessly translating a few brisk words and gestures into proper *enchaînements* had taught her how to learn as well as how to move. And what she couldn't learn in the classroom—which was much of anything about performing—she couldn't help discovering as she watched from the fringes of the stage action or from the wings.

To commemorate the post-war reopening of the Opera House ten years earlier, in February 1956 the company presented *The Sleeping Beauty* for a solid week, with a different Aurora each night. Margot Fonteyn, Violetta Elvin, Beryl Grey, Nadia Nerina, Svetlana Beriosova and Elaine Fifield inhabited the role in turn, each transforming it with her own style and manner. Revelling in their distinct personalities, Ashton increased the list by one, Rowena Jackson, bestowed a partner on each ballerina and choreographed *Birthday Offering* for the company's twenty-fifth anniversary celebration in May. Known backstage as 'Seven Brides for Seven Brothers', this glittering *pièce d'occasion* paid loving tribute to de Valois by distilling the noble classicism and glorious individuality of the dancers who then led her company. Later the same year her achievements received an even greater tribute when the Queen decreed that the Sadler's Wells Ballet should henceforth represent the nation formally as the Royal Ballet.

What an education for a young dancer, to be part of a company that could celebrate such a past and present and move forward so confidently into the future. The active repertory blazed with the classics of two centuries and with dancers of intelligence, maturity and amazingly varied qualities. Every youngster in the corps de ballet watched and listened and learned.

'But I never, ever, thought of myself in relation to what I saw on the stage,' Antoinette insists. 'If I enjoyed something I didn't think, "Oh, I'd love to do that," or "I'd love to be that." Never. It's really been like that all my life, which is why I went to Sir Fred when I was put down to learn *Daphnis and Chloe* and said, "I can't do this because I just can't see anybody fair dancing it." I'd only ever seen Margot do it, and to me she was perfect. Which is when he said, "Have you ever read the original Longus? You'll see she's fair." And when I read the book I found she was fair and sensual, so then I thought, "Maybe I can do it my way." But it had been the same from the beginning. I never saw myself in any of those roles, not even as a fairy.

'If ever I see anything well done by one particular person, I can't imagine myself doing it. Which is why I've been so fortunate in having so many roles created *on* me, because otherwise I don't think I would have got on very far. Mind you, I'm exactly the opposite with roles created by me: I'm very possessive of those. I think *The Dream* is *my* ballet! Of course other people have been wonderful in my ballets, but I still think of them as mine.

'So I didn't want to be a ballerina. Although I was doing all this hard work and although I loved dancing by now, I never thought of myself as Odette, as Aurora. I never saw myself in any of these roles. Miss Edwards and Margot and Alicia Markova and Pavlova were all the same sort of perfectionist people, and although these were the people I admired, I couldn't in any way relate this to myself. It wasn't until Pamela May came along as my teacher that I thought, "Aha. If she's a ballerina then I know I can be a ballerina." Because she wasn't perfection, she wasn't dressed all elegantly without a hair out of place. She came with long red fingernails and a cigarette in her mouth, a bit late one day or early another, always *comme ci, comme ça*, very casual, very womanly. And I thought, "That's it. That's how I see it." And when [Galina] Ulanova arrived, she got off the plane in Manchester, or somewhere dreary and she had a mackintosh on and no makeup! This was completely unknown in my experience of ballerinas. Always up to now they were dark, elegant, amazingly groomed, as if they'd stepped out of Vogue. Then Ulanova comes onto the scene, and she's fair and makeup isn't even important.

'Violetta Elvin also had a great effect on me; again, she was so glamorous but in a very womanly way, not the perfection of Margot or Markova, but glamour for glamour's sake. I very much remember Violetta's last performance at the Royal Opera House. It was the end of the season before we joined the company and it was *The Sleeping Beauty*, which was not a ballet she was particularly suited to—if only it had been a *Swan Lake*. But I loved Violetta as a person and I learned a lot from her. Of course I kept up a relationship with her; Michael and I used to stay at her husband's hotel in Italy on our holidays.

'I was very lucky with ballerinas, always. I've had nothing but a great deal of help from them since I was a baby in the company. Beryl Grey was most encouraging when she came and danced with us as a guest, and I became very good pals with Fifield, even from my very first tour, up to the Edinburgh Festival in '56. She was a junior ballerina, but what a ballerina; she'd been at the top of the other company and one of my stars because I'd always watched that company. She sat with me on the train and we used to play cards and drink Advocaat—that was her favourite. Well, to be playing cards at that age with a ballerina but to be treated as an equal . . . I took that to be a great honour.

'It must have been not long after that that I became friendly with Svetlana, which is a friendship I treasure and that's lived all my life with me—we still speak on the phone at least once a fortnight. She gave me classes and helped me back after my cartilage operation, and I've gone to her for coaching since I've been back this time. I think she was a unique talent, as was Lynn. And if you think of it, Svetlana wasn't in the Margot mould either. She was someone I could identify with.

It's so stupid—why should I? But I always have to do this, even with roles. I have to find my own way, and if I can't see it I don't particularly want to do it. I don't want to be a second somebody else. But when I saw all those other people I realized there were other kinds of ballerina and I would fit in somewhere.

'The first thing I remember about the Bolshoi is seeing these pictures of Ulanova arriving at the airport. Suddenly there appeared this Ulanova, who looked old—I don't know how old she actually was, whether she was my age now—and who was the antithesis of everything I had been taught to expect of a ballerina. And this was just from the photographs.

'We were dancing at the time—it was the autumn of '56—in Croydon, and they were rehearsing Romeo late at night at Covent Garden prior to their opening the following night. We were invited to watch their final dress rehearsal, so our whole company travelled back to the Opera House after our performance; I suppose we got there about 11:30 and their rehearsal was in full swing. We crept into the stalls circle as the balcony *pas de deux* was going on—it was Raissa Struchkova and [Alexander] Lapauri, her husband, doing it. And then at the end this little old lady in the stalls got up, short greyish hair and wrapped in layers of wool—we all thought she was the ballet mistress. She went up and chatted to them both, and then she went up on the balcony and said something to Yuri Faier, you know, the amazing blind conductor. And then she took off her woollies and in front of our very eyes, no makeup, no costume, no help from theatrical aids whatsoever, she became fourteen years old. I've never seen any magic like that in my entire life. It was the sort of miracle that it is to have a baby, that minute when the baby's born and you realize what's actually happened—to you, to the baby, to your husband—this God-given thing. This was exactly the same, theatrically, to me. We couldn't believe it. I have no idea who she danced with; my eyes didn't leave her for one second. I can't tell you anything else about her because everything was incidental to the fact that this was Juliet and she was fourteen years old and she had no costume, no makeup, nothing. How she danced I can't even tell you because none of that was relevant. This is where she was a genius.

'Then later she did the scene where she runs off for the

67

potion. Well, we all screamed, shouted, jumped up and down—I've never known anybody as excited as we were. We had been told not to applaud or anything, but there was no way we could stop. We'd been through all her agonies, all her traumas, and then she suddenly made up her mind. And she ran across that stage so fleet of foot, so impassioned that this was the final solution, that we all just shouted. She was very surprised because she hadn't known anyone was out front, so after she'd done it she popped her head round the wings and looked.

'I never thought she did that run across the stage the same again. I think we took that moment from her. Once something has been said and everyone's brought it to your notice, it's awfully hard then to repeat it quite the same. But I'll never forget it, and every time I did Juliet myself, I saw this vision in front of me of what she had done. At least I did in the rehearsals: in the performance I was carried away with *my* thoughts. It was quite extraordinary, so moving, and for me the whole idea of dance became quite a different thing then.

'It was such a natural way of dancing. You'd never think you could do anything like that, but just to see what *could* be made of dancing, in a naturalistic way ... Not like the beautiful pictures one had seen of Pavlova, not like Markova, this light, ethereal feather. Or Margot, with her figure and her musicality and everything about her so perfect. There wasn't much perfect about Ulanova, quite frankly. She didn't look particularly beautiful, her figure wasn't that wonderful, she certainly wasn't elegant. All the ideals that one had so far fixed in one's mind went by the board that night. This was somebody who was totally ... well, natural is wrong, because it isn't. It's an illusion of naturalness.

'And the next thing I saw her do was Giselle. Here she was with her hair in bunches, her shoulders a bit humped—it sounds cruel, but they weren't down—and she cut the variation. But again, the point of the performance was none of those things. It was the most delicious interpretation, quite modern. Nothing to do with the Romantic era that I'd been brought up to believe in—she could have been a peasant girl today. Amazingly shy, so charming, absolutely eye-opening. I was bowled over by her. And I actually met her, for God's sakes. We all went up and shook hands, probably after their first night—that's all. I just remember the peaceful expression of her face. I found her entrancing.

'The *Romeo and Juliet* was the first production we'd seen where the most minor character was as important to the artist doing it as Juliet was to Galina Ulanova. The little page boys, all the people in the market scenes, they were all *stars* to themselves; they gave 150 per cent of their concentration and verve. They did it as to die, everybody pulling their weight, giving these blood performances of their soul. Everything they had, they gave. And the funny thing was she did so many things we'd all been told not to do. The shoulders were raised and she didn't have a line, but she was such a personality in her own right. Not *her* as a personality, that's wrong, but the role she was performing was such a personality. You never thought, "This is Galina Ulanova performing Giselle." This *was* Giselle. There was no other interpretation at all once you were seeing her.

'The *Romeo* was the Lavrovsky production which overwhelmed us because, remember, there wasn't another *Romeo and Juliet* production around at the time. We were all one in our admiration. Whenever we weren't on in Croydon, we'd be there at Covent Garden, standing, watching or watching a rehearsal.'

When the Bolshoi left London after three weeks of inspiring performances, the Royal Ballet completed its tour to Coventry and Oxford and then settled down in the Opera House for a long winter season which twirled the corps de ballet through a kaleidoscopic schedule of rehearsals and performances as parts of the repertory changed nearly every month. Antoinette appeared with two groups in the first performance of Cranko's *The Prince of the Pagodas* on 1 January 1957, and with three groups in the third performance. In February she was one of three Naiads in the three-act *Sylvia* and one of Sylvia's eight attendants. When Ashton's *Les Patineurs* was revived in March she danced in the *pas de huit;* in May she went into Balanchine's *Ballet Imperial* and Cranko's *The Shadow*. By June she had become one of Aurora's eight friends in Act I of *The Sleeping Beauty* and often danced as a Maid of Honour and with the corps de ballet as well.

The company launched its fifth American tour, the longest to date, on 8 September. Twenty weeks and eighteen cities later, Antoinette had had her first taste of life 'on the road', which would eventually take her below the equator, behind the Iron Curtain, before the crowned heads of Europe and into theatres around the world.

'I went to New York for the first time ever in '57. The company was doing *Cinderella* for television, so all the people who were involved just flew to New York—can you imagine this today?—purely to make the film. We had no performances; we just went for that. All I was was the vision that ran across the back and dropped the shoe, Margot's vision, and I had to wear black hair. I got more nervous for that, I think, than for the Autumn page, where I had to throw the bloody leaves. I don't think I was an Autumn page for the film; I only remember going for the vision.

'Then every two years we started in New York and went right the way across America and back through Canada on our own train. We'd always get into the train after a performance; we'd first have a meal and then climb aboard, and at 1:00 or 2:00 off we'd shunt. I never slept. I can't sleep on anything that moves. I need a bed, and I need a bed that's still, so for five months on these tours I never slept properly until I got into a hotel room. But I loved it, and you can imagine the fun. Doreen Wells and I were on top bunks, and we got up to all kinds of tricks. We were very *femme fatale* and all the boys used to climb up into our 'lairs'. Talk about experience for an eighteen-year-old, getting to know the world and about things. You soon learned on those five-month tours.

'Everybody was on our train, it was like a circus. It wasn't just the dancers; it was the musicians, the propmen, scenery, electricians, wardrobe staff, everyone travelled together, all of us, playing cards, reading, eating. It was like a moving town, and you got to know people as you moved around, sat with different people at different meals, flashing past the country-side. It was very romantic, albeit one didn't sleep for five months, and we really did see the country. To go through Connecticut and to Philadelphia, in the fall, is something you'll never forget. Who else has a chance to travel across the whole of America on a train? Then to go from Chicago to L.A. took us three days, and we'd stop in the desert and get out just to use the legs. It's a terrible thing that trains like that have died out.

'It's funny how little one can remember of the performances on the early tours, though I must have been given quite a bit to do. My pals were Doreen, Petrus Bosman, Graham Usher, Gary Burne, and I can remember going out to see places that they'd arranged. I've been lucky all my life always to be with men who have been frightfully energetic in organizing things. Left to myself I'd never do it, and Anthony's a bit like me. In latter years, if we weren't being entertained at a reception, we'd always go back to our hotel room. We both adore the telly, so we'd have that on and just slouch down in front of it, having our meal.

'I remember at receptions the food was always gone, because the audience and other guests arrived before we did and they always ate it before we came. They never think of the dancers. But there was always a drugstore, you could always pick up a sandwich and a milkshake. And another thing about those tours: it was the thing, if you were going out, to look smart, and all of us wore hats and gloves—remember, it was '57 or '60. It would be very bad if you didn't show up at the airport in a wonderful hat and gloves. But one was so young in the company. There were so many people who were above you and who were on display. We weren't important—we were the babies.

'We had the most wonderful company manager, Michael Wood, very knowledgeable, and every time we would arrive in a new town I would ask if he could take me to a museum or an art gallery. Goodness knows how I used to walk round, being so tired, but one must have been so inspired. I was frightfully lucky with that—he taught me such a lot. I was also lucky at home with the opera, my other passion. An elderly man used to take me, Mr George Swift. He was a ballet fan but opera was also a great passion of his. He'd send me the programmes before we'd go so I could read all about it. I was exhausted because I was on every night, but when I wasn't dancing I was there at the opera, sitting up in the gods on those wooden benches without any backs to them.

'Obviously in more recent times I would go places on tour with Anthony or Derek Rencher. In Munich, Anthony and I went around to all the castles. We had to learn Cranko's version of *Swan Lake*, which was frightfully hard, completely different from ours, and we thought instead of having two rehearsals we'd better learn it in one. That would give us one free day to rush round all our castles. Of course New York's different. One would live in the shops and one's there longer—it's a home from home in a way. But all these other places I'd just eat in the hotel and on with the television and go to bed because one's so tired.

'You see, Lynn and Merle [Park] and I, on those later tours, had a very exhausting and responsible time. The top ballerinas were flashing forward and back; Margot, Nadia, Svetlana would do so many months and go back, but we were literally the ones that held it all together, and it was months and months of gruelling work. I can remember the three of us going to ask [David] Webster for a raise because of all of this, and how nervous we were to go and ask, and honestly I don't think he knew who we were. We were too nervous to go to him alone—in those days you never said boo to a goose—and yet we'd been the backbone of the whole tour. But that was later. In those early days one wasn't doing important roles; it was travelling all the time and not sleeping and partying, burning the candle in every direction.'

Back home in London, even Antoinette's conception of home was beginning to change. Keeping their shop in Bromley, her parents had moved to Downe, where Charles Darwin lived for forty years, and taken a flat in Down House, where he had written *The Origin of Species*. 'I must have been going home every night after performances to Bromley—I had no place in London—but Downe was impossible. You couldn't get there directly; you got a train to Bromley, then you had to wait for a bus to Downe and then walk to the other end. One of my great friends when I came into the company was Gary Burne, who is dead unfortunately. He lived at Barons Court and I stayed on odd occasions with him, and he said, "It's ridiculous, you travelling around like this." So he talked to *his* friend Rosemary Winckley and somebody had left her flat; I think Patricia, her twin, had left to marry Clive [Barnes], and Gary said, "Maybe Antoinette could take her place."

'There were four of them: Patricia, Rosemary, Joyce Tinlin and Sheila, who was head of the flat, head girl so to speak. Gary asked Sheila and she said, No, she'd absolutely hate a ballet dancer, all those wet tights hanging up and the strange hours. I remember very well walking down to Downe, to the village—I don't know why. Maybe we didn't have a phone in Down House—to make the phonecall to see if it was going to be all right for me to stay in this flat, and how excited I was because this was really my first flat as a grownup.

'Anyway, Sheila relented in the end so I went to stay in Jacob's Well Mews, just off George Street, a wonderful little mews flat. Rosemary was in the sitting room, I had my own room and Sheila and Joyce had a *tiny* room, where you could literally just squeeze in two beds, which we all had to troop through to go to the bathroom and the loo. But as they were never in, it didn't matter. Rosemary was my friend of the bunch because I never saw the others; they were out on the town every single night so they came in long after I did, and they were up and out to work before I got up in the morning. And then after a certain time Joyce went back to Canada and that's when I got to know Sheila. We got to be very good friends, and she's still my best friend now.

'She's probably the first person I ever really confided in and developed my ideas with. She was my anchor then and has remained so all these years. She's been through everything with me, good and bad: husbands, lovers, my pregnancies, births—she's godmother to both my children—all my career ups and downs, injuries and all. I can trust her absolutely with her advice, and she is a great source of strength and security for me. We're in touch most days, we laugh such a lot together and she's been my special friend for thirty years.'

Those early days are still fresh in Sheila Bloom's mind: 'I remember very distinctly her ringing me, and I think I wasn't very nice because I thought dancers are always mad as hatters. I said, "Quite frankly, I just don't want a dancer, I just feel it's wrong for our flat." And then she said the magic words: she said, "But actually, I'm on every night and I'm away every weekend." And I said, "Fine. Come along then."

'The flat was dead centre, W.1, we paid £7.10s. in rent, and we were all terribly happy there. Everyone was doing their own thing, and Antoinette was sort of there and not there, which was wonderful in the beginning. I don't think I used to notice her very much. My first impression was that she was very tiny and very scared, tremendously quiet and shy and introverted. Mavis Osborn came once and stayed at the flat and I remember the two of them, stark naked, tippy-toe-ing around not to make any noise. They looked like a couple of field mice.

'The only way I can sum up our life there without being boring . . . Because of her schedule, Antoinette found it very difficult to cope with the household chores, to put it in the nicest way we can, and one night I came home to a whole lot of dirty dishes. I thought, "This is it," and I blew a fuse to one of the other girls. I said, "It's enough. I don't care what she is or who she is, when she's in this flat she's just another member of the flat. She's got a bad schedule? Well, I've got a bad schedule. So when she comes home, I'm going to tell her, 'Go on, get your things, out . . . or pull your weight.' "

'I was going out with someone and when I came home very late Antoinette was a bit upset. I said, "What's the problem?" and she said, "Apart from anything else, Sheebee, I get you tickets for the Garden and you never even bother to come." You must understand, she was very childlike in those days, unspoiled, sheltered, very timid. Eighteen going on fourteen. She was almost like a girl in a convent. So I said, "For heaven's sake, I never really thought much about it one way or the other." I was far too busy with other things and I had barely talked to her because, honestly, she *was* out every night and she *was* home at the weekends. I was about to go at her about this household scene when she said, "Would you come tomorrow?" She seemed upset that no one had been to see her, so I said, "OK."

'I went with Joyce, and she came on and did whatever she was doing—I'd seen her do little things but this was some-thing bigger. And halfway through I turned to Joyce and said, "Who cares whether she does the dishes or not? Let her *not* do the dishes." Because suddenly you thought, "This deserves her time." But I never said that to Antoinette; when she came home I said, "By the way, wash your dishes next time."

'In those days, she was scared spitless of everything, *every-thing*, and she was very vulnerable to everything. And gradu-ally, like we all do, she had to learn to grow another layer. She didn't learn that very quickly and I think that was one of the reasons her health took such a beating. Because she was so vulnerable, she took things to heart that would brush

74

off other people. Because she took some of it so deeply, it did have this terrible effect on her physical health, and it made her highly neurotic at times. And in a profession where the body is all, it was very difficult.

'Antoinette had no time for a social life when she first came to the flat. I was out and about, but she was literally on every night, and when she wasn't on she was in bed because she was so tired. She used to come home tired out of her mind and just go to bed, because in the morning she had to be up and in class, whatever happened. And then there was rehearsal and then there was lunch and then there was more rehearsal and then she'd go to Covent Garden and do a performance. And then she'd come back at 11:00 at night and go straight to bed. Bless her heart, I don't think she ever really stopped to think what she was doing.

'I was the most unpopular woman in London because as Antoinette got to be known she was asked out to various things. We'd made a lot of friends and we were all asked out after the performance, and before we'd go she'd say to me, "Sheebee, at about twelve o'clock, turn to me and say, 'Antoinette, don't you have class tomorrow?'" And I'd say, "I can't do that. Good God, I'm not your keeper," and she'd say, "No, no, I can't do it myself,"—this shows how frightened she was of people—"I can't. But you *must* do it because I've got to get up for class. And it doesn't matter what I say to you, you just keep saying, 'You must go. You've got a class.'" I got quite a bad reputation in that way for being over-protective, but what they didn't know was that it was a play-game that Antoinette had practised for weeks. And she'd often play it to the full: she'd say, "No, I don't want to go. I'm enjoying myself," and then I'd have to play the heavy again.

'Her career made her selfish, but you have to be selfish—you can't succeed and not be selfish. All the time you're thinking of your class and your rehearsal and your body. That body has to be controlled. It has to be in prime condition, it has to be looked after, you have to study it to know what it likes and doesn't like, like having a steak or not being able to eat certain fruits. And even if you're doing everything right you're going to be injured.

'Antoinette used to say "My foot is hurting" or my this is hurting, and one day I got a call from her . . . I was in with

75

my boss and the buzzer was going: "It's urgent, urgent, Sheila. On the other phone." I picked it up and it was Antoinette, and she said, "Sheebee, I'm in the middle of a rehearsal and I've come in to Beryl Dunn"—that's the physio-therapist—"and my foot is out and she can't do anything about it. You've got to come down here and put it back in again." I said, "But, darling, I'm right in the middle of . . ." And she said, "It's life and death. I've got a rehearsal. If I don't do it, I'm going to lose the performance." This is ab-solutely true. So I said again, "Would you excuse me for just a moment?" and I left my boss, rushed out, jumped into a taxi to Barons Court, rushed in the door, rushed downstairs to the physio and Antoinette was lying on the table. And she whispered, "Don't do it in here or she'll have a stroke." I said, "OK. Where?" "In the loo." So in we went. I said, "Quick. Give me your foot," and I gave it a twist. "There—it's back." And I ran—back in the car, back to the office in Piccadilly. And when I came home very late, there was a note on my pillow. It said, "Dear Sheebee, Thank you very much for putting my foot back in. P.S. It's out again now."

'It was hurtful sometimes when *I* might have come to a crisis. I used to come in after an unhappy evening with a boyfriend, but you couldn't talk to Antoinette because she had to have that rest. Once or twice I made the mistake of waking her up to talk! But her rest was sacred. I didn't understand it initially, but I did eventually. We also learned, as a flat, that you couldn't bring a boy back and create a noise, because Antoinette was sleeping. It became slightly difficult for all of us—if you were going with a chap it had to be at his place rather than yours.

'But she wasn't devoting all this to "a career". She wasn't thinking, "I'm going to make it. I'm going to get there." It was the day-to-day thing of getting through, of always thinking, "I'm never going to get through." And she *wouldn't* have got through, she *would* be ill if she didn't have that sleep.

'There was a period when she was finding the journeying difficult. She'd sometimes get a break of an hour or two but it was too far to get to Marylebone and back again, so she took a flat in Barons Court to be close, and she'd go there and sleep. The girl who then replaced her in our flat was a brilliant student who was teaching law at Oxford at twenty-three, and she was selfish in exactly the same way: everything was devoted to the future. We got in endless arguments about housework and once she said, "One day, Sheila, you're going to have a lovely tidy home, and I'm going to be called to the Bar." It did make me think of Antoinette.'

Antoinette was not only 'getting through'; for a girl in the corps de ballet she was doing very well indeed. The American tour ended in Montreal in January 1958 and the company returned to the Opera House in the middle of February. In March Antoinette appeared with the corps in *Sylvia, Firebird, Les Sylphides, Coppélia, Solitaire, Les Patineurs, Scènes de Ballet*, and for the first time as a Pirate Woman in *Daphnis and Chloe*, as the solo peasant girl in Act I of *Swan Lake*, and as Red Riding Hood in the last act of *The Sleeping Beauty*. She began attracting attention even before these tiny solos extracted her from the ranks. The critic Mary Clarke remembers noting her initially 'when she was a Lilac Fairy attendant, and all the students from the school, all those little green jobs, were packed at the back of the stalls circle, so excited, waiting to see her.'

'But look,' de Valois exclaims impatiently, 'one of the things people don't understand . . . I noticed this recently, with the French dancers from the Paris Opéra. They're in the corps de ballet, but they don't just zip their dresses up the back and go onto the stage. They dress themselves as if they were going to a party, and they go on as individuals in the roles they've got to do. It doesn't worry them if the one in front of them or the one behind has been told to behave in the same way, as long as they look good as *themselves*. This is something the less intelligent ones cannot understand, that the discipline of the corps de ballet is not a question of turning yourself into a dumb little machine. It's a tremendous development inside. The most flattering thing that can happen to an artist is to be exactly the same as everybody else, arms the same height and everything, and have someone say, "Who is that fourth girl?" *Not* because her arms or her legs have gone higher, but because of what she feels inside. I'm not talking about people who are going to be great dancers. Of course you pick them out at once in the corps de ballet.'

Antoinette sees her own departure from the corps from

quite a different angle: 'I was always so nervous being in the corps de ballet, which I'm sure is why I was taken out so soon and put as a soloist, and I forget things when I get nervous. I once got into the most terrible trouble. It was in the *Beauty* and it was Margot Fonteyn doing Aurora. Margot wasn't like Anthony and me, talking during a performance—it's very bad, but we always have done. Margot would never consider talking on the stage; it really was *verboten*. And there I was as a nymph, and I couldn't remember all of a sudden whether it was I who was supposed to set this line off to kneel or whether I had to take it from the girl at the end of the row. So after a while I thought, "I'm sure we should kneel now," so I knelt. Then of course the girl next to me did, then the girl next, and then the next, and I suddenly looked at the other side and they hadn't knelt. So I stood up again and we all started to get up. And then I thought, "Christ! Now we're up, *they're* going down," which was probably the right time, so down I went. And I got completely hysterical, which I do with Anthony, which is so dangerous. I don't just laugh: I shake with laughter. It's like being in church or, even worse, at a funeral, where the last thing you're supposed to do is laugh and you get completely hysterical. I was right in the front, absolutely collapsed with laughter, going up and down—it was like a Danny Kaye or a Charlie Chaplin film. And there was Margot, dancing through it all, and every time she passed she'd go, "Stop that noise!" Whatever she said, she *remarked* as she went by. And when we came running off, de Valois, Babs Phillips, Jack Hart, everybody was in the wings to give you the chop. Naturally they were furious.

'But I think this is why I didn't do that much in the corps. I was much better in a role by myself because I could use my own imagination, whereas in the corps circumstances either it seemed terribly funny or I was literally going wrong because I got so nervous. I was less dangerous on my own.

'I suppose I must have been competing against my own generation—Christine Beckley, Mavis Osborn, people like that—but I didn't think of it like that. My really competitive years didn't come till later when I came up against Lynn and Merle. But Lynn wasn't in our company then, she was in the touring company, and I wouldn't feel myself competing against Merle, who was two years older and had been in the company much longer than me.

'The first thing I ever had to do as a soloist was Red Riding Hood, which I went into like Method acting. I thought every possible thought the little girl could have. And apparently it was frightfully funny because when I did do it—with Gary Burne—Babs said I looked like Red Riding Hood's grandmother. My face is so small and I had all these fair curls and this big red hood, and for all the thought that had gone into it, you couldn't see me among the mass of curls. As you know, all she does is nothing, but that was my first ordeal.

'Then the next soloist role I was given was the Crystal Fountain Fairy. John Hart took the call in the studio and it was the most nerve-wracking thing I'd ever had to do in my life, but I came through that and the whole company clapped me. It's so rewarding when the company applaud you.

'I was doing it for the first time at the matinée performance, and on the day before Margaret Hill was doing her first performance. I'd admired her so much in the second company—she was first cast of *Solitaire*—and she was a friend of mine. Well, I was frightfully nervous when it came to my matinée, and I went and sat down with her in the canteen and I said, "Look, I'm awfully sorry but you'll have to do it again. I honestly can't go on the stage and do it. I'll have to go home now." I'd been thinking for hours, all the time I was making up, Should I? Shouldn't I? and in the end I came to know I couldn't possibly go through with it, I'd have to go home. I would have to say I was ill and she would have to go do it. But she said, "Don't be silly. I'll tell you how to get on. I'll just get you a drink, you have a little drink like I have a little drink and I know you'll be fine." So I had my first whisky before a performance—that started me off on drinking the whisky before every performance—and then I went on and did it. I did it completely my own way, and I was pleased with the way it was. It was good; I've always had rather good arms. And I always take things apart, and I worked out an elaborate story about the fountain to make it work for me, when I was the water and when I wasn't the water and when I was just looking at it. I loved doing this fairy.

'That was really the first thing I was noticed for, and then I was given the Bluebird *because* of that. And the Bluebird . . .

I couldn't understand why she was called Princess Florine and he was a bluebird, so I went along to the doyen of critics at the time, Cyril Beaumont, to ask about the story. Always on the notice board it was called "The Bluebirds", but it isn't at all bluebirds, and once I knew what it was about, that's how I interpreted it. He explained to me that the Bluebird was really a prince who'd had a wicked spell put on him that turned him into a bird, and she was kept up in the tower, as a princess still, by the same magician. The Bluebird came to rescue her, so he was teaching her how to fly to escape from the tower, which is why he's the one who's fluttering and then she repeats it, she copies him. She listens to what he's saying, she tries her wings, she's learning to fly.

'I never ever did Florestan; I know both the solos very well but I never had the chance to do it, which I would love to have done, because I was always doing the Bluebird or Aurora from then on. I also did the hoppy-hoppy fairy a lot, the Glade Fairy. I did the Bird Fairy at one time, I did the Vine a lot, and I was supposed to do the Lilac Fairy. I'd learned it and done it in rehearsals, but as my Aurora was supposed to be Beryl Grey I think in the end even Madam saw that it was ridiculous, because of my being so tiny.'

If the opportunity to dance these classical miniatures is one indication of a young dancer's development, what she makes of the opportunity is an even better one. There is safety in numbers in the corps de ballet; you can forget your steps or miss your cue and still recover without making a fool of yourself. But dancing a fairy in the Prologue of *The Sleeping Beauty*, or the Bluebird in Act III, you are all alone and fully exposed. For a few minutes, everyone in the theatre will concentrate his eyes and attention solely on you, and that includes your teachers, your colleagues, the administration, the critics, the public . . . everyone whose judgment will determine your future. You must execute all the steps without faltering or forgetting, mould yourself to the conductor's tempo even if it differs from what was set in rehearsal, fuse movement and reason so you resemble a convincing character rather than a smiling automaton. You may not have had a stage call—a rehearsal on the stage—so you will have to adjust your movements to the space, your eyes to the lights, and your ears to the orchestral setting of what's always been

Top: Aged about thirteen, with sister, Georgina

Below: Winifred and George Sibley and Georgina, 1977

Royal Ballet School,
1949. AS at far right

With Winifred Edwards,
summer 1955

Top: *Swan Lake* corps de ballet. AS leads centre row

Below: Corps de ballet, autumn 1957. AS fifth from right,
Christine Beckley third from right

Bluebird *pas de deux* with Graham Usher

Ballet Imperial with Pirmin Trecu

Top: *Harlequin in April* with David Blair at right

Below: *Coppélia*. First Royal Ballet School performance,
March 21, 1959

Top: Rehearsing *Swan Lake* with Michael Somes

Below: *Swan Lake*. October 24, 1959

Right: Outside Jacob's Well Mews

Le Baiser de la Fée

<u>Below:</u> Leaving for South Africa, 1960. AS, Michael Somes, teacher Errol Addison

Top: During a *Napoli* rehearsal

Below: Birthday Offering. Soloists (clockwise from lower left) Merle Park,
Lynn Seymour, AS, Georgina Parkinson

The Rake's Progress

Above and far right:
Swan Lake with Anthony Dowell

Right:
Ashton's *pas de quatre* in
Swan Lake

The Dream

OPPOSITE
Top: Rehearsing *La Bayadère* with Rudolf Nureyev

Below: Romeo and Juliet

Song of the Earth with Anthony Dowell. Third Song

piano music in the studio. In the darkness on the other side of the pit is a vast, staring audience, and the solos are not simple. Even the strongest technicians cannot simply toss them off, since their effect depends as much on musical nuance and dramatic subtlety as on individual steps.

Every dancer knows she must meet these demands but when you are nineteen, as Antoinette was in 1958, you don't yet know what it's like to be on stage all by yourself. Once there your choices are limited: you can make your mark or you can blow it. No one disputes that Antoinette Sibley made her mark. According to her close friend Svetlana Beriosova, who was then one of the company's principal ballerinas and an exquisite classicist, 'I was aware of her all the time. There was potential star quality from the very word go. I don't think she spent long in the corps, and in the smallest soloist role she danced, she always stood out. You knew straightaway that there was a ballerina in the making—you can tell. They've either got something or they haven't, a particular quality, and it eventually makes an artist-ballerina. Some ballerinas get there on technical merit alone, and others are all-round artists, which is what Antoinette is. And a great one now, a very great ballerina.'

The press was equally enthusiastic and even more precise. The *Dancing Times* review of her debut as the Fairy of the Crystal Fountain, at the 3 May matinée, commented on her 'interesting lyrical qualities and beautifully flowing line' and commended her for 'greater musicality and sense of phrasing than some of the older members of the company'.

Her delicate features and darting, sparkling style made her a natural for such jewel-like setpieces, but she also had years of preparation to draw on and lots of careful assistance. 'After all,' says Ailne Phillips with asperity, 'they're in the corps de ballet, they've seen all these big artists come on and do the roles and the solos. If they don't take something from them, when they're sitting on the stage for hours, it's no good, is it? And when they're given a solo, they get the freedom and if there's anything in them it'll come out.

'I did a lot of coaching, mostly in solos and in things I used to dance when I was young. Now if they're doing a solo, they all think they know what they want to express but they're not quite sure how to get it going. So you have to help them according to their physique; some have long arms, some have long legs, some are quick, some are slow. Depending on the dance, you have to bring out the best you can in that girl in that special lesson. Some will respond quickly; others will fight a little and say, "I want to do it this way." And I'll say, "I don't think it suits you that way, still, go ahead." '

Winifred Edwards had held their futures just as firmly in mind: 'I detest theatricality in the classroom. I think it's totally odious. You don't teach them how to act; you teach the instrument to play. You are the living picture within your own frame, and that's where you learn projection, by doing everything within the frame. You use, as Madam always said, your brain, your eyes, your movement. I'd try to teach them to dance *for* the audience but not *at* the audience. But you don't have to teach an Antoinette Sibley or a Lynn Seymour to express herself—she can't help it. It's completely instinctive.

'Antoinette's never been afraid of the stage. She's musical but not a prodigy, intelligent but not brilliant. Not Pavlova, not a genius. But somewhere in there is an inflexible determination, absolutely cloaked in a natural theatrical gift. People come to life on the stage—Ellen Terry, Bernhardt—and Antoinette saw her road and she followed it.'

Following that road through 1958, Antoinette continued to dance with the corps de ballet, adding the Red Pawns in *Checkmate* and the Enchanted Princesses in *Firebird* to a still lengthening list and appearing in the premières of MacMillan's *Agon* and Ashton's *Ondine*. She continued to dance Red Riding Hood, the Crystal Fountain Fairy and the Bluebird in *The Sleeping Beauty*, often performing the latter two roles in a single performance. When *Cinderella* returned to the repertory at Christmas, she found herself cast for the first time as the languorous Fairy Summer.

'She was given all the classical things to begin with,' Beriosova observes, 'but we all were, to begin with. But I sensed she could do other things as well because of her great musicality, her wonderfully supple body and her intelligence.'

Other people sensed it too, and one of them gambled boldly on his intuition in March 1959 when he revived a work at Covent Garden that he'd made for the Sadler's Wells Theatre Ballet eight years earlier. Selecting Antoinette for the central role, he exposed a piquant innocence in her dancing that her twinkling classical solos had never revealed.

'Johnny Cranko was the first person to give me a chance, after de Valois of course, so he's very special in my mind. He gave me a chance to prove myself. Well, how grateful can one be to that first person who has chosen you so other people can see what you can make out of a role? After that it's too easy: somebody else can say, Oh yes, she does do this or that well, but he gave me that chance *not* knowing. And it came with *Harlequin in April*, which had been created on Patricia Miller, David Blair and Pirmin Trecu. David and Pirmin, who were going to dance their original roles in the remounting of the work, were now stars in our company—I mean, David Blair was the dancer under Michael Somes, very important—so it was a real thing for him to give it to me.

'Johnny was the most wonderful, amazing man. He was built on enthusiasm and overflowing with love of the dance; it bubbled out of him like champagne. Just like Rudolf or Madam: when you spend half an hour with either of them you love it and you can think of nothing else that's important in the whole world but dancing. He was like this: he made dancing the most wonderful thing that it's possible to do. And he gave me such courage.

'I was frightfully scared at first working with David and Pirmin, but in the end they turned out such close allies of mine. Later on David was doing a whole series of *pas de deux* for television and he chose me for quite a few of them, which was a great feather in my hat. I'd done them on tour but not at home, at the Opera House, so I wasn't considered a ballerina here. I wasn't like the people above me who he *could* have chosen, so it was a big honour. And I got to know Pirmin very well. I adored him, and we would go to country houses and do things like the *Don Quixote pas de deux*. I can't even remember where, but I know the first time I did *Don Q.* was on one of these slippery ballroom floors in some stately home. But you can imagine the lack of confidence, the shyness, of my working with them at first, all of which Johnny was able to eradicate, because if anybody could give me confidence it was him, or Madam, somebody with that outgoing temperament.'

Although *Harlequin in April* was not particularly well

received, Antoinette came away from it in triumph. The *Daily Telegraph* said, 'Antoinette Sibley danced the dual role of Flower and Columbine with technical ease and a neat charm.' The *Manchester Guardian* said, 'Miss Sibley is so young and so promising that the pundits scarcely dare to talk about the achievements which may lie ahead of her.' Yet the lack of confidence she felt in the initial rehearsals did not quickly dissipate. In fact, she wrestled with some form of the same self-doubt right up to the day of her retirement.

'Antoinette's always been nervous of performances,' Beriosova grants. 'If she were in the backwoods of beyond she'd get nervous, because that's the kind of pro she is. That *is* the mark of a real pro, because they respect their audience and they want to give their best. She is always doubting herself, criticizing herself, swearing that the next performance will be better.'

Sheila Bloom adds, 'I always remember Johnny Cranko saying to her once, "Your humility about your talent is the most wonderful thing about you, but it's also the most destructive." She repeated that to me and she said, "I don't understand what he means. Do you?" Well, then I didn't but I do now, because she had no confidence in herself and still has none. She has more now because of Panton and the children, but she never thought she was good enough, and if you go on thinking that it does destroy you. She's always saying things to me about what isn't good about herself rather than what she has.'

If Antoinette was never convinced she could accomplish whatever was set before her, she was in a minuscule minority. De Valois certainly believed in her, as the honour she bestowed on Antoinette two weeks after the first performance of *Harlequin in April* emphatically proved. For the first time since the founding of the company in 1926, Madam decided to allow the students of her school to perform before the public.

Winifred Sibley supplies some background to the occasion: 'Throughout the school there was never a performance. Madam thought it was completely wrong. The girls got the wrong idea, the parents got the wrong idea, it all got far too important. What she did have was a Parents Day when you heard the choir and wandered around and saw their work, such as their paintings and their sculptures, but not their dancing. And I think she was very wise because if you're running a school where you expect at least a percentage of the children to become professionals, you don't want to foster too much . . . not self-conceit, but self-importance perhaps.

'Then after Antoinette became a fully fledged member of the company, de Valois decided that her students were sufficiently advanced to warrant putting on a show. She wanted to do the thing properly and she made the whole school wait until she felt she'd got the talent there and they could put on something worthwhile, not silly little bits. It was going to be a proper ballet, and she would borrow Antoinette and a young chap of her own year, Graham Usher, and they would do *Coppélia*'.

'That was the very first performance given by the school,' Madam recalls, 'that famous *Coppélia*, and the idea was to have the two leads done by two promising people in the corps that hadn't come out yet. That's what they should do every year, go down into the corps and take a brilliant girl that's got to wait for those roles. Never mind if she doesn't do it well; the critics will immediately get interested in her and watch her. Sibley was more than ready for it and so was the boy. They gave a lovely performance of it. I'll always remember that first *Coppélia*.'

So will Antoinette. 'We had hardly any time to get it on, just two or three weeks, and I was working with the company so I would always start rehearsing this at five or six at night. When I'd finished all my company calls, I'd just nip over to the school and supposedly get *Coppélia* on. I don't remember Madam ever telling me about it. If anybody had—and of course Graham Usher's dead and he would remember—it would have been Ailne Phillips, because she taught me in the company and she was in fact the person who rehearsed me in Swanilda. Peggy [van Praagh] must have taken us for some rehearsals as well; she did the production of it all and possibly did all the school side of it. That I don't know, because I didn't get to do anything with the school as the only people I really come up against are the Friends. Otherwise it's Graham, who I did rehearse with, with Babs, and Dr Coppélius. But I was mainly learning my steps. There wasn't much time.

'The occasion was simply wonderful. Probably if I'd thought about it, I would have expected it to be Graham and me. As they were going to use two people who had been right through the school, it really had to be us. I didn't accept that I'd been given an honour in that, frankly, nobody else had been right through the school from ten years old. An honour, of course, to do it, but I wouldn't have thought it was an unusual choice or because I was very good that I'd been given it, but merely that I was the only possibility in that respect.'

Miss Phillips argues today that 'You can be a *demi-caractère* dancer or a classical dancer, and you have to keep within your sphere. *Coppélia*'s a *demi-caractère* ballet and a classical dancer that does *Lac* and *Beauty* may not be suitable to do it. And a *Coppélia* person can't do *Beauty*. Antoinette's not that *Coppélia* type; she hasn't got the physique or the approach of a soubrette. It's in her makeup, in her body, to be a classical dancer.' Like Antoinette's self-doubt, this argument would crop up constantly throughout her career, and every time one person stated it, another would refute it just as vehemently. In 1959, however, Antoinette was still too young—and relatively inexperienced—for it to apply, and the press wasn't interested in splitting hairs. Reviewing the school performance in the *Financial Times*, Andrew Porter wrote that 'Miss Sibley is by general consent a future *Etoile*.' And Clive Barnes pointed out in *Dance and Dancers* that she 'seems to have inherited [Merle] Park's old position of *corps de ballerina assoluta*'.

'Her *Coppélia* was not a surprise,' Mary Clarke claims today, 'although Swanilda's not easy. But we were all bowled over by the fact, not that Sibley and Usher could do it, but that the school could. It was very difficult to get into the Royal Ballet school then; you were never asked and one saw very little of the kids. But you would not have known if you'd walked in off the street that it *was* the school. Madam wouldn't have risked it otherwise.'

You didn't have to be in London to know that the Royal Ballet had a fledgling ballerina waiting in the wings: anyone who opened a copy of the *Dancing Times* anywhere in the world could have told you. The legendary Tamara Karsavina had been writing occasional articles for that monthly magazine since the Twenties, first for Philip Richardson, the publication's founder and her close friend, and then for Arthur

Franks, who became editor after Richardson. In April 1959 she began a new series, her last one on classical technique, entitled 'The Flow of Movement', which ran in fourteen parts through the issue of May 1960. The model in the illustrative photographs was Antoinette Sibley.

'She was just beginning to get classical variations when Arthur Franks was planning that series,' explains Mary Clarke, who succeeded Franks as the magazine's editor, 'and after seeing her do that Crystal Fairy variation, I distinctly remember his excitement. "A classical dancer," he said. That's when he asked Madam for permission, and then Sibley was asked. The pictures were taken in Kathleen Crofton's studios, where the old Max Rivers studios were in Great Newport Street, and Katie Crofton was there for nearly all of them. She worshipped Karsavina, and the privilege of being there was like a thank you for using her studio. Arthur Franks was there and I was there, armed with the typescript, just checking that we were illustrating what Karsavina talked about in the text. But she did all the posing herself.'

Antoinette remembers that 'they wanted to have an up-and-coming dancer to do the illustrations, the right and the wrong side of classical ballet, you know, the correct and incorrect. So I worked with her a long time on that. The book [later made from those articles and another short series, entitled 'From the Classroom to the Stage', in which Donald MacLeary partnered Antoinette] is called *Classical Ballet*, and as I was thought of as the classical one coming up, my name probably would have been suggested, in that Lynn wasn't considered the classical ballerina and Merle at that time was considered more soubrette.

'So this is how my love of Karsavina all started off. Mary Clarke came to all the get-togethers and that tall man who ran the *Dancing Times*, and we always went out to meals afterwards—it was for me the most wonderful time. After this, Karsavina invited me to her house in Hampstead, and she cooked me a steak . . . she cooked it for me. I just worshipped her.'

What finally detached Antoinette from the throng of young 'promising' soloists once and for all was a series of events so remarkable that they read, in the end, either as clichés or as the first chapters of a ridiculously romantic fiction. Turning her thoughts back to those few months in 1959, Antoinette

87

doesn't immediately focus on the acclaim they brought her, but, characteristically, on the responsibility she felt, the impossible schedule and the hard work. It's not that she doesn't remember the glory, but that twenty-five years later she can place it in some perspective.

'Around that time I really had a big decision, because I was offered Rumer Godden's film *The Greengage Summer*, the role Susannah York then did. Maybe I would have been hopeless anyway, but who knows? I had the script and I was frightfully tempted but, funnily enough, more impressed by the car which arrived to take me to see the director. This amazing navy blue Bentley with a cream lining arrived for me outside Barons Court, and I was whisked off, either to Grosvenor House or to the Dorchester, and up into a suite to chat about the film.

'But I was literally on the threshold of everything. I did my first *Ballet Imperial* at twenty, and I had only three weeks to learn it, not months. And I was never taught it. We didn't have videos or notaters in those days; you learned it from the ballerina who was rehearsing it in front, you picked it up. I would have been down to be at Nadia's rehearsals, to be in the back watching. I had been in the ballet before—I did one of the side girls in the second movement—but this was the first ballet I was given to lead other than *Harlequin in April*—can you imagine? They're always saying how hard-working people are *now*, but we just didn't have the time to learn the things. We'd come back from the summer holidays, and we were doing it at the beginning of the season.'

Antoinette's first performance of *Ballet Imperial* fell on 25 August 1959; she would continue to dance the ballerina role, with ever greater authority and élan, throughout her career. But she never appeared in another ballet by Balanchine, although several graced the repertory as the years passed. Was she perhaps too small and light for his lean, sharp style, too flowing and lyrical, too 'English'?

Ninette de Valois dismisses that speculation with one of her own: 'I think Balanchine could have made a Balanchine dancer of her. She was very well made and of course he loved well-made girls. But I don't think she'd have liked it; I think she had more to say and feel. She was a really good little actress and he didn't want that. I think she could have done it, but of the two of them, she might have been the one who found she wasn't getting enough out of it. His is a very different school of thought.

'But, oh yes, she would have been a great dancer in America, I'm quite certain of that. If you're going to be a great dancer, it doesn't matter what school you go to, you'll still be a great dancer. Like a singer: if you've got a great voice, whether you come from Italy or Russia or France you'll be a great singer. But I think she was in her element in England, frankly, because she had a versatile repertory.'

'And I think it was because of my success in *Ballet Imperial*,' Antoinette continues, 'that de Valois called me to the office and said would I, in a few weeks time, do *Swan Lake*? On tour, in Golders Green. I said, "How can I learn the whole of *Swan Lake* . . . ?" not just the white act, this is the whole ballet. And she said, 'I know this is very short notice, but Michael Somes has very kindly said he would do it with you.' Well, he was the *premier danseur* and such a wonderful partner, and of course I jumped at it. Who wouldn't?

'But I also didn't know how the hell I was going to get it on in those few weeks. Particularly because, although I had been in *Swan Lake* all those years, I have never, from child-hood, learned anything from watching because I never envis-aged myself in any of these roles. Although I'd been a page and a swan and I'd seen Margot Fonteyn and everybody a million times, I didn't actually know it because I'd never anticipated that I'd ever do it. I hadn't thought that far ahead—I never think that far ahead. So I did actually have to rush to learn it, and I learned the whole thing in just two weeks. When I was a swan I'd be looking at the principal, and I'd run round asking people what comes after this and what happens around there. And the *pas de deux* Michael Somes taught me as I went along.

'We were on tour so I would have to come in at 8:45 or 9:00, do a barre with Michael and rehearse up to the 10:15 class, and then I was involved in the calls all day. And in the same two weeks before it I had my first *Coppélia* ever with the company; I'd only done it before for the school performance. I had to get that together, a full-length ballet, which was hard cheese, and then I also had to get it together to do my first *Fête Etrange*, which was a week before my *Swan Lake*. I would have been learning *that* at the same time I was learning *Ballet Imperial*, because we knew that was coming on the tour, and at the same time rehearsing *Coppélia*. Unfortunately the first *Fête Etrange* was a complete disaster because of the nerves I was going through preparing for the *Swan Lake*.

'One always rehearses three or four different ballets together anyway—that wasn't the problem. The problem was the proximity of the performances and that they were all important first things. It's nothing to do those three ballets if you've got them on already, but this was my first ever *Swan Lake*. And *Coppélia* is a hard ballet. And I think *Ballet Imperial* is the hardest classical ballet. That, *Scènes de Ballet*, *Bayadère*, these are really hard classical ballets. It's not like getting on in your first big ballet in . . . well, even *The Dream*, where you can get lost in the interpretation. *Ballet Imperial*, you've got to get up there and just perform these really difficult steps.

'And then I had longed to do *Fête Etrange* because I'd never been given the chance to do acting roles. My first thing was Bluebird, my next first thing was *Ballet Imperial*, *Swan Lake* coming up . . . I hadn't ever been given the chance to do a mood ballet or a dramatic ballet. So the one thing I really didn't want to go down the drain, which *did* go down the drain, most definitely, was *Fête Etrange*, something I'm actually very suited to. It's the most beautiful ballet, sheer poetry, lyrical, not classical at all. Think of Beriosova and you've got it. It was something I personally wanted to achieve, but it was impossible to carry it off with everything else I had to do at the time.

'It wouldn't have been so bad if we'd been on at the Opera House, where we only appeared two or three times a week, but we were on tour outside London and on every night. *And* I was learning *Swan Lake*. I'm sure it wasn't the right way to do it, but we had a different way of looking at it in those days. We were so pleased with the opportunity, you just picked up what you could and did your very best. But I must have died a thousand deaths, and I think it must be why my nerves packed in on me a few years later.

'But I don't know which is the cart and which is the horse. Because now when I rehearse things, if I allow myself a lot of time I start getting bored halfway through. Whereas when I've only got a little bit of time, I'm better. I don't know whether that's because I've always done it that way because, all my life, never having the time I *had* to make myself get up and do it, or whether that's my nature anyway. But now, because I don't do so many ballets and I have to rehearse to keep my stamina up, my only way is to start early so I know that I know it and I know where the pitfalls are, then cut it out in the middle and then push myself hard again at the end. If I keep slogging through, day in, day out, every single day, not only do I get bored but it completely falls apart. I start forgetting the steps and I go quite crazy.

'A few weeks for *Swan Lake* was obviously too short. It's not so much the technique because de Valois always told us that, for goodness sake, if you're on in other classical ballets, doing things like the *pas de trois* and *Coppélia*, the steps are the same—you were just putting them together in a different order. Classical steps are classical steps. In that respect she was absolutely right, although you do meet absolutely horrific things in the black act. The solo is the worst, the *pas de bourrée*, *attitude* step and all that. I always found it easier to do doubles, one and a half *attitudes* actually and then swizzle round the last bit, instead of the controlled one. And it was easier to do a double pirouette after the *renversé* in the middle step, instead of the *assemblé*. I had quite a reliable technique under me—I had to. I hadn't got time for it to fall apart. So it was a matter of getting the stamina up to do it, with the *fouettés* and all.

'Of course what was impossible in that time was to get an inkling of what Odette's about. And Odette is a role anyway that you only feel and know when you're in your thirties or forties. A young, ingenue reading of it doesn't work.'

'I partnered her only in *Swan Lake*,' says Michael Somes. 'I was well at the end of my career, but she was just starting. Antoinette's a very hard worker. You have the impetus to work because your career is ahead of you and you have yet to make it. And dancing on the stage and putting those steps to their proper use is not something everyone can finally do. You know, having gone to Sainsbury's and bought all the goods for the cooking, some people can't cook it. But she had an extraordinary combination of physique—the right shape, height and looks, which you start off with—and a marvellous ability to put it to good use. And she did have a good personality for dancing, for pure dancing and for classical roles. She had a good idea of presentation: *Ballet Imperial*, for example, she did very well because she could make those steps, which were not very much in themselves, look interesting by an artistic presentation of them.

'When she found that she could make an effect, possibly better than people around her, then your confidence grows and you begin, quite literally, to make your mark. You start out somewhere in the corps de ballet and then you're moved forward to the front line, and then even further forward. She had warmth on stage, she was friendly to the audience, never aloof. And she also had the inestimable benefit of watching a great ballerina like Margot, which sadly today they haven't got. That was always there, in front of you, and you had to fight against it, but having it there before you all the time also paid great dividends.'

In a certain way, such performances are meant to pass unnoticed, except by the company and the person dancing them. They give the dancer the opportunity to 'open out of town', to find—or fall over—her feet, to take her first tentative steps towards a role that, if she's lucky, she'll develop and refine for the rest of her dancing days. Antoinette danced her first *Swan Lake* in the London suburb of Golders Green at the matinée on 26 September 1959, with Michael Somes as her partner, and her second performance, with Bryan Ashbridge, on 10 October in Streatham.

'And then *Swan Lake* was completely off my list, because now we were back at Covent Garden and there was no way I was going to do it at Covent Garden. Then several weeks later, in London, Michael Somes rang me one morning. I was married to him subsequently but I wasn't married to him then and I didn't know him very well other than having danced with him on this one occasion and he'd rehearsed me. And he said, "You're on tonight." I thought it was a rather odd thing to say, because of course I was on that night—I was dancing the *pas de trois* in *Swan Lake*. He said, "Nadia's off and you're doing Odette-Odile." I really was absolutely shattered. I think I went straight back to bed, thinking it was all a nightmare and would go away. However, I went along later and rehearsed it, and that was that; I went on and did it that night. It really was a tremendous ordeal.

'And it was Margot who said I could use her rehearsal time— this is how long I've really known her. When I came to the call, of course the last person in the entire world I would have wanted watching *me*, stumbling through a rehearsal when I was going to do it in a few hours, was Margot Fonteyn. The prima ballerina assoluta and somebody I idolized . . . It was like God Almighty sitting there on the window sill at Barons Court.

'I always remember her with the *fouettés*, saying, "Don't worry, I never know that I can get through them. But when you go on, you just *know* that you're going to get through them and you just go *1-2-3, 1-2-3, 1-2-3*, with each one." And I've always done that ever since. But apart from it being an embryo state of a *Swan Lake*, for an idol to see a *panic* person trying to do an embryo state of a *Swan Lake* . . . it was horrendous. But she's never been anything but wonderful to me, all the way along in my career.'

On the day of the performance, 24 October, the *Evening Standard* quoted a spokesman for the Royal Opera House as saying, 'It will be the first time that a dancer who is not a ballerina has been given this role at Covent Garden. It is quite unprecedented but the company has been so impressed with young Antoinette that it was decided to give her this chance to see what she can really do. She is destined to reach the top for she is a brilliant girl and now her chance of a lifetime has come.' The critic A. V. Coton hazarded this guess: 'Although lower in the company's billing than half-a-dozen other soloists, Miss Sibley was probably chosen to fill this emergency because of the highly lyrical quality she displayed in all her dancing since first coming to notice.'

Sheila Bloom remembers the phone ringing that Saturday morning: 'I was in bed in the next room and I suddenly heard, "There's no way. I can't. No, no." I said, "What is it?" "It's Michael and he says Nadia's off and I've got to go on." And I said, "Well, fine. Then *go* on," and then all hell broke loose. I rushed round to try to get the *Swan Lake* record which, believe it or not, we hadn't got, and I ran around buying steaks because she always had to have red, bleeding steaks. And then I rushed around and got her shoes, because she hadn't got the shoes, and of course I put the shoes in with the steak and the blood came out of the meat onto the ballet slippers. Oh, we got it out, but there was a hell of a lot to do in that day: "I haven't got the ribbons" and "The ribbons don't match my shoes" and "What about the tights? I need some tights. My tights are too white," and then dyeing them in tea to change the colour.

'It was a madhouse. She had to have a bath, so we turned the music on in the bathroom and talked it through while she was in the bath. She'd say, "Sheebee, what do you think? How do you think she feels when she comes on? How do you think she should come on?" She didn't want to be like anybody else. And then of course Michael was wonderful because he took her for rehearsal; we got her to the studio, and he was endlessly patient going over it. By the time the performance came she was . . . highly strung, to say the least, but the minute she steps on she's different. I went out to the front and I knew she was going to be all right the minute she stepped on. Then she was composed, because her head had got control.'

'It was very much a last minute press,' Mary Clarke recalls, 'it must have been. It was last minute for them so it was last minute for us, but everybody got in somehow, by hook or by crook. The fact they got the press in on the Saturday night—and *Swan Lake* is always a sell-out—there was no question they wanted us in. I think I cancelled a dinner engagement to go, and I think I was in a box. It was an overall triumph without question. She did more than get through it. It was one of those evenings where there might have been little blemishes, but it didn't matter.'

'All the time you're searching for the next generation,' explains de Valois. 'You don't ever say "I've got to have somebody who looks exactly like . . . " somebody else, or "I must find someone for those four ballets." You can't do that. You choose them entirely as individuals at the beginning, because their first appearance in a ballet that's been danced by somebody else will be quite a revelation from a different angle. And that's very important.

'But I'll tell you how much they do fall into categories: sopranos, contraltos and mezzo sopranos, if you go into the music world. We have our classical, *demi-caractère* and character dancers. You can't help but see it. It's in their build, it's all physical, basically. The *demi-caractère* dancer can go both ways; they can be a character dancer or they can be classical—they're very lucky. But pure classicism is like a prima donna with that great high note no one else has got.'

Four

'Becoming a ballerina is a very long-term job . . . Charm and
youth and talent will often ensure the success of a first performance and win the encouragement of applause and good notices.
But afterwards there must come, in Karsavina's phrase, "the
ripening of the intellect." '   *A. H. Franks*

'I was front page news. On the Sunday morning after the
performance at the Opera House, about twenty-five newspaper people all descended on my house in Downe. It really
was that "star overnight" business, "star is born" time, crazy.
It was a big strain for a young girl because of course de Valois
hated stars, hated people being promoted like this.'

'It was a madhouse,' Sheila Bloom agrees. 'We couldn't
get in or out of the mews all week because of the photographers. They wanted to know who she went out with, what
she did, the usual stuff, and they took pictures in the house
of Antoinette actually washing up—which was novel in
itself—and they pursued her. I was driving her to Barons
Court because she couldn't get on the subway because of the
photographers. It was murder.

'Madam wasn't very pleased about it, because in those days
the policy was that it was the company and not the individual
that mattered. I think they felt she had courted that publicity,
which she hadn't at all, bless her heart; she'd just gone there
and done what she had to do. When the photographers came
along, yes, she'd pose, because she wouldn't not; if somebody
said to Antoinette "Sit there," she'd sit there. And they did:
they said "Sit there, and would you mind holding a pair of
ballet shoes?" Madam was absolutely furious, but it wasn't

Antoinette's fault. She said, "If anyone phones up, for God's sake don't say anything, don't speak, tell them I'm not talking to anybody," and we had to calm it all down.'

Antoinette waited six weeks after her triumph in *Swan Lake* to dance another full-evening ballet, which turned out to be another *Coppélia*, and then her situation changed completely. In keeping with the dictates of Madam's unassailable logic, she was neither transferred to the star dressing room at Covent Garden nor displayed on the cozy stages of the familiar suburbs, but hustled straight out of town, as far from the London limelight and the purple prose of the press as she could possibly get, all the way to South Africa. Don't imagine she was being punished. By sending her along with the touring company as a junior ballerina, Madam was rewarding her with the inestimable compliment of further responsibility. The twelve-week tour of Johannesburg, Durban, Pietermaritzburg and Cape Town would feature the great nineteenth-century classics—*Swan Lake, The Sleeping Beauty* and *Giselle*—for which the Royal Ballet had such a fondness and affinity, and focus, inevitably, on the ballerinas who took the leading roles. Those ballerinas would be Svetlana Beriosova, Beryl Grey, Nadia Nerina, Susan Alexander and Antoinette Sibley.

'She went for the experience of it,' Madam asserts briskly. 'She wasn't going to learn anything: she was going to get the performances. Remember, we only had three performances a week at Covent Garden. When she went to South Africa, Fonteyn and people like that were still with us, so it was very hard to get a young girl as much opportunity as you'd like to give her. She went to South Africa for the sheer experience of it, and repeated the performances she'd done in London. And she did her first Giselle out there and her first Aurora. Well, why not? As long as she *got* the *Giselles*. Oh, all those things are calculated, definitely. Let her get on with it in South Africa this year if she won't have a chance to do it with us until next year.

'You see, if you're a really good first dancer you are automatically given all the classical roles. And it's up to you, or life, or fate, to say which you're really the best in. Provided you reach the peak that's needed for all of them, you have a right to do them all. You obviously have one or two that you're better in than all the others. But it would be disastrous to say that someone's so wonderful in those two, she needn't do the other four—that's nonsense.'

In South Africa, Antoinette did everything. With no build-up and very little rehearsal, she was suddenly dancing the roles that form the foundation and the crowning glory of every classical ballerina's repertory and reputation. And dancing them not once or twice, not as a last-minute substitute, but night after night. 'But I was never given any time,' she sighs. 'I did have a whole month for *Beauty*, but then I was doing my first *Giselle and* I was doing *Swan Lake and* I was doing Bluebird *and* I was doing my first *Rake's Progress*, all at the same time in this month.'

Read that last sentence again. Now read the actual schedule: Antoinette made her debut as the Betrayed Girl in de Valois' *The Rake's Progress* on 18 February 1960, as Giselle at the matinée on 20 February and as Aurora in *The Sleeping Beauty* at the matineé on 2 March. In the course of the tour she danced six performances each of her new nineteenth-century touchstone roles, five each of *The Rake's Progress* and Ashton's *Les Patineurs*, in which she'd already made her debut in London, six *Swan Lake*s and ten Bluebirds, with a sprinkling of *Don Quixote pas de deux* and *Les Sylphides* performances tossed in for good measure. All together, it adds up to a matchless definition for 'coming of age'. Within two months of her twenty-first birthday, Antoinette began to disappear into Sibley, a name with its own resonance, a name that came to stand for an individual style and qualities of technical clarity and musical sensitivity as well as for a face and body.

Meeting the physical challenges and penetrating the dramatic and musical depths of those three great classical roles demands years of study and effort. Sibley's comments about them today, understandably, combine the notions of the girl who first attempted them with the mature insights of the dancer who lived with them, and through them, all her working life.

'Now when I got Aurora together in South Africa, I was very fortunate because for the first time in my life I was working with the same partner. Up 'til now, every ballet I did, I had a different partner every time I did a performance. My *Ballet Imperial*s I did with Pirmin Trecu, then my first *Swan Lake* was with Michael, then I went to Bryan Ashbridge

97

for the next one, then I came back to Michael for the one at the Opera House. But when I got out to South Africa it was simply wonderful because I danced with Desmond Doyle all the time. So for the first time I was able to consolidate something. I did the *Beauty* and *Lac* and *Giselle* on that tour, everything with him.

'As Aurora I felt completely steeped in the ballet—I always have done. Of all the ballets, I felt most at home in that as I was always standing on the stage, from a very young age. Before I became a fairy I was always one of the fairy pages at the back; I seemed to be on in every act. So I always felt happy doing *The Sleeping Beauty* because I'd done almost everything in it, and whenever I did a performance of Aurora I'd go and watch every variation through—I'd been practically every fairy and I felt very close to those variations.

'I went through various stages with *Beauty* because when I first did it I was a child and I thought, "What a silly role this is. She's just a goody-goody and there's nothing to get your teeth into. Just got to do the steps, which are fiendish, *and* do them four times." There was nothing to grasp onto. In *Giselle* you have got the wonderful story, but Aurora's nothing but good. She's been blessed with beauty, poise, a golden personality, all the gifts, and I thought this was just awful—you know, you go through a stage where the last thing you want to be is just good and lovely and right. And you do actually have to do the steps. At least with *Swan Lake* you can cover something up with a gesture or eyes, and in *Giselle* you certainly can—I mean, the story's more important than the steps in a way. But in Aurora the steps are the character of the girl, so you can't smudge anything. And everything is four times. It's mind-blowing! I find the first-act solo after the Rose *adage*, that long long solo, is the hardest solo I've had to do in any ballet. Whereas the last-act solo is my favourite solo in any of the classics, so one pays the other one off.

'But the more I did it, the more I understood the fairy tale. And I did understand, before I stopped doing *Beauty*, what an amazing ballet it is. You come to a time in life when fairy stories have their validity because you realize what a balm they are for everybody, including yourself. When you're living real life, and the older you get the corners you find yourself in are quite tough and hard, love-wise and career-wise or any other wise, it's wonderful to escape into a fairy story. The audience sees it as an escape, you see it as an escape, and it doesn't seem so silly. And that has to be some of the most splendid ballet music ever written, and the classical choreography is unbeatable. I could understand Aurora in the end.'

Svetlana Beriosova declares that Sibley's portrayal of Aurora, 'apart from Margot Fonteyn's, is my favourite of all times. A great Aurora—unsurpassed. It's a combination of her musicality, her radiance, her assured technique and something she emanates, that she gives to the public, which is obviously reciprocal. Sometimes I watch a performance and technically it's fine and the ballerina is smiling, but she doesn't shine. And Antoinette shone; she still does, in whatever she does on the stage.

'We got to know each other better on tour somehow than in England. I've shared a room with her on more than one occasion, and she's a perfect roommate, very considerate. And now we keep up our friendship and she remembers birthdays, Christmas . . . With so much to do, a family, a husband, a career, she'll still remember her close chums and come whipping around with a present. Generous to a fault, always, and it shows in her performing—it's part of the radiance.'

Following Sibley's first *Beauty* at the Royal Opera House, Mary Clarke wrote that 'Her Aurora, already enchanting, promises to be for her generation what Fonteyn's has been for mine. She dances it joyfully and beautifully.'

'When I was doing *The Sleeping Beauty* in New York once,' Sibley muses, 'I had these terrible calves and Margot asked me round to her apartment at the Navarro—I always longed to stay at the Navarro after going round that day. She lent me this hot water bottle thing to put on my calves, and she was arranging all her flowers after the first night; the doorbell kept ringing and the orchids would come in. I remember her saying, "I wish that I would have time . . . I often think how wonderful it would be to be a lady of leisure, to be just arranging my flowers." And she turned to me and she said, "Would you like to do that?" And I went, "I never really thought about it. Oh no, I don't really think so." But of course it's something I absolutely adore doing now, and whenever I do my flowers I always think of Margot.

'She very kindly taught me *Giselle*, not the second act, the first act. I can't think why. I don't know how that came about. I can't imagine that I would just go up and ask her, although she's always been very nice and pleasant. Maybe Michael was taking me for a call of it and she had the next call . . . I don't know. I only know that she showed me the whole first act. The steps I more or less knew, but it wasn't so much that—it was the mad scene and things.

'Margot's Giselle had always been one of the things I'd liked the best. I remember hoicking up from Bromley and queuing for hours to stand to see her *Giselle*s because they always said these were going to be her last ones. Oh, this was before I was in the company; I must have been a student. I found it so warm, so moving, and she looked so beautiful. Very vulnerable. I could believe in her totally. And yet one was always told about her *Swan Lake* or *Sleeping Beauty*, which of course were also wonderful, but she wasn't talked about like Markova or Ulanova for *Giselle*.

'I'd seen Markova do it, I think with the Pat Dolin company at Earl's Court, and I do remember her doing *Les Sylphides* as a guest with us, at the end of her career. She was as light as thistledown and very much the Romantic ballerina, a lithograph come to life. No hair was ever out of place, very gentle, and no effort whatsoever. She just took off; with no preparation she was up in the air. This is why I would love to have seen her do *Les Rendezvous* or the Polka in *Façade*, to see that quality. She had this phenomenal technique as well, but the main thing for me was it was like watching a Romantic lithograph.

'And then we come to Margot's Giselle, which was more—I see now—how I was going to do it, which isn't really thought of as "the right way". One thinks usually of the great Giselles as the Romantic ballerinas: Carla Fracci's a wonderful Giselle and Makarova, and of course Markova herself. You think of Ulanova, but this is on to my way of doing it, the naturalistic way. Margot wasn't quite as removed from the Romantic as Ulanova or the way I hoped that I did it.

'When I first did *Giselle* I did what Margot taught me, and it didn't fit like a glove—of course not—because it wasn't my personality. But even at that stage I realized that I wasn't a Romantic ballerina so there was no point my attempting to do it that way. And as I loved the way Margot did it, naturally I took in and tried to do as much as I could of what she had shown me. Sad to say, it was the ballet that I then didn't do for years because the policy was for the younger soloists-*cum*-young ballerinas only to have two full-length ballets to their credit because there were so many ballerinas. At the time we had five or six ballerinas, and then another layer, and *then* us. So although we were supposed to be really very good, we had to wait our turn.

'We were all given two: I was given *Swan Lake* first and *The Sleeping Beauty*, which was obviously the next one to do. Merle didn't do *Swan Lake* for ages; I think her two would probably have been considered the *Beauty* and *Giselle*. And Lynn never got the chance for the *Beauty* until she was I don't know how old—hers were *Lac* and *Giselle*.

'So I was never given *Giselle* with our company, but I did in fact do it. Madam rang me up at Jacob's Well Mews and said, Could I, the next day, go down and do *Giselle* with Walter Gore's company at Brighton, because Paula Hinton was ill? And I said, yes, but I haven't done *Giselle* in two years—this was April of '62—and I'd only ever done it those few times on the tour. And she said, "Well, it would really be helping out if you'd do it." So this was my first one in England. You see how my life has been? What short notice. She rang me the night before, and on the day, it was a Saturday, we were rehearsing either *Ondine* or *Napoli*, I can't remember which, on stage. I was in the whole call, and they wouldn't give me that off although that night I was doing my first *Giselle* ever in England. I did it with Alexis Rassine at the Theatre Royal—an important theatre, not any old where. He had been in the company but so much above me; he danced a great deal with Nadia.

'So I did my stage call—I was flogged out when I'd done that—and then around lunchtime I went down to rehearse in that tiny room next to the canteen where you can't do anything full out, and you certainly can't do any jumps for *Giselle*. Michael came down with me and I think Julia [Farron]. And then I went on the train down to Brighton—I suppose it was now four or five o'clock in the afternoon. I did my rehearsal on the stage with Rassine and the company, and then that night I did it. You certainly don't think about the role . . . how could you? When would I have the time?

'But I still didn't do it with our company. The first time I was given the opportunity was in New York, which again was very difficult because one's on every night in New York and really having to show our paces, because at this stage we weren't there every year as we had been when I was young.' To herald that long-awaited first performance, at the matinée on 10 May 1970, an usher at the Metropolitan Opera House greeted each of his 'regulars' in the Grand Tier with a daisy. 'I did it with Donald MacLeary, and again I had not much time to prepare because we were on every night in the big ballets. So it was silly, really, but in a funny way that's how I'd always been used to it. I did have to sink or swim.

'Lynn, for instance, was in the fortunate position of first being in the touring company, so she wasn't in the goldfish bowl of Covent Garden for every first performance she did. She was on tour, doing them three or four times a week, which physically was exhausting but nevertheless you had the rhythm of being on all the time and not being *pounced* upon, by all the critics, by everybody. The relief when one was away and could try things out a bit and experiment, knowing you had two or three of them coming up. Whereas we would have one performance or so a year, and we were judged on that. And also, when Lynn first did *Lac*, she just did the white act—she didn't do the whole ballet, bang, for her first one.

'I did have this to cope with, but maybe I'm better that way. With injuries, for instance, which I was so prone to, I couldn't possibly have done what I did do—like being off, coming back and two days later getting up and doing *Cinderella*—had I not been used, in the first place, to going on with very little rehearsal. And I probably wouldn't have been able to do what I did now, come back five years after the event and take on these roles, if I hadn't known that when I'd first done them . . .

'For instance, my first *Bayadère* . . . I think only Margot and Svetlana did it at the time, and maybe Annette Page—this was in 1965. Rudolf came to me and he said, "So-and-so's off. I'd like you to be the next one to do it." Which was a great surprise because he had been very slow in coming round to liking me. I wasn't even first cast for the soloists: I was second cast in the second solo, the quick one. So I was thrilled to bits that he was giving me the lead, and I was going to do it with him, even more wonderful.

'But I had to learn it that day. There was no such thing as a stage call, nothing like that. We were in Baltimore in some studio, wherever we'd been put up to do class. I don't remember going to Baltimore that often, so we wouldn't have had an established place to work. We had a rehearsal room rather like this room, one space with a smaller bit tacked on but with actual pillars in between, and I had the day with Rudolf to learn it through the pillars. And he wanted me to do I think it was Plisetskaya's version, doing the turns with the scarf to the right *and* the left. And instead of what I do now, finishing the double pirouette in arabesque *fondu*, which is what Margot and Svetlana did, he wanted me to stay up on pointe at the end of the pirouettes. So obviously we were doing it round and about, in and out the pillars, there was no room. I think it probably was the first time I'd danced with Rudolf.

'But just to finish off *Giselle*. So that was New York. And then, after all this, I was given the first night of Peter Wright's new production, which I did with Anthony at the Opera House the next year. This was completely my own version; having waited so long in between and had all my own thoughts over all these years of how I really saw the role, and not being able to put them into practice properly for New York because of lack of rehearsal time, now I actually had time to rehearse it and get it together. It was a success, but critically speaking not the kind of Giselle most people were looking for.

'It wasn't Romantic or old-fashioned, but I think I did a very good Giselle. My Giselle was simpler, more natural, than many, but I think I understood her. As I'd been ill quite a bit of my life and was a very nervous person and highly romantic, I feel I could have died of a broken heart. I never died on the sword: I died of a broken heart. Being a very frail person physically but full of vitality and life, obviously this was something I recognized in myself. I didn't have to act this. So *Giselle* wasn't a problem once I found my way of doing it; I had confidence in it, and also in my *Beauty*.

'But with *Swan Lake* I did have a problem. I asked Karsavina if she would teach me Act II and the mad scene from *Giselle*, and it was fascinating. The interpretation I have always admired most, which is why I never considered myself particularly wonderful in *Swan Lake*'—she said with a laugh—'was Beriosova's: wonderful extensions, expansive generous gestures, great warmth, such majesty and beauty. A curvaceous way of dancing, not a straight, simple way. Plisetskaya and Makarova could also get into these amazing positions, not strictly classical but with the wrists bent and the legs curved up. They had the length of limb and languorous amplitude to make these swan shapes. But of course my body was straight classical, with a simple line. I asked Karsavina to teach me their way and she quite rightly said it wouldn't suit me at all, and that she saw it as a rather pure ballet. I said, '*The Sleeping Beauty* must be the purest. In *Swan Lake*, surely the exaggerated line, the wrists and legs bent . . .' But she wouldn't, absolutely not. She said that wasn't right for me.

'So since nobody would teach me the way I wanted to do it, I did it the pure way, and I was always fighting against what I liked to see with my own eyes. But funnily enough, only the other day somebody sent me a video from America of a little bit of my second act and more or less the whole of the third act, from 1972. And on looking at it, I could see with my more mature eye that I wasn't as ghastly in it as I had always imagined. I was a seductress and vile as Odile, really powerful, and Odette I can see now was very vulnerable with just a simplicity of line. And there's something touching in a simple way of doing it, but it's like Bach: you can't really appreciate things like that when you're young. Now I see why Miss Edwards sent Lynn and me to see Margot do *Swan Lake*, because Margot was obviously the purest of us all. I didn't appreciate that either—isn't it maddening?'

'Those big roles demand the ultimate,' Beriosova declares. 'A hundred per cent. The lot. Technically you've got to be at your peak. You can't go for more than an hour and a half if you're rehearsing, say, *Swan Lake*, or you'd be flat out. Usually they allot you three-quarters of an hour or an hour, and if you go from the opening to the *pas de deux* to the variation to the coda to the end, *and* then you do the third act, the entrée, the *pas de deux*, the variation, the thirty-two *fouettés* to the end,

and then you do the last act . . . Well, by the time you've
gone through the *pas de deux* and all the bits in between with
Rothbart, you're exhausted.

'And it's a question of such incredible discipline, preparing
yourself mentally as well. You've got to live yourself into the
role for days in advance. Or if you have *The Sleeping Beauty*
on the Tuesday and *Swan Lake* on the Thursday, by God you
work on *Swan Lake* on Wednesday. You start towards that
performance; you can't just expect the 'Half-Hour' to go and
then suddenly there's an Odette on the stage.

'You weren't told you must feel this or feel that. It was
presumed that you *knew* what to feel when your partner kissed
your hand in Black Swan and you took it away, or when you
took the roses from the four suitors and you didn't really like
any of them and finally gave them to Mum—so much for the
suitors. We had a *répétiteur* whom we respected and admired,
but I think we had some leeway by way of interpretation.
You couldn't go bananas, but ballerinas are not that dumb.
One's got to believe in fairy tales up to a point, but I think
it's better if you've really lived, seen the harsher side of life,
if you've been hurt, if you've cried a little, if you've laughed
a lot, if you've loved a lot. It makes a difference if you know
everything, the lows and the heights, and love.'

By the time Sibley came to dance these landmark roles at
Covent Garden—Aurora for the first time on 27 December
1961 and Odette-Odile in her official Opera House debut on
28 March 1962 (she waited nine years to dance *Giselle* there),
she had been forced to learn about the harsher side of life.
She had also fallen deeply in love.

'And it must have been around this time, after the tour,
that I found faith in God. I was brought up as an agnostic
by my parents, and I did feel the odd one out at Barons Court
when everyone except me and a very few Jews and Roman
Catholics went in to prayers. I didn't give religion much
thought, but I just felt odd and conspicuous when the few of
us trooped in afterwards for assembly. Before that, at boarding
school, it was even worse because everyone went out in croco-
dile to the local church for Sunday school and I was left
behind. I think in the end my parents let me join them.

'When I got to be about eighteen or twenty, I obviously
did talk about religion with my friends, but it wasn't until I

was twenty-one and going through a crisis—nothing to do with dancing—that I prayed for help and it came in the form of words I would never normally use. From that moment I have believed wholeheartedly.

'Now, after South Africa the knee was awful, but I had done *such* a lot of work. I don't know anybody of that age who'd done that amount of work in those heavy ballets in that short a time, so I put it down just to that. Unfortunately it's the left knee, which is the side you really need to have a good knee on. If your chronic injury's on your right foot or leg you're more or less all right, but it's very bad news to have it on the supporting foot or leg. That's always the one you stand on, you promenade on, you turn on—it's the one that gets all the work.

'I remember I got home and the tour had been such a success that de Valois was giving me this wonderful opportunity to go off to Dublin, again with the touring company. But I knew I couldn't do it because the knee was so bad. By then I didn't seem to be able to straighten it properly at all.'

So the Aurora scheduled for Dublin in May 1960 went by the boards, as did the rescheduled performance in London in June. But Sibley was back on her feet, in Nerina's role in *Birthday Offering*, that August, and sufficiently rested and recovered by September to fly to America with the company for another long tour. Fonteyn opened the season with *The Sleeping Beauty*, Beriosova danced the first *Swan Lake* and Nerina the first *Fille mal gardée*. Sibley was seen as the Crystal Fountain and Songbird Fairies and as the Bluebird, week in and week out for the entire fifteen weeks, but as she'd been promoted to principal in July, de Valois gave her an occasional crack at the coveted principal roles as well. A very occasional crack: she danced the second act of *Swan Lake* twice, in Denver and Atlanta; the third act of *The Sleeping Beauty* once, in Washington; and two complete *Swan Lake*s, on matinées in Cleveland and San Francisco.

Her 'still junior' status was even more clearly confirmed the following June when, after years of planning, the company made a one-month visit to Moscow and Leningrad. But neither surprise nor disappointment surface with her recollections.

'In South Africa I was doing *Swan Lake*, *The Sleeping Beauty*,

Giselle, Bluebird, *Rake's Progress, Patineurs*. But now, a year and a quarter later, we go to Russia and we're all put in our places. All our junior ballerinas went down as soloists—I never did any role bigger than the Bluebird—because it was great guns for Russia and we had all our top ballerinas with us, of course, Margot, Svetlana, Nadia. On a tour like that, no way would one *expect* to get an opportunity to dance *The Sleeping Beauty*.

'Dancing in the Bolshoi Theatre and in the Maryinsky—I have to call it that because for us it will always be the Maryinsky—was such a great honour. And the Russians were really clued up on all of us; although we'd never been there, they knew exactly who we all were. And they're very much like the Americans in their approach to ballet. They love it and they're going to *tell* you they love it, and because they love you you love them back, and you'll do anything because they're so enthusiastic.

'We were all keyed up and we did our best . . . but the food was abysmal. The only meat we could get we used to call rhinoceros meat, it was so tough. You couldn't eat it actually; you'd chew and then you'd spit it out. A few of us bravely found a marvellous Georgian restaurant that had some meat we could eat. I don't know how we found that place. I remember also the queues. We'd go into a shop to get some fruit: first you'd have to queue at the counter to say what you wanted and get a ticket, then you'd take your ticket to the counter to show what you wanted, then you'd have to go and pay at another counter. It would take you an hour to get two oranges. They spent their whole time in those days queuing, and there was such drabness, everything was drab.

'Ah, but what else we saw—Tsarkoe Seloe, and Peterhof, the palace on the Baltic with all the beautiful fountains. The Tsar had trick fountains everywhere, so you'd sit down on a lovely seat and the water would suddenly shoot up around you, or you'd be ambling across a lawn and up would come another fountain to surprise you. And the Hermitage, and another ravishing palace with the roofs all done in gold leaf.'

Regardless of her title or the roles she'd been allocated, Sibley knew as well as anybody how much she still had to learn. And de Valois knew, as usual, not only what the young dancer needed but where she was going to get it:

'The best *répétiteur* in the world she ever had was Michael Somes. He partnered her also, of course. But you see at her age, naturally she was ambitious, and most artists like the old Svengali idea; they're always looking for someone who will bring them out. They have an instinct for the person who will do it for them, they're drawn towards it, and they work very badly with the ones who can't. We often have to say, "Oh, don't send her to rehearse with so-and-so. She can't get anything out of it, she doesn't like it, it's no good." It's not just naughtiness; it's a psychological thing and you've got to accept it. Of course you can't give in to them completely. There must be discipline in the company, and they must accept certain things they don't want to do that way. They have to listen. But you watch to see who's getting the most out of them, and you're just being tiresome if you don't recognize it.

'She was a joy to work with from the point of view of a coach,' Somes declares, 'because she had the basic material and understanding of what it's all about, so you don't have to flog yourself into the ground trying to teach her that. As a coach you have to make them aware of their special abilities and make them learn to think for themselves rather than relying on all the things fed to them.

'Antoinette had everything it takes to be a very good dancer, but God moves in mysterious ways, there's always an Achilles heel somewhere, and she did have physical problems. Although she had a strong body and an enormous capacity for dancing, she had a certain weakness in her general health, in stamina. She had a weak chest, which made her susceptible to colds. But these are things to fight, which is almost always a good idea for a dancer because if it all comes too easily you don't develop attack, the ability to fight.

'Very often, through no fault of anybody, a dancer may develop some difficulty technically, something they can't do or think they can't do, but each fault has its compensations. Antoinette was not the loosest kind of dancer; her speciality on the technical side was speed and lightness. Because she was small, she could exploit that. She hadn't got the greatest jump or the highest arabesque. If you've got a side that's below what you'd wish it to be—figuring numerically, say sixty-nine out of a hundred—that's fine, but you must keep it to sixty-nine, you must never let it be less than the best you can make it. Only the best you can do is good enough.

'Antoinette had capability, she was able to criticize herself, not big-headed. On the contrary, she had the fault, an endearing fault but one that could also be irritating, of under-valuing herself, under-estimating herself—'Oh, I can't do that. I'll never be able to do that. Why can't I do that?'—which then makes her tense, so in the end she puts herself off it. Every dancer must care, but not worry so much that you think mountains will collapse and you will be consigned to everlasting damnation if you fail. They all get over-wrapped with their sense of failure.

'Failure always is and should be the largest part of a dancer's life. The better, the greater dancer you're eventually going to be, the greater sense of failure you're going to suffer, because the knowledge of what you might accomplish makes the failing all the sharper. You think to yourself, "I have to master it by tomorrow but I can't, and I have to do a rehearsal and then a performance in the evening . . . " and the nervous tension builds up. Dancers are living with failure all the time, and they must learn to overcome what seems like failure at any given time. If Antoinette did something hard, she overworried about it, not so much when she was younger but as she got older and knew more. It was difficult to make her let herself go, though on the stage she was always able to tackle it and have the nerve.

'As a coach you must approach every single person differ-ently; some need to be jolted and pushed, others encouraged and drawn. You must change your approach for every one, and even change how you approach any one depending on the situation. You must be very patient. With Antoinette, you'd give her an idea of something that could be done better but she would have difficulty seeing what you wanted. Until she'd absorbed it into her own mind, accepted it herself, she was a bit rebellious of it. She'd argue about it, which you'd understand was her process of accepting it, of arguing herself into it. By tomorrow she'd be doing what you wanted—and what she'd said was impossible—but without ever admitting that she was doing it. You couldn't press it too hard; you'd just let her gestate it herself, and if you had any sense you wouldn't say "I told you so." She could be stubborn, but that's no disgrace—sometimes it's a good thing to be like that though it's hard on everyone else.'

One specific instance springs to Ailne Phillips' mind: 'Antoinette was always a delight to teach, but she could be obstinate on many occasions, with a determination to get her own way which I cannot agree was always to her advantage. For instance, she had trouble with pointe shoes at one time, couldn't get the right pair. And she had to go on for *The Sleeping Beauty*. She said she couldn't go on, she hadn't got any shoes. No shoes were any good, and unless she got proper shoes she wasn't going on. So. We had all the shoes up from Freed's, great big boxes of shoes, and boxes from somebody else, and we all turned out in the office and made her try them on. She came into the room and said, "There's not a scrap of use me putting any of those on—they won't fit and they're no good." She was determined she was not going on for that performance. And she didn't—she didn't do it.'

'The terrible thing,' Sheila Bloom protests, 'is that she set a standard for herself and then everybody began to expect her to be able to pull it out of the bag. Starting quite early—I mean, she went into the company with a great sort of fanfare before she ever got there, which is lovely in one way and a drawback in another, because I think she came in to a fair amount of hostility. And I remember, when I was working and she was on tour, she used to phone me and say, "I am not going to get through this performance. I have to have somebody up here." She was a scared little person, and she always had this insecurity about being alone, without somebody she could trust to be there and to be honest.

'She had endless little red books over the years, and she used to write everything in them. Apart from her budget—she wrote systematically every single thing she spent—she'd also write about any influences of the day or the performance or some little thing that would happen in the country, "Must phone such-and-such" all mingled in with "What does Aurora see?" I think she put things down there for reference and sometimes to believe something had happened. It had to be down there before it actually was real. She was complex, but I've often said to her, "If you were straightforward your performance wouldn't be what it is."

'But to make Antoinette have any confidence took endless

days and nights of saying, "Yes, you can do it. It's got to be you. It can't be anybody else." She was always herself in things like Bluebird, small things, but in big things it took a long time. For instance in *Beauty*, where it's sometimes difficult to make Aurora anything but a little wooden, she'd say, "What do you think I'm feeling now?" And I'd say, "It's not what *I* think, darling, it's what *you* think. It's *you* they want, not me. It's in *you*." And she'd say, "But I'm such a strange, mixed-up . . ." and I'd say, "*That's* why it works. Because you are not like the others, you *are* a bit odd, you *are* strange. If I tell you the way I see it, I'm dead ordinary. But the way you see life is *bizarre*, so go up there and *be* bizarre. Be you, Antoinette. That's when it's your performance." And after a time she'd relax and decide to just feel the way *she'd* feel given that set of circumstances. And she had the confidence, at last, to say, "I can be me and it's acceptable."

'Of course Michael certainly affected her performance; he gave her confidence too. But I remember, when Makarova was with the Kirov, Antoinette and I went backstage to see her, and Makarova said to Antoinette, "You're all I'd ever want to be." That was *Makarova*. And afterwards I said, "Now, do I still have to go through the routine every time: You are good at this. You can do it. Do we still have to go through all this?" And she said, "Oh, Sheebee, she doesn't mean that. They just say those things." You'll never convince her and in a way, as Cranko said, that's what makes her so wonderful, because she's not up there thinking she's doing it beautifully.'

Michael Somes was one of the most important and lasting influences in Sibley's life, as she herself is the first to admit. 'The first time I ever saw Michael was the first ballet I ever saw at the Opera House, *The Fairy Queen*, and the only person I remembered later was Moira Shearer. Michael thought it was a bit bad that I hadn't remembered Margot and him, because obviously they must have had the leads. I had all the books about them, naturally, and I saw him also when Lynn and I went to see the *Swan Lake* with Miss Edwards. I must have seen him all the time, and I was a great friend of Deirdre [Dixon, Somes' first wife]. She was older than me, but I dressed near her in the dressing room at Barons Court.

'The first time he rehearsed me he took Graham and me for Bluebirds. He wouldn't have taken much notice of me; it was probably Graham that he was helping. But the main thing was, after Deirdre died he'd gone off to dance with Margot to try to get over it, in Brazil or somewhere. Madam had thought it would be a good idea if he started rehearsing people, maybe it would help him, when he got back. He was still dancing, but as *Ballet Imperial* had been done on him, he came back and rehearsed me for it. That was the first thing.

'He was a very hard taskmaster—he would say the same—and he sought perfection. He was very . . . I suppose strict would be the word, determined and strict, and he didn't want anything smudged. And in fact he made me cry, I can remember it. I couldn't produce the goods that he desired for *Ballet Imperial*—it was my first big assignment, of course. I did do what he wanted eventually, in the performance, but I'm usually better in performance than I am in rehearsal—I'm speaking of technique as opposed to theatre. If I'm very nervous, I usually pull off some things that I wouldn't expect to be able to do, and I think I did in my first *Ballet Imperial*s.

'He certainly was the toughest person I'd ever worked with. You see, some days I really can't dance at all. Now I've worked with that and I now *don't* dance when I can't dance—unless there's a performance and I have to—and I don't rehearse because it gets me too depressed. But then I didn't realize it, and as most people get better the more they rehearse, I assumed that's what would happen with me. In fact I now realize I don't necessarily get better. I don't mean that I don't need lots of rehearsals, but I can't do them consecutively, day after day after day, the way most people do and can. And whether it was that, in those days, I don't know, but certainly he was very demanding.

'Naturally with any sort of relationship, with choreographer or partner or coach or anything, you're finding out about each other for quite a long time, so of course the pressures might be too great at certain points along the line. At the beginning I didn't know the fruits that would come of all this, and at first, because he was also new at rehearsing people, he was feeling his way as well. So what I'm talking about at the beginning is not exactly what I'm talking about at the end because over the years he would come up to it a different way. It's a gradual process, all this. But certainly in the end what came, apart from the enormous respect because he could give you the idea of the theatre and the build-up of something, was a tremendous trust. Of course he knew me then so well; he knew the difficulties that I had and the things that I could do. He is innately musical, and he knew the things—again, in the end—that I myself would bring to it, where he didn't need to push me.

'I trusted him absolutely in the way he went about things and he could correct me always in a marvellous way. When you've worked with somebody, as indeed I did from then on, he could get very good results, the best results, out of me. He did give me confidence; once I had done the performances and realized that what he said worked, then I trusted him, after *Ballet Imperial* and the *Lac*. Oh, but that was quite a different thing because he was partnering me too.'

The critic G. B. L. Wilson once reported that while Karsavina was rehearsing Fonteyn and Somes in one of her ballets from the Diaghilev era, she had said to Fonteyn, 'How lucky you are to have Michael to partner you—I only had Nijinsky.'

'And the great falling in love was with the *Swan Lake*,' Sibley continues. 'Apart from relying 150 per cent on somebody under such a stressful condition, what a romantic situation. Remember, I'd been with the company then for however many years, and every girl was affected by him, all of us, everybody was a little bit in love with Michael. He was the top dancer, the most handsome man—he was like Rock Hudson, Paul Newman, his looks were like a film star. So you can imagine working on something that exposes your own emotions so much you're raw, Odette-Odile. From then till November one's feet . . . of course touched the ground because one was working so hard, but it really was the most extraordinary time for a young girl. And of course Michael was all part of it and helped me cope with it. It was big ordeal time on both sides—he had been through the most huge ordeal himself with Deirdre dying—but he was wonderful to me. And it was a big passionate wonderful romance.

'I had loved other people; I had been around a bit with other boys. I've always loved men all my life, from my father onwards. They've always made me feel good, they've always given me confidence. I can't think of a time when I haven't adored them. And I was always at boarding school with girls, girls, girls, and then when I got to the Royal Ballet school I loved the boys. I didn't have brothers so I wasn't used to boys being awful and rough. Brothers are ghastly and they bash you on the head, but always the boy next door was my boyfriend. So I idolized them.

'Michael and I lived together before we were married, on and off, for five years. Not necessarily living in the same flat, but we were known as a twosome. We were together from about '60 to '69 all told.'

'It was the most marvellous relationship in its own way,' Sheila Bloom murmurs. 'Michael used to say to me, "You'll expect them to play *Beauty* when we're coming down the aisle," and I always did. He was so romantic, so good-looking, and he gave her confidence because he thought she was so marvellous.'

So did many other people, even those who weren't, coincidentally, in love with her. It would have taken a much less realistic woman than Sibley to argue otherwise, given the repertory entrusted to her and the fulsome praise her performances regularly inspired in the press. In October 1961 she was permitted to create her first leading role, in a short-lived ballet called *Jabez and the Devil* by Alfred Rodrigues. In the several years that followed, she was privileged to work with some of the most renowned figures of twentieth-century ballet. Serge Grigoriev, who for twenty years had been Diaghilev's *régisseur*, and his wife, the dramatic ballerina Ljubov Tchernicheva, were together passing on to the Royal Ballet the distinguished repertory Fokine had created for the Ballets Russes. Erik Bruhn staged a *divertissement* from Bournonville's *Napoli* in May 1962, and Léonide Massine mounted his witty work, *The Good-Humoured Ladies*, two months later. Having succeeded de Valois as director of the company, Frederick Ashton invited Bronislava Nijinska, in whose troupe he had once danced himself, to teach his dancers *Les Biches*, her masterpiece of manners, which they first performed at the Royal Opera House in December 1964.

Once again, Sibley's star rose more by chance than by choice as circumstance fashioned a priceless setting to display the facets of every dancer's acquired skills and innate talents.

'The person after Cranko to seek me out was Rodrigues, with *Jabez*, my first created role. He had been ballet master with the company, but I knew him because I went away with him and his group during my summer holidays, probably for two weeks, to Grenada or Nervi—this must have been in '58 and '59. The group included David Blair, Pirmin Trecu, Shirley Grahame, Margaret Hill, Maryon [Lane], Ronnie Hynd and Annette [Page], and me—I was the baby of the group. The first year Beriosova was with us, and I did things like the Mirlitons in *Nutcracker* with Shirley and the background people in his [*Ile des*] *Sirènes*. Then the next year Beriosova or somebody couldn't come at the last minute, so Rodrigues gave me the opportunity to dance the lead in *Sirènes*. He gave *me* that chance, and I really loved it—she's the wicked woman who lures the men to the island, and once she'd got them there she kills them.

'I had to learn it frightfully quickly, as usual, because my parents were going away on holiday—they only ever had a week—so I took over the shop with my sister. I never had holidays as such because when I wasn't dancing I was working in the shop in Bromley. It was quite a worrying time for me because I had to be in charge of the money and the cooking, the lot, and my sister was only young and so she wasn't up to much. I remember I wrote *Sirènes* down, so all the time I was in the shop I was going over it in my mind. When we arrived in Nervi, I think we only had the one day to get it on, so I didn't have time to think of interpretation or anything—I was still busy with the steps. But I'd been in the corps so I knew the music, and I did it with David, who was a great help to me.

'Up till then the roles I'd been given by de Valois were the classical roles. I was never given dramatic roles but Rodrigues noticed this other side of me, the seductive, sensual side, and from the moment he gave it to me it felt absolutely natural. It came more easily to me than the classical. The *Manon*s and the *Dream*s, all my roles were that sort of thing in the end really, but he discovered it right here. *Jabez* was absolutely that: I'm Mary, the sweet, uncomplaining wife of MacLeary, but I'm also a demon-woman, a seductress, in the next scene. It was most demanding, all quick changes, and I remember I was on pointe in black boots, right up to the knee. He was very much a man of the theatre so he liked theatrical effects, rather than just steps being done. I can't remember any of it now—but I wouldn't unless I heard the music again anyway—and it wasn't a successful ballet, but I'm very grateful to have been given that role.

'I first must have worked with Tchernicheva on *Petrouchka*, in '57. I was nothing important, just a cadet, but I certainly did classes with her and I was absolutely mad about her. Apart from that she was so beautiful, she gave the most wonderful *dance* classes; they moved so well, freely, not so controlled or set. She was utterly charming and she liked me very much from very early on. I'd not been in the ballets they had produced so I think it was from the classes, although I'm not good at doing steps absolutely correctly. I can move rather well, but class is usually a static thing . . . which hers wasn't, which is why I suppose I could do it well.

'Her husband I didn't see so much of at first because he didn't take classes: he put on the ballets. However once I'd gone into *Firebird* and been a Wife and then a Princess, then I knew him very well too from rehearsals. Grigoriev was like a wonderful bear, a big, growly type of man but very cuddly. He looked stern and at first you could be quite frightened, but he wasn't at all; he was soft as a huge puppy dog—an enchanting man. Of course Michael worshipped both of them, and once I'd married Michael I got to know them very well. We used to go along to their flat in High Street Kensington. On one of the visits, Madame Tchernicheva did two or three of her favourite roles for me in her sitting room—she portrayed these roles sitting on the couch, and she was magnificent. She told me about *Thamar*—I'd never seen *Thamar*—and she got this scarf out for a veil and did it all, beckoned on all the men, very seductive. Other roles too, but this is the one that stuck in my mind.

'Then in later years when he was so gravely ill, I went to visit him in St George's Hospital. He was a gentleman to the last degree, with old-fashioned manners and courtesy that are fast disappearing from the world. Ill as he was, the moment I came in he sat up in bed, spruced himself up and was polite, trying to speak English. Madame Tchernicheva said after that that I mustn't visit him again because it took too much out of him. He put on such an act for me, but he wouldn't think of just lying in bed, being ill. One doesn't see this any more—it's a thing of the past.

'The ballets they were putting on were so great—I did

Sylphides with him at a later date—and they were there when those ballets were created, so they knew the essence of it all, as I would about the ballets Fred's done on me. Grigoriev had a photographic memory, and everything that you had to do was absolutely precise.

'Monica Mason told me she was watching a performance of *Firebird* the other day and she saw one of the Indian girls *smiling* when she arrived in Kostchei's den. So Monica said, "Why are you smiling?" and the girl said, "Oh, I thought I was happy." And Monica said, "How can you be happy? You're waiting for Kostchei to come in." But the girl didn't know what it was all about. Of course she should have jolly well looked up and seen what it was all about. She thought this music was by Tchaikovsky as well. I mean, this was completely unheard of in our time.

'I always did immense research into everything—I'm a great digger. I don't ever accept anything as it's shown to me because unless I understand it for myself, so that I can interpret it my way, I'm not interested. Unless I can feel the skeleton of anything, I don't know how to do it. I don't like to copy people because it feels awkward on me, and I can only make it my own if I can go back to the skeleton and build my own flesh on it.

'And I never think of just getting up and performing steps, because if I thought of that I wouldn't dance. That's why I never liked dancing until I *could* make something out of it. That's why I hate class and I'd do anything not to do it; having a wonderful teacher is the only thing that makes it endurable. I don't find it fun, I really don't, because steps don't fascinate me as such. I play with steps a lot and I do some things well, but maybe they're not classically perfect. I don't know. I prefer to dance than to do steps.

'Now unfortunately I didn't actually work with Nijinska at all. I was supposed to, in *Biches*, but one of my wretched illnesses intervened. But again, Michael worshipped the ground she walked on, and he brought her home to our house in Earl's Court and we gave her a meal, with her husband. We had a new kitten at the time and she so adored that cat, she hardly spoke to any of us during the whole meal. She just sat with this cat on her lap. It was a black cat so Michael had called her something like the White Beauty, in Russian, but Nijinska said, "No, you must call her *dushka*, darling", so she was always Dushka after that.

'I rehearsed the Blue Girl in *Biches* quite a lot—but not with her, this was some time later—and then for some reason I didn't do it. I certainly did do the Grey Girls, in New York. We did a programme of three short ballets, two of which were *Biches* and *Patineurs*. For both of them they wanted Merle and me on, and I'd done neither of them. I'd done the White girl in *Patineurs* but I'd never done the Blue girls, and I'd never been in *Les Biches* at all. It was a hell of a thing to get both on in the same night; it was just to make a splash, I suppose, but it was a nightmare-ish splash. And I think it's the only time we ever did either of them together—it would have been fun to do them again.

'Massine came over for *Good-Humoured Ladies*, and he chose me to do Mariuccia. I used to go in every Sunday to work with him, because he liked to work very slowly and everything had to be absolutely precise. He was very particular whether you tapped your finger on the middle of the other palm or on the end of the palm. But he was very charming and one understood immediately what he wanted. It was . . . not mannered, but the style was very intricate, like with Fred, a lot of shoulders and *épaulement*. It was miming at the same time as dancing—you eat a meal while you're dancing. Fascinating. And those eyes of his, like spaniel's eyes, deep fathoms of blackness. He was very demanding but also very encouraging. It was his ballet and one was hearing it from the horse's mouth, so one knew exactly how to do it.

'I don't remember how I felt being chosen; I only remember how I finished up loving all those people—love is the word. Very giving people, full of heart, and they seemed very pleased with what one was doing. And they each gave you a different style, a different way of doing things, which is what builds the building of oneself. You pick up little bits from everybody.

'Doing *Napoli* was not really that much of a surprise in that it was all my contemporaries: Lynn, Merle, myself, Georgina [Parkinson]. We would be the obvious choice to do it. But the funny thing was that we *all* fell in love with Erik. He has to be the most handsome man that's ever been, *ever*, followed closely by Desmond Kelly. Even now, at this age, when I meet Erik I blush. I don't think we'd seen him dance, but each and every one of us did every rehearsal with a heartbeat missing—we were all at that age. And if he stood in the wings, which he always did because he would do *Flower Festival [at Genzano]* with Nadia afterwards, we could hardly dance. We were half-embarrassed, half-shy, half wanting to do our best because we wanted to give him everything we could. We were all knocked out by him.

'There's a church off Earl's Court where Lynn and I used to do private lessons with Miss Edwards later, and when we rehearsed with Erik we used this hall quite a lot. We didn't each learn every dance and then he chose when he saw us, as we did with Jerry [Robbins] on *Dances at a Gathering*. I only learned my dance—that's the dance Erik chose for me—and each of us was very suited to our own variation, that's where *he* was so clever. Mine was the balancing one with a lot of swizzling body movement.

'We all adored *Napoli* and we all did it very well. It wasn't exactly as it was done by the Danes; I think he made it more complicated. Certainly, having seen the real veritable version recently, ours was more complicated. Bournonville is extremely difficult and it was a different style for us; we weren't really brought up on that kind of beating and the light jump with the quick take-off. But we all worked very hard to get it right for him, because we all loved him—it was that simple.

'And Fred adored the whole thing. In fact, there's a step in my variation that he fell in love with and wanted me in some way to incorporate in *Enigma*. So we've got a step in Dorabella with the same feel to it; it's also got a *rond de jambe* in it, with that wide *port de bras* thing and then a lightning little *pas de bourrée*.

'There's a lovely story that goes with *Napoli*. None of us was happy with the colour of our costume, so at one perform-ance at the Opera House we all decided to change to the costumes we'd always wanted to wear. I gave up my pink one and went into the yellow—I've always loved yellow. We didn't come onstage at "Beginners" like we normally do, to warm up and all, but we'd done it quite a lot by then and nobody thought anything of it, and by the time we did show up it was too late. Well, the staff went absolutely crazy from the moment the curtain went up. They all looked at us—de Valois, the lot—and they realized we were not in our costumes, and of course they thought we were going to change variations too! So they were really in a panic. But they couldn't get to us until we came off at the end, because we hardly leave the stage. Remember, you stand on the side to watch or you run round to go on in the next wing while the other person's dancing. So they'd had it, but of course there was trouble afterwards. They were livid and told us so, that we were all ghastly and we would all be given the sack, but we knew they couldn't get rid of all of us. I think I'm right in saying it remained ours for quite a long time.

'But I must say that one of the few things that's unfulfilled is that I have never danced with Erik. If you think about it, I've danced with all the great male dancers but I've never had that chance. He wasn't here a great deal and I think he'd retired by the time I started dancing away with people, but I would have loved to.

'Oh, Rudolf's there through all this. Rudolf's very much around in the rehearsals when *Napoli* is going on, because he loved doing all that Bournonville himself. When he first came, one saw him as a "newspaper person", a star in that respect, and we all thought he was incredible when he started working with the company. But I had slightly different feelings from most people because of Michael. At that stage, he'd really taken over from Michael with Margot, if you know what I mean. Margot was always going to retire with Michael and then didn't. When Michael retired, she says in her book she was really thinking that there were not many years ahead, and then this genius had come along and taken his position. Obviously this was a wonderful thing for her because it inspired her so much, and he was so inspired by her—it was a marvellous partnership.

'And de Valois would do anything for him. If Rudolf asked for the lights to be changed, the lights would be changed. It didn't matter that we'd all been asking, or that Michael or the top people had all been asking for years. The moment Rudolf said it, it was done—he had that effect on Madam. So many things in life are on personalities, aren't they, on what makes personalities click.

'Well, being close to Michael I obviously thought at first, "Gosh, it must be hard for him to see this young whipper-snapper coming on and doing all this." It was a tricky . . . not a begrudging sort of thing, but one just felt a bit hurt for

Michael. This was such an exciting thing happening, such sparks and fireworks, yet Michael had done all that he had done quite quietly. So of course I felt all that, 'til I realized it simply wasn't the case at all. Michael wasn't in any way jealous, he's the most generous person ever, and he so admired what Rudolf was doing. And I admired Rudolf as well, enormously, but Erik was there at the same time and Erik was the one that knocked me out—this is again just a personality thing. And the same with Rudolf; Rudolf never showed much interest in me either. It was later that we really understood each other and worked together so well.

'I don't know what happened, but suddenly on that American tour I was told that Rudolf wanted me to do the *Bayadère* and *Les Sylphides* with him—I can't remember which he asked me to do first. I had always sworn I'd never do *Les Sylphides* again because it was the one ballet that I honestly couldn't be serious through. I never particularly liked doing it. I was in the corps originally, then the first part I got was the Waltz and I was simply horrendous in it. It was one role I never ever got right. I did the most abortive performance of it in New Orleans where on those *arabesques penchées*, on the diagonal, the dress was so long or I was so bad that I kept walking up the skirt and falling down. Every time I started the arabesque I got caught in the dress and went down, three times in the variation, and at the end when I went off the audience laughed. They thought I was the comic turn. I was simply dreadful in it.

'I was, I think, quite good in the *pas de deux*. I've never done it with Anthony, but I did it with Pirmin and with John Gilpin. But although I found it a very hard ballet to do, I immediately jumped at it when Rudolf asked because I'd never done anything with him, I hadn't had an immediate rapport with him, and I was amazed he asked for me. And I loved doing it with him, I loved dancing with him.

'So, you see, I worked with every choreographer—I was so lucky. Cranko used me, Rodrigues, Kenneth, Massine picked me for Mariuccia, Antony Tudor used me later for *Lilac Garden*. The only one who didn't was Fred. Think of anybody, any choreographer that arrived, Jerry Robbins, van Dantzig, Hans van Manen wanted to do something for me and even Neumeier—his ballet [*The Fourth Symphony*] was going to be for me, but I left before he started rehearsals. This is where I got my big opportunities . . . Helpmann with *Hamlet*. So it's only Ashton that was my stickler—it's so strange, the way it's turned out.

'He hadn't let me do any of his roles and Madam was somebody you didn't go and ask for things. She ran that place and it was more or less up to her. The first thing I ever did ask for . . . I did go to Sir Fred, who didn't really like me at the time, and I did ask him if I could do *Two Pigeons*. I wasn't asking to do it for the first time; I had been doing it on tour with the other company and supposedly everybody had been very pleased. But I don't think Fred had ever seen it—why should he go on tour? But then it came into the Opera House, with our company, and, blow it, I wasn't down to do it. And I was heartbroken, I just couldn't understand it.

'I went to his home in Marlborough Street to ask him—never been so frightened in my life, because I was very frightened of him anyway—and I blurted it all out. I said, "It's just that I've done it so often. Obviously if you've seen me do it and don't like me doing it, then that's fine. But I would like to know it from you." He was absolutely sweet but he said, "I can't be sure of you. I've never seen you do this ballet. Whereas I have seen other people do my work, I admire them in my work and I can rely on them. And I can't on you." And I said, "Oh, I absolutely understand that." So that's how it was left, and at least I knew where I stood.

'I did come to do it later so obviously he did risk it on me, but I hadn't done many of his things, he didn't know me, so he didn't trust me in his work. He'd never given me my chances, you see: my chances had come in the classics, but that was from de Valois. And in a funny sort of way . . . I don't know, but so many of his friends liked me so well that I think it might have prejudiced him slightly the other way. I always got on very well with Alec Grant, and of course Somes. But anyway, he certainly didn't like me up 'til this time.

'It was soon after this conversation that he did give me the White girl in *Patineurs* to do, at Covent Garden. I'd done it *ad infinitum* on tour with Desmond Doyle, so it was very much in my rep, but Fred had never seen me do it. I could easily have done it earlier at the Opera House, but as the last cast, so he wouldn't necessarily have seen it. It's a tricky *pas de deux* at the best of times, though it doesn't look it, but I didn't falter around too much. I was good in it, I didn't have many difficulties. But when I came to do it this time at the Opera House, it was with Ronnie Hynd and we hadn't done it together before. And I got so nervous when I saw Fred walk across the stage before I went on. I thought, "Oh my God, this is the first thing he's ever seen me do of his as a soloist," and, honestly, I couldn't stand up. I was so frightened because I thought he wasn't sure of me or didn't trust me, and so I was appalling. I was hardly ever up on my feet—I spent most of my time on the floor. I don't think I accomplished half the *pas de deux*. It was the most embarrassing thing I'd ever done in my life: everything that could go wrong did go wrong.

'In fact it was so appalling . . . At the end, you're dragged off backwards into the wings, and then you automatically skate back on for the call. It's like part of the dance; you don't listen for the applause—you skate on, do your bow, and off you skate again. So we skated on and there was no applause. I don't think it had ever happened before—literally no applause, just an embarrassed silence. So you can imagine where I went in Fred's estimation.'

Frederick Ashton allows a flicker of amusement to cross his face as he fondly recalls his first encounters with Sibley more than twenty-five years ago. 'I didn't realize that she was terrified of me, and I don't think I disliked her. I didn't know her well. You see, if she was on tour I wasn't necessarily on tour with them, because I didn't go around with them. I was with the main company really.

'There were lots of rising dancers at that time and she was one of them. Well, I thought she was a very pretty girl. She was also extraordinary in that she's always been a great theorizer, she's always had theories about this, that and the other, sometimes in quite a confused way, not really rationally thought out. She may have had theories about dancing, but she didn't expose them to me. I remember once going up in the lift with her in Covent Garden tube, and her telling me she was an atheist. I said, "Oh, really? How interesting," and I thought, "That's rather astonishing. She doesn't look like anybody who's thought a great deal about religion or things like that." And I thought, "Well, perhaps there's something different to her."

'And she was different. She's always had something to give as a performer. You give her some material and she'll make the most of it. You don't have to drag it out of her—if anything, you sometimes have to quieten her down, because she can be too ecstatic . . . I don't mean calm her down . . . restrain her.'

'My turning point with him,' Sibley confides, 'was the *Giselle* Peasant *pas de deux* with his new solo, which I absolutely adored and wanted to do almost more than anything. At that time I had done Giselle herself on tour, I'd done *Swan Lake* and *The Sleeping Beauty* at the Opera House, and I still wasn't getting the *Giselle pas de deux* with Fred's new solo. He hadn't chosen me for it. Everyone did it before me; he choreographed it for Maryon, then Annette did it, then Merle, I think, and Doreen—I was the last one to go on. And it was a most important performance because it was one of Margot and Rudolf's first *Giselle*s. I know that gorgeous Erik Bruhn was sitting in a box, so we must have been near to the *Napoli* time.

'Well, I worked myself round the twist on this when I did get it because I'd always loved it and I thought it was very "me". I didn't do it the Romantic, olde-worlde style most people did. Again, I had my own way of thinking about it—I couldn't put it into words because it would sound so stupid—but I did it all my own way. I simply can't remember doing it at the Opera House before that night. Of course I danced the *pas de deux* all the time, but not with this new solo, which is why it's so significant with Fred. I know I had stage time to work on it before that performance, and I was so nervous I rehearsed right up to the half-hour. I did it with Brian Shaw, and that particular night it really did bring the house down. And that was the changing of things as far as Sir Fred and I were concerned.

'When I was so shy and nervous of him, I was working against myself all the time because I was frightened, and I boobed everything up instead of doing anything well. But from then on . . .well, from then on all sorts of things happened, *The Dream* being the most important, of course.

'Already by the time we choreographed the *pas de quatre* in *Swan Lake* I knew he liked me quite well. By then he must have seen me do a lot of his rep and he must have got confidence in me. I'd done *Fille* at some point and I'd done the Summer Fairy for years in *Cinderella*, which was one of my favourite roles, and that was a clinch-deal with Sir Fred. But certainly by the time I came to the *pas de quatre* I must have been on a fairly . . . well, very good relationship because I was able to discuss changing the end of the solo with him. I seem to have worked with him over a lot of things, but in those days, you see, he took all the calls before you went on in his ballets. So it wasn't like my going into a room and suddenly working with a stranger. He had worked with me on all his ballets by now, so I was very familiar with him and he with me, with my way of working. So it was an honour, of course, to create the *pas de quatre* but not a strange thing at all.

'It was for this big new production of *Lac* being done by Fred and Bobby Helpmann, and I was doing Odette too, with Christopher Gable. Fred set the fourth act on Margot and Rudolf, but I was worked on a great deal by Bobby as Odette-Odile, so I was merely going from one room to another. That's why, in fact, when everyone comes to do the *pas de quatre* now, they could kill me, because my pace is so exhausting. I'm the last solo, a very controlled, very tiring solo. Now the coda is much easier but when we did it, I come straight off after my solo, the music starts the minute I've taken my bow, the boys do the first phrase, and I run round and Merle and I come straight back on from the back wing. So while the boys are starting, I'm just running from the front wing to the back wing to come on. The girls don't do that any more. They've changed it so that my girl has time to get herself prepared just to come on for the *fouettés*. But still it's an absolute killer.

'I knew I was exhausted throughout and when I came to do the pirouettes at the end I was in another world, I was on remote control. But I thought it was because I was literally going from the Odette-Odile rehearsals straight into this, and back to Odette-Odile . . . I never stopped. It was one or the other. That's why I didn't say . . . Nowadays I would say, "This is killing, it's exhausting. Can we change something?" but I didn't And that's why everybody now is suffering like mad even though it's been cut.

'Merle's dance is based on the Charleston and mine's on

the Cha-cha-cha, because I always did the Cha-cha-cha, it was my best thing at parties. Alec Grant and me and Doreen and Gary Burne were all wonderful at the Cha-cha-cha. It was just coming in and it was really "our thing"; the four of us used to get up and do it wherever we could, and of course Fred had seen this at all the parties in New York. He's made it completely classical, but it was definitely based on those rhythms, with the swing of the hips. We spent quite a time on setting the last step because we had a lot of the swing of the hips and the Cha-cha-cha and it didn't really build up. So I must have known him a lot by then to be able to discuss this and alter things a bit.

'But you see, the same year, 1963, Kenneth was creating *Symphony* on Lynn, and I was the second cast so I was at all the rehearsals. I was going to do my performance with Donald [MacLeary] and Desmond [Doyle] when Lynn had done hers—there were no second-cast boys. So I had nobody to work with, and it was very, very complicated. In the end I had to do the first night, and I'd never done it with these people till the day before . . . 'til the *day*. But when I came to one of the full calls I saw this young boy—who I really didn't know—just sitting, not doing anything, so because it was quite impossible to do this by myself I thought, "Could he just hold me up?"

'So he did. He said, "Yes, yes," and he stood up, and it was quite extraordinary. It just felt so right and so easy. I really was amazed because I had worked with so many other people by now and I knew the very good ones and the ones who weren't so good. I'm not saying he was a wonderful partner because at that time of course he wasn't. He was a young boy and not very powerfully built, but it was his timing and I suppose his height with my height and where our hands reached—it just was natural. Yet he wasn't like MacLeary or Doyle or Somes, these unbelievably wonderful partners, experienced but also natural partners. This was something quite else: it was just how we worked together. When he turned me under it felt right and I finished up exactly right and our arms reached the right height together. Everything was just . . . right, and I do remember thinking that right then and there.

'Obviously, this was Anthony. I knew he was a very good

dancer from his solo in *Napoli*, but I certainly didn't think of him as anything to do with me. Why would I? I was working with Christopher and Donald and Desmond and Michael, so it was for no idea of that that I asked him to get up and work with me. It was absolute chance, like my coming back, all chance.

'I got on as easily with him after this occasion. I'd chat with him in the canteen, and it was the same humour, same jokes, we were very relaxed with each other. So when we came to *The Dream*, it again wasn't something odd. It was magic, and I was most aware of it. He was very much more withdrawn in those young days and frightfully shy, a little bit like Princess Diana, looking up from under the lashes, the head down and the eyes up. I was able to draw him out in a way, before he found his own feet and started being himself, and also because I suppose I'd had more experience. But it did work remarkably well—it was exactly like it is now. But it was the same *then*, that's what I'm trying to say. It's not just through experience and working together. I know when he's nervous, he knows when I'm nervous, I can see the way he's thinking, and it was no different then. And it was Fred who obviously saw this thing working, the lines and the proportions and our reactions to each other and I suppose our natures. In the beginning it was completely Fred's intuition.'

Anthony Dowell looks straight into his dressing room mirror as he looks back over his entire performing career to his early days with Sibley. 'Ashton putting us together at that time in her life was far more important to her than it seemed to me. I'd been in the corps, and I had no structure to my working life in that I was put with this partner and that. I was still finding out, whereas she'd danced maybe three of the classics, already before we'd met, and had been put with every partner in the book. And because Fred saw that these two bodies were going to work together and we did complement each other, I suppose she felt comfortable and this was suddenly right for the first time.

'I took it as the norm—it sounds blasé in a way. Here I was, dancing with the next up-and-coming ballerina, but I just took it for granted that this was how it would feel. I hadn't ever been put with someone where it was all awkward, so not having that to judge against I thought this was normal.

I don't remember being shy particularly of her—I think I just was a shy person. Or maybe people read shyness from my rather reserved qualities. Friends have often said that in my early days they never knew quite whether to approach or not. I wasn't conscious of doing that; it was just my way. As to actual classical partnering, I'd merely handled the girls in the corps de ballet, like in *Patineurs* and *Swan Lake*, just the regular lifts.

'Oh, I knew her dancing. One got to know all the ballerinas of the company. In the *Beauty*, for instance, we'd all be standing on the steps seeing the Rose *adage*, so one was seeing Fonteyn—still very much at the top of the tree then—Beriosova, Nerina, everyone. At that time there were so many established ballerinas that we were all up there thinking, "Oh, it's that one tonight," and one enjoyed each one in her own right.

'I had *no* ambition to do any of the roles. But, I suppose being terribly lucky or talented at an early age, they just came anyway. The biggest thing for her, ever, was to have a role created by Ashton, because naturally Margot had been his muse for so many years. That was Titania. I took it almost as the natural course. I thought, "Oh, this is lovely," but it wasn't such a big, big thing to me.

'It was Ashton who put us together—it wasn't accidental. He knew. With his amazing eye, he knew that those were the two people to come. Maybe not—maybe he just saw that she was right for Titania and I was right for Oberon. So maybe it could be accidental in some respect.'

'She was absolutely the one I wanted for *Dream*,' Ashton confirms amiably, 'because I thought she was a queen of the fairies. She had this very pretty appearance and she also had something *farouche* in her. What is this in English? Wild, yes, a little bit wild, and that's what I liked in it. She had this kind of wildness in her, and I didn't want just a sweet fairy. And then also, at the same time I'd seen Dowell; I thought he would be an ideal Oberon and she would be an ideal Titania. They were the perfect two separately, and I just brought them together. And started off their partnership, union.

'We were all perfectly comfortable together, but if I'm working with them they have to approach it in my way. But she's very responsive as an interpreter and as an instrument to work with. She's technically very well equipped, always has been, and she's very musical, and she feels what she's doing—sometimes, as I say, even to excess. You see, the joy of working with them is that they're *both* so musical.'

'It's quite well known now,' Sibley admits, "but when we started with *The Dream* we really didn't know that we were Titania and Oberon. That is absolute fact. We knew it was *Midsummer Night's Dream*, but I don't know whether it had *The Dream* up on the callsheet. It would have said "Ashton", then "Sibley, Dowell, Park, [Austin] Bennett", no cast list, and Ashton taking it. And as we started with a quarrel, we assumed we were one pair of lovers and Merle and Austin were the other pair. The fact that they were doing it behind us didn't mean anything in that we thought we'd be learning each others' parts. We were never told . . . we have never ever been told to this day that we were Titania and Oberon.

'When I first realized it was Titania I was going to do, I was slightly upset. It sounds ridiculous in retrospect but I was, because I thought maybe the first big role with Sir Fred . . . I just had hoped . . . I thought Titania seemed such a bore. A fairy, a proud fairy: I thought "Oh, how boring." I really wanted some meat, something I could get my teeth into. Until I realized what a delicious person she was, so volatile and proud and angry and so . . . well, womanly. After all, a lot of that last *pas de deux* is giving in, and all we women do, because it's the best way for our end result. There's a lot in her that's really wonderful, not wonderful as a person but so true to womankind. Oberon's not really winning the battle totally: she's letting him win for the final result, so that she keeps the boy as well, they both can have him. I just adore her. When you look at the role and all that one can do in it, it's not just a fairy. I think of her as wild and sensual and tempestuous and yet giving in when she wants to.'

Michael Somes believes that '*The Dream* was the most important and memorable thing done for her by Fred. Titania embodies the best of what she does: brilliance and softness, nobility and the quality of the fairy queen, tongue-in-cheek humour in the donkey bits, which in my books adds up to charm—those things can be so dull and dreary without that. And of course she was very pretty, in her face and her figure.'

'The usual hair-raising things happened at the dress rehearsal,' Sibley groans, 'which we weren't, either of us, used to. The costumes were too long, I had a wig but Fred wasn't happy with that so I dyed my hair green . . . Yes, the first night I wore my own hair dyed green. It was all these last moment things, which can throw you when you're that young and inexperienced.

'Before the first night we were absolutely terrified. Remember, already at that time Sir Fred was exactly like he is now, I mean, the king. It wasn't as if he was down the ladder a step or two: he wasn't. Margot of course went up the ladder with him, but not us, and so we were naturally worried we wouldn't produce the goods or we would make it a flop. What would we do letting the king down, so to speak? And *he's* frightfully nervous before a first night.

'But one also has to put the first night in perspective. It was the quatercentenary of Shakespeare's birth, so we weren't the only new thing going on. Kenneth had done *Images of Love* and Rudolf was in it, so really the occasion was not us and Sir Fred. Rudolf, who was such a mega-star, and of course none of us were, was doing two numbers—I think the opening number was Bobby's *Hamlet*—so he was who everyone was really coming to see. But for us the responsibility was just as great because we hadn't had that responsibility before with Sir Fred.'

The Dream, which stands today among Ashton's most memorable achievements and among the cherished treasures of the Royal Ballet repertory, opened at Covent Garden on 2 April 1964 to a decidedly mixed reception. According to David Vaughan's authoritative book on Ashton, 'the general tenor of reviews . . . [was] that Ashton had come up with another *pièce d'occasion*, pretty enough but without lasting value.' Andrew Porter, however, reported with insight and fervour in the *Financial Times* that *The Dream* was 'purest lyric poetry' and Ashton 'one of the great English lyrical poets whose medium happens to be choreography'. Sibley's enchanting characterization drew handsome praise from Mary Clarke in the *Dancing Times*: 'Antoinette Sibley, who can shine coolly like the moon as beautifully as she can shine radiantly like the sun, is exactly right for proud Titania. She succeeds in looking like an immortal and she dominates the other fairies as one born to rule.' And nearly everyone noticed the auspicious pairing of Sibley and Anthony Dowell, which would quickly develop into a partnership of rare sympathy.

Gathering momentum as they revolve around *The Dream*, Sibley's thoughts fly effortlessly through time, to the ballet's first appearance in America a year later: 'The extraordinary thing that I remember even more vividly is the first night in New York, when we really *weren't* nervous. We were rehearsing it upstairs in the Met, giggling our way through it in our usual stupid way, and this was a *huge* night, the first night in New York for a new Ashton ballet, and there weren't any new ballets going on that night as well, like Rudolf doing *Images of Love*. I'm the most nervous person in the world always, but I really wasn't until, again, I saw Fred walk across that stage before it began and, honestly, he was so nervous he was shaking. And the responsibility came looming down upon us again.

'But then it did go like a bomb. I always have a lovely time because I lie for so long in my bower by myself, after my first solo, and I can judge the whole way the performance is going—and I've judged it all over the world—by the way the audience receives the lovers. And New York got hysterical; the minute Derek [Rencher] went "Go sit over there" and blew the kiss, the place fell down. I knew right then and there that *The Dream* had made it in New York.'

'I'm not a basher,' Ashton observes quietly. 'I'm not one of those people who do just terrific lifts and all this kind of thing. I don't knock the audience on the head, if you know what I mean. It has to saturate slowly into people's consciousness. What is surprising to me is that although my approach is so thoroughly English, nevertheless it seems to me that I had more *réclame* in New York than I had in England at that time. Nobody's a prophet in their own country, so it was only after the successes that I had in New York that people began to think, "Oh, well perhaps there is something to him after all."

'What is so wonderful in New York is that you *feel* it. In England you can be a success or not and it's no different, but in New York if you're a success you're *really* made to feel it. Mind you, if you're a flop they rush away from you too. But

I like that, I like that positive reaction one way or the other. It's not indifference.'

The American critic Lillian Moore wrote, 'For many balletomanes here, this season will be remembered as the one in which they discovered Sibley and Dowell.' 'The two of us really took flight,' Sibley grins, 'because New York took us to their hearts, as only New York can. It always has been far warmer in New York than in London for us; although they love us in London, in New York it's quite a different thing, quite a personal thing for two foreigners, and that night was the first time that happened to us. And then we went on the Ed Sullivan Show with *The Dream pas de deux*, like the next day, with Diana Ross and the Supremes. It must have been a big hit for us to be picked up the next day for television. So we really made it in New York and it was *The Dream* that did it all.'

'Sibley was established by the time of *The Dream*,' reckons Mary Clarke. 'To any dancer in the Royal Ballet, to have an Ashton role created on you in a major work like *The Dream* must be the most wonderful accolade. It's a wonderful sense of recognition, of really arriving, if Ashton wants to use you. I seem to remember that she couldn't believe it.'

Ashton mentions neither recognition nor accolades as he remarks, 'If I'm doing a ballet I think, "Now, who do I think is the right person for it?" Whether it's an established ballerina or somebody out of the corps de ballet. I first of all think of the right ingredient for the pudding. Possibly when I used her I could have used all sorts of other people, but I thought she would be ideal. It wasn't a risk at all. I was perfectly confident that she would be good in it, which indeed she was.'

Five

'I . . . am trying to catch the expression of ballet from various points of view. Unless you can catch it in motion, you don't catch it at all.' *Edwin Denby*

'I can't remember when I thought, "Oh, I'm now a ballerina." It was so long ago that I got to that position. I'm forty-six—I've been a ballerina longer than I haven't been a ballerina. I suppose the thrill wouldn't have been getting the title as much as doing the ballerina roles. But those first ones were all such ordeals: no time to prepare the first *Swan Lake*, no time for the *Ballet Imperial*. It was like a nightmare to get them on, so I certainly didn't have the time to think, "My God, isn't this amazing! I'm going to do *Swan Lake!*"

'I must have felt like a ballerina when I went out on tour in '60 to South Africa, because then I was doing the ballerina roles every single night. But of course the moment I got back all that went, and if I had anything it was once a year. So I never had that minute of thinking, "Ah, now I've made it. Now I'm a ballerina." First I was too busy and too worried, and then when I did become one, when I got back in my own company I wasn't: I was absolutely back on the treadmill. And then it seemed just automatic that one *was* one somehow. It was such a long time happening and also too quick in certain ways, in the rush of getting the roles, and slow in getting the title, so in a way there never was that moment.

'It's hard to explain. Maybe when I'd done *The Dream*, when I'd had that created for me . . . Ashton is so important. But certainly by the time all this started happening in New York and we were doing all our *Lacs* . . . I suppose then one realized one was a . . . ballerina. Ballerina. Principal they call you.'

Ninette de Valois doesn't concern herself with distinctions of time and title. In her experienced opinion you can tell a dancer has arrived 'by the way she dances certain big roles and the reception she gets. You can't *not* get over, you know. But this is an "inside" thing—it's inside the dancer that you get over. It's not a question of throwing yourself, but of feeling it. Personal.' If it's that simple, and Madam can be trusted to know these things, then Sibley's position as a fully fledged ballerina was indisputably established when the public saw her as Titania, whether one argues that that creation defined her status or only enhanced it.

In which case, an interesting change occurs in the telling of her story: chronology becomes all but irrelevant. Not because progress ceases once a title is conferred and generally acknowledged—far from it—but because the more obvious milestones of debuts and promotions have all been passed. The substance of Sibley's life and career after *The Dream* lies much more in what happened than in when it happened.

For a start, she was swiftly recognized as the supreme classicist of her generation, both by her ever more avid public and by the even more discriminating members of the press, who were quite prepared to write their recognition into the record. In 1965 her *Swan Lake* prompted the American critic Walter Terry to announce, 'She is of the rare stuff from which prima ballerinas are made . . . I use the term "prima ballerina" not as press agents do—to describe any filly who can stagger about in toe shoes—but in its proper sense, and that means there are barely more than a handful of prima ballerinas in the entire world.'

She was lucky, as she puts it, 'that our company's mainly based on the classics and Madam's syllabus is purely classical, so I had my root set clear.' She was also lucky that when Ashton inherited the director's chair from de Valois in 1963, he declared, 'One must preserve the nineteenth-century classics because people, dancers and audience, measure themselves by them. A dancer that does not qualify in the classics is only half a dancer.' Two years before he ceded the company's leadership to Kenneth MacMillan in 1970, Ashton fortified the repertory with both Peter Wright's staging of *The Sleeping*

Beauty, for which he choreographed several selections himself, and Nureyev's *Nutcracker*. Under MacMillan the company gained Peter Wright's production of *Giselle*, which transferred from the touring company to Covent Garden in 1971, and the director's own rendering of *The Sleeping Beauty* in 1973. In all but *The Nutcracker*, Sibley was awarded the first performance.

Leslie Edwards has been dancing with the Royal Ballet since 1933, primarily in mime and character roles, and has watched the development of every ballerina the company has produced. His eyes glow with enthusiasm as he says, 'Classical ballerinas are like choreographers: rare birds. And classical dancing is very cruel, it shows up every tiny detail, it demands perfection. So you need intelligence and diligence. Antoinette works very hard to achieve her style, which is obviously deeply thought out. She has no carelessness at all and she's very intelligent. The great ones are. You couldn't become a ballerina . . . you wouldn't survive without it.'

Peter Wright proves the point by example: 'When she was doing the Aurora *pas de deux* for some gala recently, she came to me and said, "I've got to have someone to work with me on this. Can you please help me with it?" Well, you can't keep doing it just the same all the time, and dancers can never see themselves. The interpretation of the big roles is something we have lost. With Aurora and even with *Nutcracker*, dancers today don't quite look at it the same way. They're desperately upset now if a pirouette doesn't come off, if it's not quite perfect from the technical point of view. The upset then was if they felt they hadn't given it the right embellishment and the right nuances.

'When I did *Nutcracker* for television with Margot, she said to me, "For God's sake, look at me all the time and tell me what I'm doing and what I'm not doing." Those are the great ones and Antoinette's like that too. Those great ballerinas need to be watched all the time, and controlled in a certain way. They all seek out the ones that can help them, that they can rely on. Of course you get to the stage where you become a prima ballerina and you're fairly self-sufficient. You have to go out and do your own thing on your own when you're a star. But all creative people may put on a front of being rather tough and confident, but all of them feel desperately insecure about things at times, and self-questioning.

'The marvellous thing about ballet, and I think Lincoln Kirstein said this, is that it's full of hazards. You've got to have that knife-edge of performance in the solos and the *pas de deux*. If it looks too easy, you lose the thrill. You don't want to see the horrible nervousness but the nervous excitement when you know it's all there. Antoinette always generated excitement. She was a very classical, very Petipa dancer, and very musical. And she had a strong temperament, but those are the ones who look at what you give them and really think about it. Antoinette could never be just a yes-lady, but she is completely open to any suggestion—she never closes doors. There's a nervousness about her too, a nervous edge, and you have to be like that.'

'The nerves are slightly cancelled out when it's a role that's been created on you,' Dowell observes, grinning a bit nervously as he approaches the subject. 'The worst nerves are always the classics since you're following in so many footsteps and you're treading on so many people's memories of their particular favourite. And you want to do well, and they expose you more too than a role you've created.

'The black act in *Swan Lake* always is my execution time. I get the nearest to what it's like for someone going onto the scaffold—that's how I feel waiting while the character dances count down and it gets nearer and nearer. I suppose because one's so nervous you don't like to admit it to each other. You try to get a strength from the other being all right. If you suddenly both went, "Oh God, we've got to do . . ." you'd cancel each other out. Luckily, once I'm on I'm OK, but then I could be a ventriloquist. Antoinette and I talk all the time, but it's not a conversation. It's little remarks, or jokes, and sometimes they break the nervous tension.

'Basically the nerves were when we were apart—her variation, her *fouettés*, my solo, my coda—unless it was a number like the *pas de deux* that Kenneth did for us in *Anastasia*. That was a very tricky, long, tiring piece, so that's where we would be nervous and tired together. And the big *Nutcracker pas de deux*, as well as its solos, was quite terrifying. But I get my worst nerves ever before a tele-recorded performance, i.e. all these videos we now make, because the day of the legend's over now and we can no longer be mysterious legends. We are there for every student: "Who is this Sibley and Dowell?"'

Slot it in and look. So if you were slightly off in that perform-ance, you are down there forever. It kills me.

'Of course Michael taught me a lot, all of the technical side of it. I was with him for years, and really—what's unusual nowadays—we had him all our working lives. It was very rarely anyone else would rehearse Antoinette and me, in all of it. We always had him, for everything, all Ashton's works down to the classics, and of course he would spot everything. Sometimes rehearsals were pretty heavy going because of different moods, but what was marvellous was that the last two rehearsals or the last one, one would always do it as a performance. He would say, "Now we're going to do it right through and you're going to live with your mistakes," and that was *so* valuable. Because when you go on stage you *know*, because you did it in the studio, that whatever happens you can get through it, and also if things go wrong you've been able to check them and live with them. We'd finish and he'd simulate the applause and wait so we would do a bow . . . you know, with a setpiece, Black Swan, where you needed the strength.

'So that was invaluable. And of course all the technical things: where the hands should be in relation to the girl for certain balances, all that. Some rehearsals can be absolute hell for the male dancer because the ballerina will be saying, "Oh, no. Push here. I don't feel right here," and to try to partner with all that is very hard. But Michael very rarely let Antoinette express an opinion of "I don't feel right on this." He was *very* much in control of both of us.'

'I think he could see very early on what Anthony and I had together,' Sibley asserts, 'which again, if you think about it, was a wonderful generosity of *his* spirit. After all, I was on the verge of being married to him, yet he could see that this was another great relationship, and it was his bigness of person that wanted to develop that.

'On *The Dream* he wasn't teaching us so much about us together, as a unit, because Ashton was creating that, and then not on *Romeo and Juliet* either, though I'm sure he took us for rehearsals, but certainly when he started on the classics. I can remember loving doing *Swan Lake* again because for the first time I had time to think about the role and develop it. There wasn't ever time to develop it, as opposed to just learning the steps, until I first did it with Anthony. He had only just started dancing it and he certainly hadn't done it at the Opera House, so this was when Michael began giving him all the benefit of his knowledge and passing on what Plucis had taught him. Anthony of course is so receptive, such a quick learner . . . it all worked out very well.'

Nearly five years after their first romantic encounter over *Swan Lake*, and just three months after the première of *The Dream*, Sibley and Somes were married. On 22 July 1964, they had a tiny wedding, with fourteen guests and Leslie Edwards as best man, at St Peter's Church in Milden, Suffolk. Because Sibley wanted to be wed in the country, her close friends Murray Arbeid and Frederick Fox helped arrange for the ceremony to take place in their local parish. The bride was twenty-five and the groom forty-six.

'On our honeymoon we went to Italy, to Violetta Elvin's hotel, where we went on holiday several times after that. Mainly we went to France on holiday. Michael introduced me to the south of France when I was twenty—we went to Beaulieu then—and we had quite a few holidays there, in Monte Carlo, Villefranche, St Jean. I go back year after year—it's almost an obsession with me. It has a bit of everything that I love: the heat, the colours, beauty, elegance, sophistication, plus you can go up to the mountains and have the wine and cheese and bread and unsalted butter. You can have everything there: the sea, the sun, French language, French culture . . . I love it.

'Then we had a sweet little house, Child's Cottage, in Child's Street off Earl's Court, and of course the awful thing was that I went straight down with glandular fever the moment we arrived. Michael was obviously busy, he was at performances at night and couldn't look after me, and Miss Edwards so kindly offered to have me in her flat. It was at the beginning of the season, and they were doing *Serenade* which I was frightfully upset to miss. I remember doing a rehearsal and feeling very tired at the end, and I thought to myself, "It's just because it's the first ballet back at the beginning of the season. And it's a new ballet, and I always get tired learning new things." I put all these excuses, but the next day I was hardly able to walk I was so exhausted.

'It takes months for them to be able to know you've actually got glandular fever—it's hard to diagnose. But when I realized I was ill and had to do nothing, it was far better . . . Well, it was absolutely wonderful, I can think of nothing better than as it turned out, being looked after by Miss Edwards. If I'd been in my own house, with Michael coming back reporting on what was going on—because after all that's his life as it was mine—I think it probably would have been difficult and upsetting. I would also not have been getting meals for him, not that he expected it, but *I* would have felt badly not being able to do it. It's a frightfully bad way to start off a marriage, isn't it?

'At my worst point, I couldn't brush my hair from my parting right down to the end. I got the brush as far as my ear and my hand fell down. The effort of keeping my arm up . . . I just couldn't do it. So it was very bad, and I *just* made it back for the *Romeo and Juliet* in February.'

This bout of glandular fever robbed Sibley of time, strength and momentum, and marked the beginning of a debilitating cycle. Given her talent and determination, her career might easily have unfurled smoothly, flowingly, without a hitch. Instead it was pleated at irregular intervals with illness and injury. Having begun 1964 joyfully, with *The Dream* and a dream of a marriage, she finished it in bed. The next pleat would come in 1966 with her first knee operation and the nervous collapse it induced. Each time she left the stage for months; each time she returned to it weakened and thus more prone to injury. She withdrew from an American tour in 1972 because of illness, she succumbed to an inflamed hip in 1974, and then, for several years, she scarcely danced at all.

But in between the months of pain and invisibility, there was almost nothing she couldn't do. Gertrude Stein once wrote that 'English dancers, when they dance, dance with freshness and agility and they know what drama is.' That was Sibley, when she danced, more and more Sibley as the years passed.

Kenneth MacMillan's sumptuous *Romeo and Juliet* opened in London on 9 February 1965. Down the line, after Fonteyn and Nureyev who danced the first night and Seymour and Gable for whom the work was choreographed, came Sibley and Dowell, the company's youngest pair of star-crossed lovers. Writing in the *Express* Clive Barnes commented that

'Neither acted out the roles with any great power or passion. But when you can dance as perfectly and eloquently as they did who, frankly, cares?' That's perfect, eloquent dancing after several months of glandular fever. Now read what James Monahan wrote in 1973, and you'll have an inkling of the effort expended by a ballerina and the rewards garnered:

'Sibley's Juliet is the one who grows. She always danced the role beautifully, easily, but what so impressed me . . . was her apparently tireless self-dissatisfaction; she seemed to be probing, thinking about the role, trying this and that emphasis, always in terms of dance movement rather than just mime and always, it seemed, trying to replace the good by the best . . . Her interpretation of eight years ago [was] a scaffolding of lovely dancing around which the full expressiveness—the palace—has since been growing and still grows.'

It's fortunate that critics provide such descriptive rhetoric since dancers lack both the time and the inclination for it. In 1965 Sibley was concentrating on the more practical side of dancing: 'With *Romeo*, I was scheduled to dance with Christopher Gable, but as Lynn was doing the performance with him about three days before mine, it would have been totally impossible for me to get that whole ballet together with nobody to rehearse. So I asked Kenneth if I could work with Anthony, who was dancing Benvolio—he had no performance as Romeo, he wasn't scheduled to do it, he merely understudied it. And Kenneth quite rightly said, "Could he get through it? He hasn't done anything as taxing as that." It's a killer. That first act is really gruelling for the man, and he hadn't done *Swan Lake*, *Giselle*, nothing at that point. So I said, "We do work terribly well together. Can we have a go at it? See what you think." Well, the rest is sort of history.

'I wasn't looking for a partner, but when I realized it was so happy and working so well, I immediately thought, "How marvellous. Maybe I can do more things with him." But I didn't think "partnership" in the way of Margot and Rudolf or Margot and Michael or Karsavina and Nijinsky. When you meet someone, you don't immediately think of marrying them; you just know you get on terribly well with them. I was amazed at the ease with which we worked and our compatibility, and happy that it was working, but I don't work things out in advance. They merely happen, they evolve, as my life has done. It's not thinking "That's what I want" and go after it and get it. Nothing's been planned. There have been rare exceptions, like my second child. I would have done anything to have it and I could think of nothing else. But I have never worked out any of these other things like my partnership with Anthony or my coming back.

'I don't remember a response to us after *The Dream*. I suppose there was one, but the only thing that people here were interested in that night was that Rudolf appeared in two ballets. But in America they're always making stars, and they adored us, from *The Dream* onwards, and hailed us and kept promoting us. In America we were very much a pair, sort of the young hero and heroine following Margot and Rudolf, and had very much our own audience.'

'New York *was* very special,' Dowell agrees. 'All the people in show biz in England say this—I'm not the first: if you're going to make it you've got to make it somewhere else before they'll accept you back here. And really, although you'll probably get a lot of the ballet fans saying "Of course we recognized it," it was New York that took Sibley-Dowell to their hearts. One'll never get such a high from an audience as performing there, ever.'

Closer to home and in the quarters where it counted most, the response to the new partnership was far from indifferent. 'Obviously Fred was thrilled to bits,' Sibley points out, 'because it was his idea in the first place, his baby coming to realization. So in all his ballets we were together; you name them, we did them. Kenneth also; from *Romeo* onwards, as he says himself, he could see this magic work. And of course he used it in everything that he did with us: *Triad, Anastasia pas de deux, Manon, Pavane.*

'But from the company point of view originally . . . I don't think de Valois was much pleased with it at first. She loves more extrovert characters, and Anthony was frightfully shy and retiring. All his humour and suavity didn't come out when he was young or when he didn't know people very well. Now of course he can put anybody at ease but in those days he didn't, and I remember after a *Swan Lake* we did together de Valois casually saying that she didn't think it was a good idea. I don't know whether she wanted Christopher Gable, I don't know what she wanted. She merely said she didn't think that this would be right. And of course obviously she's changed her mind as well since then.'

'Antoinette always talks of her school experiences as naughty,' Dowell laughs, 'and I think, "God, no, I'd never be a person like that." I wasn't a "naughty boy". Too frightened of the consequences, where she probably wouldn't think of them.

'As characters we're very different. She's always certain that everything's either red or black. I suppose I'm a bit calmer; my mother was a very practical person and I seem to have got that streak from her. When I'm on the borderline of going slightly over, it checks me all the time, just in time. With Antoinette, more live wires are exposed at times. That's probably been the way we complement each other, on the part the audience don't see, all the working out of everything.

'The famous occasion is when we went to Pacific Ballet in San Francisco to do one of our rare stints outside the Royal Ballet—we're talking about the early Seventies. We were going to do *Thaïs pas de deux*, the *Romeo* balcony *pas de deux* and, because they wanted fireworks, the Black Swan, although we both always hate taking something out of context. And they said, "You have to dance to tape," and we said, "What if the speeds are wrong?"—you know, all the ballet recordings are either cut to ribbons or they're the wrong speed. "Don't worry. We have the most fantastic technicians here. They splice it, cut it, double it . . . you name it, they can do it. Don't worry." So over we go. For some reason the *Thaïs* and the *Romeo* were not too bad, but by the time we get to the *Swan Lake* coda—no way. Because the *fouettés* really have to be just right speedwise, she became really desperate, and between being nervous of doing this *pas de deux* out of context and being like stars brought over to sell the season, we both felt like fish out of water.

'So off we went to this Wizard of Oz technician, in his room with all the knobs and switches and lights. And of course as we both knew, if you want something faster the tone level will go up, and if you slow it down the tone will go down. There's no way anyone can alter that. So I suddenly realized that this was just impossible, and she gave up on the whole situation. That I think was where my patience was really tried to the end, because my practical streak was saying, "Yes, it is impossible. This whole thing is just terrible. But. We're here, we've accepted it, we've got to save the day. You can't just give up on it." And of course the more I got going to try to save it, the more she got "This is impossible." It was really out on the surface; all her worst qualities came out. And she just sat in this chair while I was whizzing round the room, trying to do my steps *and* her steps, going, "You see? Maybe that's it for tempo. Is that better?" Something in the end saved it; maybe we just had a good drink when we got back to the hotel. But I said, "You just don't know how near I came to putting an axe through your head."

'We've had all kinds of things go wrong. One funny one was in Australia, in *Cinderella*. After the *pas de deux*, we have to join in the coda with the Seasons. I have to lift her on my shoulder and bring her downstage, and her tutu knickers got caught on a hook on my tunic and she just hung there. I had to run off with her hanging from my front. But those are just fun.

'The most disastrous I think was when those terrible kids in New York ripped her skirt off in Rudolf's *Nutcracker*.' ('It was the last night of our New York season,' Sibley groans, 'and the Bolshoi and Plisetskaya and Sol Hurok were all out front.') 'The kids were really precocious and they must have all planned together. Antoinette's in this party dress and it's done on velcro; the rats have to grab at it and take the upper layer off, and she's left in a net skirt. Well, they not only took the top skirt off, they ripped the net skirt off. I just stood there and looked at her—I couldn't believe it. I don't think there were knickers on; it was just the pink tights up to the bodice and a shred of net. And the awful thing was that Michael took off afterwards and held her responsible. She was helpless! What could she do? She couldn't run off stage: I would have no one to dance with. That was a *terrible* performance because after the nerves of that, we had the next act with this amazing monstrous *pas de deux* . . . I mean, monstrous in a nice way. It really felt like the Grand National, every fence to get through. There we did have to pull together, and that's where I suppose I was able to help.

'I never usually thought of giving help. Naturally one's there to save things if they go wrong, but that's something you just learn to do, quickly adjust. But providing help didn't come into it. It was very much a dual thing: we just danced together.'

'Just danced together' doesn't quite do justice to the harmony these partners achieved, in their impeccable line and phrasing, in the subtlety of their musical responses, in the elegance of their carriage and the intelligence of their characterizations. Nancy Goldner wrote in 1969 that 'as a pair they form the most idealized conception of beauty possible.' The same year, reviewing their *Romeo and Juliet* in New York, Anna Kisselgoff observed, 'There are times when greatness becomes too overwhelming to be defined.'

'You need the right materials,' Leslie Edwards insists. 'You can't put a calico hem on some satin—it looks ghastly. You need two satins. Some dancers never go together; they don't all find somebody. They have to be the right consistency, like Garbo and John Gilbert or Gertie Lawrence and Noel Coward. A trust grows up between partners, mutual trust, and the public sees it too. You feel safe when you watch them. I like to think partners mature with each other, and in good partnerships one sees all the development. Together Sibley and Dowell got more magical; the latter-day performances of *The Dream* were more wonderful than the earlier ones. It was not only their marvellous line and trust of each other, but the in-between bits. What's the point of having ballets if you don't have magical moments *all* the time?'

The magic between them stretched to whole minutes, to entire performances, emerging as rapturous abandon in *Romeo and Juliet*, as luminous serenity in *Symphonic Variations*, as tender trust in the "Awakening" *pas de deux* Ashton created for them in the 1968 *Sleeping Beauty*. They could make the unreal either real, as in *The Dream* and *Swan Lake*, or true, as in *Manon* and *Daphnis and Chloe* and *Afternoon of a Faun*. Impeccable classicists one day, dreamy yearning romantics the next, their bodies and temperaments were mutually enhancing and ennobling.

Beriosova claims, 'It was obviously a partnership that was destined to the greatest heights in ballet. They were miraculous together—the chemistry between them.' Mary Clarke contends, 'They're such a good fit because of the schooling. It's the first partnership to come right through the school.' Critics groped for fresh superlatives, but couldn't explain why one Sibley and one Dowell should equal something far greater than two dancers together. But then, as George Balanchine has said, 'The trouble begins when we start to explain things that are unexplainable . . . You cannot describe with words something for which there are no words.'

Anthony Dowell doesn't even try. Leaving the ineffable to the theoreticians, he speaks only in practical, physical terms: 'Proportions did a lot to make us fit. In my early days I suffered from a bad back, and in those days the girls were larger than they are now. Being in the corps you couldn't choose who you were with; suddenly someone would come up and you'd have to lift them. Antoinette was the first person to come along where the weight seemed right to me. Slowly the back got stronger and the problems ceased. It's like when you do weight-training: you have to find the right balance for your own structure and muscles. So that was a purely technical reason why it worked.

'One of the things has to be the way we hear music. There's never any doubt as to how we're going to move, how and when. Musically we hear it together, so that takes half the battle out of it. Our performance pictures are taken in a fraction of a second, and in most of them we're almost in the identical position. It's the bodies, yes, and in a way maybe the training. She came through with Winifred Edwards who also taught me.

'But in the end, it's not necessarily going to work. I can describe all the technical side of what I think contributes, but there has to be something else too. And I can't see us on stage anyway, so I don't know.

'You see, we're not conscious of what comes across. For a dancer, and this probably destroys awful illusions, when you feel things are taking off is when things work technically. If you suddenly go for something and it feels awful, you think, "I'm not on tonight. It's all going to be such an effort now." I can honestly say that there have been two or maybe three *Swan Lake*s where I feel I've been on top of it, ever. And what you have to learn is, as in my early days with Michael, to live with your mistakes and not let some step going wrong colour the whole performance. That was the hardest thing I ever had to learn as a dancer, that you go on to the next thing and it's the performance and what you give it that matters.

'And when I need . . . When I've gone and lost it, that's when suddenly you see a different side of her. You see flashes of—I don't want this to sound wrong—a very sane and practical woman, absolutely clear and steady. That's the only time she will show it, and that's when she is always there and 800 per cent giving.'

'In twenty-two years,' Sibley says thoughtfully, 'we've grown up from youngsters into mature people. We've been through my first marriage, various relationships in my case and the same in his, the deaths of his mother and father, his aunt looked after me at one point . . . well, all our adult life we've shared together. Of course there have been upsets and jealousies with each other, of course, because we're both highly strung and we both want what we want. But we adore each other. He trusts me, I hope, as I do him and you can't have much more than that.

'If you think of the pressures we've been through together, apart from when we were younger, creating all these things and having to make them work. When Fred was leaving as director, we had to hang in there and keep the performances going. It all happened during a *Cinderella* performance; [David] Webster came to tell us, and the whole company felt abandoned—we couldn't believe it. It was a big upset for everybody, and Anthony and I had to keep dancing. We had to go on and do the *pas de deux* and our solos, and we were mind-blown by this news.

'Or in Brasilia where we had to keep that *Bayadère* going when we couldn't hear the music. We weren't scheduled to go to Brasilia but because this tour was such a huge success in Brazil, they asked us if we could open this vast sports stadium in Brasilia, the new wonder place. We were opening with Anthony and me doing the *Bayadère*, and we didn't want to go with the rest of the company because we obviously had to get to the theatre early to prepare. Theatre? Stadium—I mean, it held something like 20,000 people. It was a sports stadium, it was no arena, and we were on a platform at one end. Well, we got there and they wouldn't let us in. All the guards were around with their guns and their helmets, just like Martians everywhere, all these state police, and no way would they let us in because we had no cards. How could we show we were ballet dancers? I showed my pointe shoes. It was so frustrating and upsetting.

'Anyway, eventually the company arrived and we got in. Now we were frightfully late; you've got to really get ready early for *Bayadère*, see the stage and keep calm. And we started and what happened was . . . We were using a stage up one end, but they'd sold the tickets right round the whole stadium. So there were 2000 or 3000 people who had tickets and who weren't being allowed in because those seats could no longer be occupied because they were backstage. There was hysteria outside. We had begun the performance, and they were still trying to get into the theatre. They'd paid for their tickets, black market lots of them, and the police still wouldn't let them in; they were coshing them on the head and putting them in vans. Well, the noise was so much that it drowned the music.

'Now if you can imagine thirty-two girls coming down the ramp to no music! How do they know when to do it? We only know by the music, and not by anything else. So Anthony went one side, I went the other, and we counted it for them, singing the counts. Well, they came off and burst out crying from the strain, and then it was the *pas de trois* and we sang all their bit for them. And of course we came to go on and there was nobody to sing for us, nobody at all. They were all hysterical. We were by ourselves. We came on with no music and nobody to sing to us, and *Bayadère*'s hard enough anyway! We were in such a state afterwards I don't think we ever knew what we'd done and what we hadn't done. You see, we didn't know if people were getting killed out there. We didn't know the tickets had been sold. We thought it was a revolution going on. For us, it was just bloodcurdling screams.

'We've shared so many of these nerves and pressures: the first night of *Manon*, the first night of *Manon* in New York, opening and closing seasons as we did in New York and London. And even more so now, at this stage in our career, still having to show that we can do it and we're not just crumbling to bits. After all, people are now *really* expecting things from us, because once you've got there, there's only one way to go. And travelling around the world, in all the appearances we've done together without the company, we've had to hold our own and cope with it all and do it. So really

I think we've seen each other at our very very worst and probably at our very best.

'Now when I heard about the CBE of course I was thrilled to bits. You get a letter saying you have been nominated for this honour and will you accept it? But the thing was, Anthony and I didn't have secrets from each other, we had always shared everything, but you are specifically told not to tell anyone. It is a secret until it comes out. So I waited quite a time and then I thought, "Well, Anthony will never tell anybody." What we pass on to each other is sacrosanct. We were at the Coliseum for the summer season, and I said, "I've got the most unbelievable thing to tell you. It's an absolute secret, but I've been given the CBE." He looked at me and he smiled and he said, "So have I."

'They were absolute box office,' exclaims Winifred Edwards with pride. 'They were the natural heirs of Margot and . . . not Somes, but Somes-Nureyev, that would be accurate.'

'That was the sort of position we did reach,' Sibley nods. 'Critics would hail us here and in America as the young king and queen, or like the Prince of Wales, waiting to succeed. Obviously we'd been labelled this for quite a time, mainly because we were the classical dancers of the company and it was a classical company. It was nice for us because it gave us more prestige, but it was a big strain having to put on such big performances and be judged good or bad with so few a year. And after all, we must now be thirty, so we should now be getting to this position. And the only way to get it was when Margot and Rudolf weren't there, because when they were around they were given the performances because of the huge stars they were.

'We always lived with this. It wasn't a matter of battling against it—it was a fact of life. We were very much dominated, always, by Margot, but then when Rudolf came to the scene it added to it in that Rudolf needed to be on every night. So he would ask for more performances of everything, and therefore they had to cut down on everybody else's. And in that respect of course it slowed our progress or kept us back, of course it did.'

'When I was directing the company and Margot and Rudi were a thing,' Frederick Ashton murmurs wearily, 'everybody used to complain, "You're only using them. They're doing everything." I said, "It is part of my business to see that the houses are full." In those days, if Margot and Rudi were billed together the house was packed out, so therefore I'd got to. But I used to beg them both, "Please go away and do things abroad. Let other people have a chance." Oh, I'm much happier choreographing—I hated all that.'

'Of course we learned such a lot from watching them, and we admired and respected them so much it's nothing against their talent,' Sibley continues fervently, 'but the only ways that *we* could get through, Anthony and I, were in our own ballets or with the classics. When they weren't around, *we* got more performances and naturally we grabbed at them. We needed and wanted and had to have them at that stage, and we waited for them.'

Kenneth MacMillan remembers the situation vividly: 'I think all those three girls—Merle and Lynn and Antoinette—one day hoped to take over the company; they would have been mad not to think that. That's perfectly natural. But the charisma of Fonteyn by then was so huge that it wasn't possible at that moment. And it was a shame because it was the right moment when those girls could have zoomed up. A whole stream of dancers was eclipsed, and I don't only feel it about those three. I feel it about Svetlana Beriosova also, Nadia Nerina. But I don't know if that was anybody's fault or it just happened.'

'But there was no elbowing,' Beriosova insists, 'especially not in Dame Ninette's time or Sir Fred's. We were so different, for a start. The gallery-ites always used to say, "Ohhh, that one's having a row with that one because . . . Ohhh, they're so jealous of each other . . . Ohhh, that one's got the first night." But on the contrary, it certainly didn't exist in, shall I say, my heyday. There was Margot Fonteyn and there was myself and there was Antoinette coming up, and I was the best of friends with Margot and with Antoinette.'

'Beriosova was and is one of my great friends,' Sibley declares firmly, 'but I suppose there was a healthy rivalry with my own generation. I don't want that to sound wrong. Lynn and I have always got on very well; of all my contemporaries, Lynn and I got on the best. We are the same age but for ten days, we're both Pisces, we had the same teacher, Miss Edwards. From the age of seventeen or eighteen we saw each other a lot. And then when she went off to the touring company we were brought up in completely different spheres: me totally as a classical ballerina, she totally as a dramatic ballerina. So our paths didn't cross that much, either as rivals or anything else.

'Then when she did come over to our company, and she had *Symphony* done for her, I was always her second cast. That could have upset me, but on the other hand I was doing maybe *Ballet Imperial;* I had my roles in which she didn't even understudy me. So it was balanced up; I knew that Kenneth would use me after Lynn which I considered a big honour—Lynn was his favourite. But then Fred used me in everything. So it didn't really conflict and we've always got on frightfully well. I admire and respect her and I think she admires and respects me equally well. And if anybody tries to manufacture some aggro between us, there isn't any and never has been, so it's no point trying. Obviously we've both thought, "I wish I was doing that," but no more than an instant's thought. She never hurt me and I never hurt her.

'It's easy for me to talk about Lynn, but about Merle it's harder. In some ways it was difficult for us, but in other ways not. She has the most amazing fluency of dance; she really can get up and do anything at any time and in any way, and she's got the most extraordinary gift of musicality. And she had her own things that were very much hers. There have been differences with Merle, ups and downs, and there we are. But since I came back she has been nothing but helpful and encouraging.'

Ninette de Valois dismisses the subject breezily: 'But that competition was very good for Antoinette—she needed competition. They all need competition. She needed competition to find her own level, her own style. You learn eventually "That ballet's not for me: it *is* for so-and-so." It's awfully good for them. They had much more competition at her age than in the time of Margot. Margot and the younger ones, in the Thirties and at the beginning of the war, had it all their own way because there were fewer of them. I think it's very good to have a bunch, but it doesn't hurt to have . . . I do think Margot did a terrible lot of good, for Sibley, for everybody. They all adored her; she was too good for anyone to be jealous of.'

'Haven't I said about Margot?' Sibley gasps. 'It's hard to know where to start because she's been one's idol—well, she was prima ballerina assoluta—as far back as one can ever remember. Margot Fonteyn . . . it was like Anna Pavlova. A legend.

'There was no manner with Margot. She was very kind to everybody but she was also, and quite right . . . strict isn't the right word. For instance she would point out if there was a thread hanging from one's skirt or one's shoes weren't tied up quite properly; if your hair was a bit messy she would tell you. In *Symphonic Variations* she would whisper to you if you weren't in quite the correct position: "Over there . . . Come nearer . . . Go further . . ." I was very nervous always—we all were, the side girls—apart from the nerves of the actual ballet because in fact it's harder on the side. The middle person takes most of her positions from the conductor, because she's in the middle, whereas the side girls have to see that not only are they on line with the middle one but lined up on the right mark. We have markings on the stage for it; you're opposite this box or that bridge. So we were nervous of the ballet, but very nervous of dancing with Margot. I mean, Margot was Margot, and we were merely nothing.

'Her standards were so high, and she was perfect in every respect and you can't do better than perfect. She was what everybody thought of, what I always thought of, as a ballerina: her black hair and her silk tights, and the execution as well. It was all just right, perfect in its purity and its paring down—if you're that perfect you can take away anything extraneous, which is what she did. It's much easier to put frills on and bravura and flourishes, but not to just be absolutely pure and correct, which she was even at the end. If naturally things got harder for her, she still retained that purity.

'Now talking about hair is interesting because when we were in Italy doing *Romeo and Juliet*, we all dressed in the same room, and she asked me why I hadn't ever considered dyeing my hair black. I was so taken by surprise I couldn't really think of an answer. It hadn't entered my head to be dark. That's why I hadn't thought of myself as a ballerina, because I didn't have dark hair. But now that I *was* a ballerina, I still couldn't think of getting my hair dark. It wasn't correct for me. But she said it adds theatrically in so many of the dramatic roles, and of course she's right. Darkness is for drama, and somebody with dark hair automatically looks sadder. But if you think of a golden-haired person, they look more radiant, and that's without doing anything. I did think about it, and I thought, "No, I wouldn't feel at all right being dark," and then I luckily went back to my Ulanova thoughts and remembered it all could be done by fair people.

'I knew Margot so well . . . When I say that, I don't want it to sound presumptuous, but of course Michael was a great friend of hers so from when I started going with him I was always included in things. When we arrived in New York, for instance, she'd say, "Look, I've got a car, Michael. Come along in the car," and she'd drop us off somewhere. So there I was with Margot.

'I remember going to her house in Thurloe Square after a television thing we'd done. She'd been Aurora and I'd been the Bluebird, and she invited us back for a meal afterwards. The house was all white and clear and uncluttered and so elegant, just like she is, and I remember her giving us soup and saying how nourishing soup was, and listening to every word she spoke. So I was very fortunate in getting to know her on these terms very well.

'And she has always been really wonderful—I don't mean just balletically. I have gone to her in a couple of difficult times and asked her advice, as a woman, nothing to do with the ballet, and she's been most helpful. And I know she's always admired my work; she's always been very kind about it. She was compèring a big gala in New York recently, and Anthony and I were doing *The Dream pas de deux*. Because it was a big international gala and hard for anybody to be given the final position, it was given to dancers from the two American companies: Peter Martins, representing New York City Ballet, and Cynthia Gregory, representing ABT (American Ballet Theatre), were going to do *Don Q.* or *Corsaire* or something. Then Peter Martins hurt himself and they came out of it at the last minute, and everyone thought it would be a good thing to put Anthony and me to end it, although you wouldn't think of *The Dream* as a good ending to all these fireworks. However, we did, and it worked very well. Afterwards Margot said we'd reached new heights that night and she thought we were dancing better than she'd ever seen us. And this was after all this time off.

'Rudolf says that Margot had suggested at some point very early on that he should dance, not with her, who after all was much older than him, but with one of us younger ones. And apparently she suggested me. Rudolf, not unwisely, thought that was quite wrong—it was he who told me; he wanted to dance with Margot. And that was all right with me because the only person I was thinking of was Anthony, who I was just getting to dance with. Isn't it odd? We laugh about it, because we adore dancing together. And I've danced with him such a lot, in every ballet other than *Giselle*, which I would love to have done with him.

'You can't compare dancing with Rudolf and dancing with Anthony. Everybody of this calibre is different on every single night, and prima ballerinas too, and that's why they're where they are. Every night they throw off new feelings. That's how Anthony and I have been dancing together since 1963; we'd be bored out of our minds if we were still the same. I hope that every time we dance together there's something that sparks us off still—otherwise it would just be dead as a dodo by now. It's the same with Rudolf, with Mischa [Barysh-nikov], with Natasha [Makarova], with Haydée, and that's why it's always interesting.

'One of Rudolf's friends, Maude Lloyd, said after one of our *Swan Lake*s that it was amazing that when Rudolf was with me he became very soft, much softer than she'd ever seen him before. I don't know why, but that's obviously what I brought out in him. It would be interesting if somebody would tell me what he brought out in me, because I don't know how it appeared to other people.

'The thing with Rudolf that one goes back and back to is his absolute enthusiasm and love for dancing. That is completely the opposite to my or Anthony's kind of person-ality, and it goes right the way through class, through the barre work, through everything. He does it 110 per cent, all the time. Every single day. And if there's a performance, he does it in the morning and in the evening. He is the most extraordinary person I've ever met in that respect—it's phenomenal what he does. And he does it with a relish because he enjoys it, that's the difference. When I'm having to do it every single day and I can't see a break, I start to get claustrophobic; I can see it happening to myself and I'll look for a way out. But not Rudolf: he will double his work and then he'll still be happy. He'll work all day every day, which I can't do. Anthony and I sometimes tend to gloom around a bit and say, "I can't do this. Can't even walk today."

'Before the last *Cinderella* we did we had organized to go through a couple of things on stage, and I remember sitting in those Stepsisters' chairs and looking at each other as if we were completely mad even being made up, let alone actually appearing on the stage dancing. We looked at each other with total resignation, the feeling of "I don't know how we're going to get through." And that was one of the best performances we ever did when we finally made it up there.

'But it is wonderful when you come up against this amazingly buoyant love of the dance. And because Rudolf is so enthusiastic, the enthusiasm rubs off and you do try the most extraordinarily difficult things. Because he suggested it and he's so sure you can do it, you jolly well try it. For instance, I had *Swan Lake* coming up with Rudolf and I was going to do the *manège* I used to do instead of the *fouettés*, and he said, "Why don't you just try the *fouettés*?" I said, "No, I haven't done them for ages, because of my bad knee." And he said, "Well, if they don't work you won't do them, but just try them." And because he was *flinging* himself into these amazing things . . . It's not like Anthony, who tries them as well but not with this daredevil style. Rudolf literally throws himself into things with such risk, so you think, "OK. Why not?" And he's such a strong, firm partner, and again it gives you tremendous confidence.

'He's such a mega-star, but in all these years I've never had a temperament with Rudolf, a scene, never. I've never seen him like that. The thing is, and I know it sounds terribly stupid, we're both Pisces and all Pisces seem terribly close to each other. I don't know if that's why we don't have rows, but Pisceans are all mad and you do recognize it in another person. So he's a real comrade in that way.

'He's invited me to go and dance all over the world with him. But with my health and my injuries I could only barely keep doing what I was doing, let alone do the extras, so they've mainly had to go. I seemed to be always letting him down.'

Ever the historian, Mary Clarke casts Sibley's situation in a slightly different light: 'Guesting has never been the Royal Ballet practice. The traditions of the Royal Ballet were that you were a member of your company and you worked with your own company. You didn't zoom around the world. Sibley was very much rooted in the Royal Ballet tradition because of Somes; he's very very conscious of what he got from *his* predecessors. I think she had a mix of loyalty and the feeling that it was the right kind of setting for her kind of dancing.

'But I think it's something of a tragedy for her that she never had the chance to be the assoluta of her generation—there was a spell where she *should* have been the one. Margot was there for such a long time and then Sibley was off so much; it was a combination of the two and because of that she didn't become a "household name". In a funny way, she is now more than she was then, when she should have been.'

The same idea has occurred to Sheila Bloom: 'You see, the Garden at that time had a policy where they wouldn't allow Antoinette very much leeway to go abroad as a guest. They kept her pretty strictly to her contract, and she was getting lots of invitations to go here, there, everywhere. She had an enormous loyalty to the Royal Ballet, and she didn't want to make them feel that she would ever desert them. It was always "the company first", and she did turn down an enormous number of offers, which would have made her more of an international ballerina.'

'To me it felt like I did a *lot* of guesting,' Sibley protests. 'I went to Stuttgart by myself once or twice; I did the *Beauty* there with Ray Barra and also the Bluebird with him, and my first *Flower Festival pas de deux*, with Henning Kronstam. Anthony and I did *Swan Lake* and *Thaïs* in Munich, and the *Romeo* balcony *pas de deux* for a big gala in Amsterdam and a bit of *Dances at a Gathering* at the Aldeburgh Festival . . . It did seem to me that I was rushing around quite a lot.'

'Antoinette was a very valuable member of the company,' de Valois asserts adamantly, 'and a devoted loyalist to the morale, which is always so nice. She was sensible like that.

'Now almost every century produces only about eight international names that really go on through the centuries. I looked up the history once, and it's very interesting. There are lots of great dancers, but international means every corner of the world and an international name is a very different thing. I think you could say that this century, with Fonteyn, we reach the peak of the twentieth century's great international stars. Markova was another, Pavlova, Karsavina comes into this time, Plisetskaya, and the other Russian, Ulanova. You've got to accept it. They're single numbers, nearly always. Which isn't to say there aren't hundreds of great stars. A star of your generation, that's quite a different thing. I was talking about an international name that in two hundred years you will remember belonged to their time.'

Although Sibley danced all over Europe, North America, South America and in the Middle East, Russia, Australia and Japan, she never pretended to be 'an international name' in the sense that de Valois uses the phrase. But no one could pretend she wasn't a 'star of her generation'. It's true that her country honoured her with a CBE a year before her company honoured her with the opening *and* closing performances of the New York season, 'something for which we have waited all our dancing lives,' she said at the time. And it's true that during the same 1974 season at least one New York newspaper was still referring to Sibley and Dowell as 'new stars', although they had received twenty curtain calls on closing night in the same city a full six years earlier. The rapturous ovation for their *Nutcracker* that night went on, undiminished, for so long that the inconceivable occurred: the asbestos fire curtain, already deliberately lowered in an effort to send everyone home, had to be raised again to allow the bows to continue.

When asked what it took to be a star, Katherine Hepburn replied, 'I don't know. I've got it.' Sibley had it too, offstage as well as on. She was interviewed, photographed, filmed, painted and sketched. *Harper's Bazaar* nominated her as one of 'Britain's Most Beautiful Women'. She bought her clothes from Thea Porter and Sonia Rykiel, modelled jewels for charity galas, and was herself modelled in porcelain for a limited edition of Spode figurines. In 1973 *Woman's Own* magazine said, 'Her tip for looking chic is itself very chic: "Let everyone else do it for you.' " The same year the *Telegraph* announced that her friends included Barbra Streisand, David Hockney, Richard Chamberlain and Claire Bloom, and that 'She was about to have her legs insured for £25,000.' She danced with Dowell and Nureyev and Baryshnikov before the camera, and with ambassadors and dukes and tycoons at parties. Her baby picture went up on the wall at Drones, a chic Belgravia restaurant, and in 1974 she received the supreme English accolade of appearing as Roy Plomley's radio guest on *Desert Island Discs* (the one luxury she chose to take to the mythical island was a bed). She also went to visit the Queen.

'The honour is enormous, of course, being invited to these luncheons the Queen gives. I was the only woman guest that day; the men were Jonathan Miller, Bobby Charlton, the football player, and a top businessman, Bernard Stern, who's now a painter. I had gone in a silk dress—I remember it was an Emilio Pucci that I'd bought at Bergdorf Goodman in New York—and I sweat profusely when I'm nervous, so it was clinging to me and you could see through it.

'You have drinks first, and we all felt very nervous standing there with the drinks waiting for the Queen to come in. Everybody feels the same, full of anticipation and expectation. Not that she doesn't put you at ease, because of course she does, and the Duke of Edinburgh is very relaxing. All the corgis came in with the Queen; there must have been five of them, trotting in, and one was sort of going round in circles. Anyway, this relaxes everybody.

'So we were sitting eating and the Duke was next to me—it was a round table—and suddenly one of these corgis ended up on my foot. Well, I've always heard that corgis tend to nip you, so I said to the Duke, "Excuse me, sir, but one of your dogs is on my foot." And he said, "Oh, kick him out of the way." I said, "You must be joking. It's not worth my life to have my foot bitten off!" And he said, "No, wait a minute. *I'll* kick it out of the way," and he did. He was most charming about it.

'Now the CBE ceremony was amazing because it was like a whole production going on. There are hundreds of people on this occasion—people getting the DBE, knighthoods, all these different honours—and you're ushered into your various groups in different rooms. It's all such ritual: there are flunkeys everywhere . . . it's very beautiful. Then you queue up, waiting, in this very long corridor full of the most amazing pictures, like an art gallery, and the ballroom, the throne room, where it's held, has a gallery at one end where an orchestra's playing. It's quite overwhelming.

'The Queen had asked that we receive our CBE together, which was quite unusual, so we both went up together. We actually had a choreography: so many steps forward, curtsey, so many steps back, curtsey again. The Queen pins your honour on you and says a few words—it's very exciting. Then we went out afterwards to celebrate, to somewhere very luxurious, and I think we all got poisoned on the oysters!

'Another time at Buckingham Palace was with Rudolf when we went for the Wildlife Fund gala. We had to go first for a big drinks do, and I went in my red fox coat. It *was* the only warm coat I had and it *was* the middle of February, but it couldn't have been more stupid. A *fox* coat! There must have been five hundred . . . I don't know how many hundreds of people there shaking the Queen's hand, and she spoke to each one. She gave us her time, she had something to say to every single one of us, she was absolutely amazing. And then I noticed she had her shoes off. She was standing in her stocking feet, and I thought that was so enchanting.

'I've also been invited to 10 Downing Street—I've been two or three times. One was a dinner for the American President's daughter. Was it the peanut man or was it Nixon? Which is the one who wanted his daughter to marry Prince Charles? I sat next to Geoffrey Howe, so it was absolutely lovely for me—that was the first time I met him. And another time that I went, when Wilson was P.M., we were taken in to see the Cabinet Room, which was fascinating. I think we went in because it was the one thing Frank Sinatra particularly wanted to see.

'I've always got on well with Lord Wilson; in fact, he's been to a dinner party at my home. I first met him at a large dinner given by the Fellows of the Royal Society, where we talked for a long time. He told me that every time he went to Moscow he went to see *Swan Lake*, and he named all the different ballerinas he had seen. We spent the rest of the time talking about how to deal with insomnia without taking sleeping pills.'

'The thing about Antoinette,' says Peter Wright, laughing, 'is that she likes being a star. She likes the star thing. Good for her too.'

'We all like that,' Dowell admits, 'even the big stars. I think it's only because they've had so much of the trappings that they have the luxury of saying, "I hate it." You have to enjoy success and what goes with it—otherwise you wouldn't be a performer or a success. OK, I haven't had the mass recognition and adulation that *big* stars like Rudolf and Mischa have. Maybe I would hate that, but one would be willing to have a go at it first.'

But Sheila Bloom maintains that 'Very little changed on Antoinette's outside persona. She became a little more sophisticated, but in a funny way she really hasn't changed a great deal. Once in a while, like at dinner parties, she'll be a little grander than when it's very close friends, but on the whole she's very much herself.' And Beriosova adds, 'To this day she's extremely humble, takes nothing for granted. She's grateful for her parts, grateful for the golden days of the Royal Ballet, for the real fortune and for the teachers we had, the coaches, the great ballerinas of the past who taught us.'

'She's a devoted hard worker,' de Valois observes with evident approval, 'and she did listen to people, those that were teaching her or coaching her or producing on her. She really did listen; she wasn't a one who went all her own way as some of them can.

'Choreographically she fell under quite a lot of people. She never had that sort of label on her as, for instance, Lynn with MacMillan or Margot with Fred. I can't label her like that. Mind you, being of a slightly younger generation it was hard to get a label, because the choreographers had done so much work and there were so many ballets for them all to learn. At the beginning the labelling was very easy, because there were fewer dancers. But when they came in at her age, they had to accept a big repertoire, and they had to accept a choreographer saying, "Yes, I'd like her in that ballet of mine," and not necessarily saying, "I will do a ballet only on her." Fred accepted her. He did a lot of work on her. But when she was young, he was still working on the generation before her.'

Michael Somes sees another aspect of that situation: 'She didn't have as many opportunities to be worked on choreographically. There was a potential in her movement that was never exploited, perhaps because it wasn't what was wanted at the time. Brilliance was her forte. I don't believe in giving opinions, but she probably enjoyed doing those things with some character in them and where she could make some effect as a fast, quick dancer. I couldn't see her in languid, dreamy, droopy things. Fred built on what she could do: brilliance, sharpness, charm, characterization. He used all of that.'

Sibley herself says, 'All of Fred's ballets feel natural to me. He loves *épaulement*, shoulders, and skimming, moving at the speed of light, twisting peculiar ways, all the things that I like to do and feel happy doing. I don't feel as I start to do them, "Oh my God, it's quite impossible for me because I can't get my legs up here" or "I can't jump like that" or "I haven't got the heaviness for this." They're very difficult, but I feel quite natural doing them, and I love dancing his things.

'When Fred arrives in the studio the music is completely sunk in his whole body. He knows it inside out, and he also knows the idea that he wants to get over. He doesn't arrive with a whole lot of steps in his mind, not like Madam, or Kenneth, who really have worked out the shapes and steps that they want. Sir Fred hasn't, but he very much has the idea of a theatrical minute. He would certainly have thought out the minute where she takes the book from him at the beginning of *Enigma*, and in *Varii Capricii* he very much wanted the dark glasses used at the end. We had two or three different endings, but nevertheless he had worked that out.

'Then it usually comes from an idea. With *The Dream*, for instance, he said, "I want a fountain. I see a fountain here," and so you emulate a fountain and he goes, "Yes, yes, that's right." And of course it's very difficult because when you get up and do a fountain it's not actually a step and you can't quite remember what you did. It's not like doing *glissade, assemblé, pas de bourrée, jeté*. But this is how he works. With Dorabella in *Enigma* the main thing he had in mind was that she was stuttering throughout. So we tried whatever would look like stuttering, and of course he wanted it all hopping on pointe, which he usually gave me, I guess because he likes me hopping on pointe.'

'Of course I knew her better by *Enigma*,' Ashton explains, 'and I knew her qualities and what she could bring to something. I think she has a beautiful way of moving, an individual way of moving, which is what is important. A dancer must have an individuality. It's no good just being a machine, typed, or just having a perfect technique. There has to be an individuality in a performer to register.'

Sibley's memory makes her giggle: 'When he arrived to do *Jazz Calendar* he'd even forgotten the bloody music; he hadn't got it with him. Rudolf and I were there, and Georgina [Parkinson] and Donald [MacLeary] were the next cast, and he had the idea that Friday's Child was going to be more giving than loving, and he wanted it rather sensual. He wanted . . . lust more than anything—he had the idea very firmly in his head—and he'd get Rudolf to try 'manly' things and me being seduced and giving as much as I got. Of course it was simply wonderful doing that with Rudolf because he's very abandoned in that way. But we hadn't got the music to put the give-as-good-as-you-got steps with, so we just sang any old blues we could think of. And then when we got the actual music, we had to try to make the actual steps work to it.'

'Quite possibly the change of partners brought out something else in her,' Ashton speculates. 'She and Rudolf in *Jazz Calendar* . . . It was something quite different for both of them, to do that kind of thing. I put them together hoping that they would . . . not really unite or melt into each other . . . what is the right word? Fuse, yes, and they did. It would have been quite a different thing if Anthony had done it; it would have come out quite a different way. Of course I'm influenced by the people I work with, and I want to make them appear at their best. I don't want to hinder them or make it a struggle; I want them to melt into it and enjoy it and not have a warring element in it.

'I've always enjoyed working with her, but I just work and do it and I'm not aware whether people are bringing it out of me. I don't know about that. That's for other people to say. It's a kind of collaboration where there's nowhere where it begins or ends.'

Which is precisely how Sibley feels about it. 'What is wonderful about working with Fred, in this particular fashion, is that you are creating with him. He gives you, or we think he gives us . . . It appears to us, and we're most grateful for,

really taking part in creating it all. Maybe he's just *so* clever
or maybe he's got the whole lot worked out, but he makes
you think that you're helping him. Another choreographer
will want your body and the theatrical way that you would
produce a step, but Fred actually makes the step on you, you
make the step with him. You do it together, you work on it
together; he gives a bit, you give a bit, you turn it around,
it's very much happening right there in the studio.

'It feels just right; you neither feel fear or apprehension.
Like in *The Dream* . . . He wanted this wretched step that he'd
seen in a dream. He could actually see what he wanted us to
do, but that step had never been done before and there was
no way Anthony and I could do it. And he said, "Well, I've
seen it in my dream and I know it will work. I'm going down
to have a coffee and you work it out." It was impossible! It's
that passing under his arm and coming up, in the *pas de deux*,
and we didn't know how to do it other than cut my head off
or cut an arm out. We were equally obstinate; we said it
couldn't work unless you cut bits of the body off, things were
in the way. But he wouldn't have it; he went down to have a
cup of coffee until we'd solved it for him, and by the time he
came back we *had* solved it.

'But he gives you confidence that way. Because he *knows* it
can work and he goes and leaves it to you, it's up to you to
make it work. There are some frightfully difficult lifts in *Varii
Capricii*, swooping and turning over up onto his shoulder,
which again he could see in his mind's eye but which didn't
seem possible. And again he wasn't interested that it wasn't
possible—that's what he saw and that's what he wanted. So
it was just a matter of us getting together to make it work.
He's frightfully obstinate as well; when he knows something,
that's what he wants. Like with hops on pointe. You say,
"Oh, that's absolute agony," and he says, "No, I like that. I
like it when it's done that many times," or "That'll be all
right,' and then you just have to. He's very firm about certain
things.'

'Well, I daresay I am,' Ashton grants. 'I'm stubborn in
insisting what I want out of a dancer and how I want them
to do it, and if they're having difficulty I say, "No. That's
the way I want it." And I didn't give her just hops on
pointe—it must have been what the music indicated. Every-

thing with me comes out of the music. And if she said she couldn't do something, I'd say, "Oh, don't talk nonsense. Get on with it. *I'm* perfectly satisfied, so go on. Do it."

'But you can suggest things,' Sibley points out. 'Rudolf and I were having our *Jazz Calendar* fittings in rooms next to each other. We were both in red and blue, and I had never worn red in my life, never ever, hated red. So I said, "Look, wouldn't it be better if I was all blue and Rudolf was all red? I really can't wear red. I look appalling." And Rudolf was in the other room saying, "I can't wear . . . ." Apparently we were both being awful. And then we had skullcaps on, which we looked awful in as well. We did get rid of the skullcaps, but I didn't win out on the red and blue. And I was thrilled I didn't because it completely changed my life: I've worn red ever since.

'We ended up totally happy in our costumes, but then Fred wanted me to try my hair down, loose. Well, I'd always wanted to have a bubble cut and it was the rage at the time, so I went down to the stalls at the dress rehearsal and said, "What would you think if I wore a bubble cut?" And he said, "It sounds wonderful. Let's try it." But my way of working is that I'm very much a piece of clay. I'll try anything, do whatever they want, so they don't think I'm being rude or presumptuous if I suggest things.

'When one comes to take over roles that one *hasn't* created, which of course I've done so often—for instance, just recently in *Month in the Country*—he *also* gives you such a lot of rein. He sees the way you're doing it and he could very much put his foot down and go, "No, no, no. That isn't how it should be" or "That isn't how it was" or "That isn't how so-and-so does it. That's not right." But he sees, I suppose, that this is the best way for me, because this is my character interpreting that character. So he gives you that lead and he adds to it. He allows you to have your head and he helps the way you're thinking by adding adjectives around it, so in your mind you then see other adjectives.'

'They're all different,' acknowledges Ashton. 'Hers is maybe different from Merle's and maybe different from Marguerite's [Porter], but the role allows people to be different. And she's not different from anybody else in not wanting to be like anyone else. Don't you think each one wanted that? Each interpreter wanted to do it her own way and give out what she felt about certain things, of course.

'I don't insist one must do exactly like another did when it comes to the interpretation, of course not. I give them licence on that, but I don't give them licence in not doing the correct steps; they've got to do the steps which are set. But I can modify them; if they say, "Margot could do them, but I can't quite," well, there's always another way. They would only surprise me if they brought it off 100 per cent or 90 per cent—then I'd be pleased.

'Antoinette always tackled everything. I never felt she was intimidated, although I see that one might be, taking over a role when somebody has been sublime in it, as Margot was in *Daphnis*. But it didn't bother me; one *had* to have other people coming along, and she seemed to me the obvious choice in it.

'Of course we have fun, Antoinette and I, but another side is that she fusses, she comes fussing. I'll be in the country and she'll ring me up about a wig. I'll say, "What's the use of ringing me up? I've got to see the wig on you. Get the wig and put it on and then I'll tell you what I think." It may be nerves and, putting it at its best, it may be a desire for perfection, but that can be catching—she can fuss Anthony as well. I don't mean upset him, but, "Can we try this again from?" She can be a fusspot sometimes, and I just say, "Oh, for God's sake, get on and do it and stop fussing," because I am very practical in spite of everything.'

Following her thoughts happily through her Ashton repertory, Sibley settles her attention on a ballet she has recently created. '*Varii Capricii* was all decided very suddenly. We were going to Miami to do a whole Sir Fred programme with the Washington Ballet—Anthony was away from London even longer than I—and then just getting back I think one week before we headed off to New York for the opening. So he only had a swift three weeks to do the whole ballet, and already he must have been nearly eighty!

'The nerves in New York were really horrendous. People think *Varii Capricii* is just Anthony and I larking about, but in fact we never stop. It might only be eighteen minutes, but we are actually on all the time and it's quite difficult and tiring. We'd only had three weeks to create it in, and then this break, and then coming back and changing the things Fred thought weren't right when he'd seen it. We'd put it on Covent Garden stage once, so he could see where he'd got up to, and he wasn't happy with certain things because they got lost with that huge, very strong, Hockney backcloth. So we had to change lots of directions and steps so they'd stand out more.

'So we had no time to get this ballet on, and when we arrived in New York we had one stage call which was a disaster. A total disaster! As it was only a short ballet and as we only had the one call, we naturally assumed we were going to go right through and do it again. You always do that on your first stage call, particularly if it's eighteen minutes. And then when they suddenly called whatever the next ballet was . . . Well, I just sat down and burst out crying on stage. Fred was fuming out front; apparently he went mad and he's not someone who loses his temper in public. Anthony had a brainstorm as well. So we got our way and we did do it again, but starting at 11:30 at night or something. And then we did it the next morning as well, and thank God we got it to be what it was in New York.

'But I must say, it was such a responsibility again on our shoulders: Ashton, his new ballet, and it *was* for New York, it was, for that week's celebration of England in New York. He was sitting in my dressing room that night and he started putting his cigarette ash on my place—he smokes like a chimney. And I was so nervous, with the bloody stage calls the night before and all our tears and outbursts that I kept that ash, I kept it for the first night. And before his eightieth birthday gala, when we did *Thaïs* and the *Daphnis and Chloe* finale, I got him to give me more ash. And for *Month* he had to come to my dressing room and put all his ash there. Isn't it stupid?

'I hardly have any superstitions, but I do have one, and that is that I won't sign my name on the day of a performance. Autograph or no, I simply won't sign Antoinette Sibley, whether it's for shopping or anything. MacLeary tried to get me over it; he said it was quite absurd, which it is. We were coming in the stage door one night and I wouldn't give my autograph and he said, "How ridiculous. Why not?" and I said, "OK, I'll break it tonight." And I broke the superstition and I fell down. Whenever I sign my name I've always fallen down in performances.

'I had to sign my name up in Manchester recently because I couldn't pay my hotel bill otherwise, and I didn't fall down that time. And I actually had to do it the other night before *Birthday Offering* because somebody delivered something to the house. Well, I wouldn't write Antoinette Sibley—I wrote Antoinette Corbett—and I didn't fall down. So I don't know whether I've broken it or not. Now Anthony's got hold of it and now he doesn't sign. It's too absurd.

'But I must also say, getting back to roles, that each one Fred has given me has deepened my understanding of myself. In *Varii Capricii*, such a woman of the world, and I'm adding to her all the time. She is very much 'the Roman Spring of Mrs Stone'; she knows she's over the top, she's having a last fling, but there's a bit of humour about it. It's no longer for love; nothing's for love any more and nothing's too desperate either because you've gone past the passionate stage in life. So it's "Oh well, there's always another day. What does it matter?" It's a different thing from Juliet or Giselle where everything's so intense, so passionate. And look at Dorabella. She's enchanting, so nervous, but again the love. Always with Fred it's love, passion, warmth, in everything I've ever done, *Soupirs*, *Thaïs* . . . He's given me such a lot.

'I love to stand in the wings and watch certain ballets before I go on. Certain ballets make me feel very relaxed before mine and other things make me feel very nervous—I can feel frightfully nervous watching things I had never been anything to do with. I loved watching the *Bayadère* before the *Month in the Country*, and I always loved watching *Enigma*. I feel very soothed, whether I'm in it that night or not. I've never done a performance of Dorabella without watching what used to be Vyvyan Lorrayne's *pas de deux* and then Anthony's solo. In Vienna I did *Bayadère*, *Symphonic Variations* and *Enigma* all in one programme, and even then, when I was exhausted, I still watched Isabel Fitton.

'Dorabella is frightfully tiring; it's very long and all hops, you never stop. Now I watch lovely dancers doing Dorabella, and they all say they're exhausted when they come off after it. And I'm so relieved because that's how I am and I was when I first did it, but I thought it was because I was so under par when we were choreographing it. So many a time I say I can't do something, and many a time Fred will just walk away and smoke another cigarette and go, "Well, you work on it and when you come back with it we'll go on." He treats me like that, quite offhand.

'Of course he is a genius and I would stand on my head for him. He can be quite firm, of course he can, and I suspect I'm frightfully difficult, I'm sure I am. But he knows me, he knows how to treat me. He can be abrupt . . . Of course if he says "That's good," it means a million words to me, but he doesn't often say that. After *Month in the Country* he said, "Four times you were standing in a bad position." But it's always these things he tells me about: I haven't pointed my foot or I've stood without my foot behind or my hair's fallen down. He's always been like that.

'The wonderful thing with Sir Fred is that you can talk to him about any subject, about life, about happiness, sadness, poetry, painting, and about funny, silly things like television series. I feel privileged to have known him, apart from the fact that my dancing . . . Well, I wouldn't be back here now if it hadn't been for him. I wouldn't have done all the ballets I've done since retiring. And I wouldn't have known myself as a person, dance-wise or otherwise, if it hadn't been for him.

'You know, in Fred's original conception of *Enigma* I was in Nimrod. But it was a very sad and difficult time for me when we were creating this because it was when my marriage was breaking up with Michael. I was under such stress and ill and I couldn't cope any more.

'I had started off my marriage trying to be a 100 per cent wonderful wife, coping with my new house and making cooked breakfasts and doing all the shopping, as well as my dancing. Of course I didn't cope very well at all at first because of my glandular fever, but then I really did try to be the perfect wife. I think everyone does at that age, 'til you realize later on that everything's a compromise. Michael was a wonderful help too and we were working at the same job so obviously we did see each other during the day.

'But it was a frightfully difficult situation, if you think of it, to have your husband rehearsing you and pulling you to bits. It's hard before you're married but then it's hard on the marriage, because if somebody's telling you off, which of course they're doing, it's hard to take from your husband. So all ways round it must have been a frightful strain, but that was the situation. On the other hand, it was very good that we were together; the hours were long and hard but at least we did see each other some of the time.

'One of his most amazing and wonderful qualities is his generosity, with his time, with his effort, his spirit, with the degree he goes into things. He would rehearse you on a Sunday if you wanted, he would come in at 6:00 in the morning, he would do anything to make the end result right. For you, for the ballet, for everyone concerned. He loves the ballet. It's been his life and he's given everything to it. And his knowledge . . . He has a photographic eye, so he can remember things that he was told by Karsavina, by Grigoriev. He takes it all in like a sponge, and passes it on. He has no professional secrets—I have, I think everybody has, but he doesn't. He gives all his secrets and that's the most amazing thing about him. He's unstinting with everybody and every-thing, not just with me because of who I was to him, but with anybody.

'And of course it can come over the other way. *Because* he does that, he expects perfection back. He expects the same hard work, the same endurance, the same ability to work those hours at that pace, and of course you can't always give it.

'All my emotional turmoil always took itself out on me in illness and injuries, and for quite a while up to when we separated I wasn't able to cope strongly. So I was off, either ill or injured, time and time again.'

'It did play on her health,' Shelia Bloom concedes sadly. 'Her health suffered at that time, because if you're in love with somebody as she was, deeply in love, you become more vulnerable and you can only be hurt.'

Sibley chooses not to dwell on the subject any longer. 'After our marriage ended, and we naturally went through an unhappy time, the friendship returned, and there's still a great friendship there.

'Anthony's aunt, Joan Dowell, came and looked after me for a while in the house in Earl's Court, and then I moved to Barons Court. And what I reckoned I must do was go out and get away from the ballet world. I'd been with Michael since I was nineteen or twenty, and it was a passionate, romantic, idealized love in every way. But I then realized I was at a very low ebb and must pull myself together. How narrow my existence was, having given so much of my time to ballet, and then marrying and remaining closeted in the same world. I felt the need to acquire new experiences, so I deliberately set about meeting people, men in particular. As I was now an established ballerina, it followed that the men I wanted to meet would have achieved a similar degree of success and would be leading interesting and varied lives in which I would share.

'Up 'til now I'd always let my life lead me along, but now, for the first time, I set out to make some decisions. I decided that what I actually wanted and needed was to get out and see and do all the things I had missed in my enclosed world. I achieved my wish, and for the next few years I proceeded to have the most exciting time with people from lots of different worlds—top bankers, stockbrokers, doctors and film people. I'd rush off to Madrid to the Ritz for a weekend. I'd rush off to Paris for the afternoon. I'd be in Hollywood for my holidays. All these men to me were really fascinating because of what they'd achieved. That's what I was interested in.

'I had a wonderful time and I learned a lot. Killed myself dance-wise, burning the candle at all ends, rushing off on a Friday to Paris, rushing off for weekends, rushing back here. I really worked at it; I rang up friends who might know of people or have parties, and said that I would like to go to parties and that I was interested in meeting people, and from meeting one I'd meet more. Oh, I made it quite clear. I didn't wait for things to happen because I was determined on this run of events. I looked at myself quite straightforwardly: How many years did I have left for dancing? Was I content not to be married to someone? And I wasn't. I'm interested in marriage. I need marriage. I need to be with a man all the time; I like the permanence, the stability. I'm not happy to be by myself, living by myself—I actually can't cope. I needed a man in my life, so at that point I had lots of men.

'I was more ill than I wasn't, but I also realized that I had to find a life for myself. It couldn't just be the ballet. I had to find the other half of my personality. I couldn't go on and not have another life, with marriage and something going for me. So I *had* to burn the candle at all ends and therefore I *had* to get as ill as I got. There was no other way I could have achieved it, and I wasn't happy just to be a ballerina.

'I suppose I knew about Manon very well by the time I came to do *Manon*, absolutely. I'd experienced Manon by then. I was not the nineteen-year-old. I had been with lots of people and had a wonderful time.'

Sibley flashes a deliciously knowing grin and hugs herself in satisfaction. Then she sits back to talk about Kenneth MacMillan who in 1974 presented her with the title role in *Manon*, her first and only three-act creation. They had worked together for years, both before MacMillan left the Royal Ballet in 1966 to serve as director of the Berlin Ballet and after his return as co-director in 1970. Yet her links with Ashton were so many and her affinity for his style so great that one might logically have expected her first full-evening creation to come from him. Except for one fact, which Sibley herself astutely points out: 'Fred's never done a three-act ballet since I've been around. He's done no full-length ballet since . . . I don't know, probably *Fille* was the last. It wasn't one of the things that appealed to him, whereas I don't think Kenneth minds at all tackling these big ballets.

'I wasn't nervous of Kenneth when I first started working with him, as I was with Fred, because Kenneth is much nearer my age group. And as I saw every single ballet he did at Sadler's Wells—*Laiderette, Solitaire, Danses Concertantes*—I literally grew up on his work and with that company and with Johnny Cranko. We were all nearly the same generation, so we could chat together. There was no way I could go up and chat to Sir Fred in those early days, whereas although I was only young, Kenneth was young too and we all used to sit around together. The main person in *Agon* was Deirdre Dixon, who was Michael's first wife and a great friend of mine, and the rest of the cast were also my friends: Maggie Hill and Shirley, Pirmin and Graham Usher and Peter Clegg.

'Then there was Kchessinska *pas de deux, Triad*, also I was cast for *The Invitation* and I was to follow Lynn in the full-length *Anastasia*, which I couldn't do, again, because I was injured. But I did all the rehearsals and I was supposed to do it, and I was supposed to do *Song of the Earth* as well. Of course having such a supreme dramatic dancer with us as

Lynn, naturally when things were divided out . . . Her *Invitation* was just fantastic and I couldn't do things like she could do them, but I could do them my way given the opportunity. I'd never been thought of as a dramatic ballerina, but Kenneth was able to help me with this, as Tudor did by giving me *Lilac Garden*. This was a new side of me. Of course I wanted to try it, because I thought I could do it, and Kenneth was one of the ones to give me that opportunity, with Juliet, with everything, terminating in giving me Manon.

'Manon is my first flesh and blood role really, and it was a dramatic ballet set completely through the dance which is the way I can achieve it. It's how I work. As opposed to somebody who does it mainly through acting, my way was through dancing, which is why I always thought that in certain respects I would have been quite suited to the Russian *Romeo and Juliet*. The other thing I thought I was quite good in, in that respect, was the Betrayed Girl in Madam's *Rake's Progress;* the whole essence of her is through the dance and the movement.'

'I first noticed her,' MacMillan recalls, 'when I did my version of *Agon*. I used her in that and she'd just come from the school. She hadn't done very much in the company, but I'd seen her in class and I wanted the best girls for the corps.

'She was a wonderful dancer from the beginning, but there were two very strong personalities amongst the women in the company, and that was Fonteyn and Seymour. I felt Antoinette at that time was a bit intimidated by both these very strong ladies. She had a sort of identity crisis, and I think it took her some years to find out who she actually was on the stage. There was Ashton still creating for Fonteyn, I was predominantly working with Seymour, and there was Sibley, a wonderful girl, in the middle of both. I'm sure she was wondering, "Well, who am I? What am I doing? Nobody's looking at me except for the classics."

'I did make her second cast of *Symphony*, but I didn't think she would have to go on in it so soon—she was shoved in at a day's notice. It's always difficult when a role is created on a dancer and someone has to take over that role, even much later let alone the first performance. It was also a strange ballet because I was going through a very strange state at that time and reaching out for something I couldn't even define myself. So it's no wonder Antoinette felt a bit lost—as I was trying new things myself, it was rather unfair on her.

'In my formative years as a choreographer, a lot of pressure was brought to bear by Dame Ninette to use certain dancers. I didn't always do it—I mean, we fought, both when I was at the Wells and when I first did my ballets here at Covent Garden. Of course when I became director I did have more freedom, but Fonteyn was still dancing, that hierarchy was still going on, and beneath her were all the young kids like Sibley, Seymour and Merle, who by rights should have been really taking over. That was very difficult, both for them and for me. On the one hand everyone was clamouring for Margot because she was such a great star and a great dancer, and on the other hand I was thinking, "Fonteyn is going to go any minute because she's reaching the age when she has to. What can I do for these young kids?"

'I had different responsibilities when I came back. I could no longer just think of my own work; I had to think of the whole of the Royal Ballet. And in thinking of the whole of the Royal Ballet, there was Sibley, the supreme classical dancer of the young ones, and of course I wanted to use her in my and her own way, both.'

'Of course he's terribly easy to work with,' Sibley declares, 'in that he knows exactly what he wants and he shows you. Not only does he know the music inside out, as Fred does, but he knows the steps he wants, which of course Fred doesn't. When Kenneth comes into the room, he knows just the steps he wants. Now, if those steps don't work or they don't look good on you, he will change them. He knew the steps he wanted for the Manon solo, in the ball, but I heard it a different way, and that was fine. He'll make it look right on you and fit your body, but step-wise he's got an absolute reading. And when he comes to the *pas de deux* ... In *Manon* he had *such* an idea of those *pas de deux*. How he had that I don't know because the dancers are so controlled by each other. You hardly ever let go—it's all manipulation—and one doesn't know how he could have seen that sort of thing.

'The first I knew about *Manon* ... I was dancing the last *Sleeping Beauty* of the season. Before I did the Rose *adage* I went back to my room to get a tissue and I saw this book on my place, which Kenneth naturally hadn't thought I'd see until after the first act or he would never have put it there. It was the book of *Manon*, and there was a note saying, "Your holiday reading. I want to do the ballet next season. Love, Kenneth." Well, we knew that Kenneth was going to do a new full-length ballet, but we didn't know what and we didn't know who, we didn't have any idea. So I went down for the Rose *adage*, and there was Anthony standing in the wings—he always stood there because he felt nervous for me—and I said, "I've just been to my room. What about *Manon*?" And he said, "Yes, Kenneth's just come to see me too." And we stood there grinning at each other, and I had no fear, no worry at all, for the Rose *adage* that night. There were far more important things going on.

'This was the end of the season. So we go on holiday, we come back in September, and it's supposed to go on in March so we head straight into it. At the same time, I did the opening night here, *Swan Lake*. Then the next morning at the crack of dawn Anthony and I went up to Stansted airport, got on a plane and went to Brussels to celebrate Britain entering the Common Market. There was a stage call when we got there for us to get accustomed to the terrific rake, and then we did the *Beauty* for the gala that night. We were there three or four days, and then we came back to London and had another week or two for *Manon* and then we went off to Australia. We were supposed to be in Australia and Japan for at least a month but Kenneth, quite rightly, was rather put out, so we just went to Australia, which we couldn't cancel, which was about two weeks. But we work hammer and tongs on *Manon*, and it isn't a question of having to force it out because those *pas de deux* came frightfully easily. We'd finish one and start the next. It was just flowing out.

'So before I started getting injured, we did the first *pas de deux*, the bedroom *pas de deux*, the bracelet *pas de deux*—we call it that, where she keeps showing him the bracelet—the solo, the *pas de trois*, oh, we did a whole lot. More or less we did everything that concerned me before . . . not necessarily before I went to Australia but before I went off with my knee or my foot; I think it was all of them in the end because one went on to the other. So I had done those various numbers, but I hadn't done that *adage* with the boys and I hadn't done little bits where I'm concerned with other people because I'd never been with groups, I'd never put it together with anybody. I'd done the rest, except for the last *pas de deux*—Jenny [Penney] created that—which I never could get together. I hadn't created it, so I could never remember it.

'I know I had an awful hip, but as I say, once this knee got bad and let me down it just became a vicious circle. It wasn't a reliable knee, and as it weakened I couldn't work at all correctly because my natural balance was upset. So I had to compensate, and then the compensation would cause me to strain one thing after another. I'd come in one day, we'd do a bit and then the knee would go. Come back two days later, do a bit more, then the hip would go. And if I kept working, which I did because I realized we had no time, then the foot went and it just kept going. It was absolutely dreadful. And the pressures were so great: if you think how long Kenneth took over *Isadora*, over *Mayerling*, like a year, and we had only these few months to get this three-act ballet on. That's all the time we had before Anthony and I went away, before I got injured, before anything.'

Anthony Dowell remembers that 'It was a very difficult time for her. It started off . . . Well, one naturally loved Kenneth's ballets and we did do *Romeo* and everything, but we'd been very much the Ashton couple and Kenneth had been with Lynn and Christopher. So suddenly to have a big work created on us by Kenneth was tremendously exciting. We started work, and we just seemed to create *pas de deux* in two or three goes. There are a lot of *pas de deux* in *Manon;* so we created the first act, and we created the second act, the packing and the bracelet, and then she had trouble with her hip.

'I went over to see her—she was in bed, at Barons Court—and she said, "Please, if you can do anything, I beg you, make him not work on the last *pas de deux* till I'm back. Please, please." All the time Kenneth was anxious to get on, and with Antoinette being away, we were starting to run the acts. Jenny Penney had started to stand in and we were doing all the *pas de deux* together, and he just couldn't wait. There was nothing I could do—he couldn't—and I think this just about finished her off. But as a true pro, when she got better she came back and learned it. But I suppose that's one thing that's seriously missing to her in the ballet, that that *pas de deux* wasn't her.'

'I wasn't sure what her ailment was,' MacMillan admits. 'I never knew and I never found out. The thing is, when you do a ballet it's announced and you have to finish it by a certain date. So I had to finish it and Antoinette wasn't around, but the whole stimulus for doing it was her.'

'Well, the trauma of the actual first performance was tremendous,' Sibley sighs, 'because I had only got back from all my illnesses a week or two beforehand. So although I'd done all the initial work except for those few things that I mentioned, I hadn't done anything in front of the company. I hadn't been part of the ballet that had been put together until I came to a stage call. Not that I have a lot to do with anybody else, actually—the main parts are the *pas de deux*—but going straight into the stage call isn't the best way to go into anything. So it was very nervewracking from everybody's point of view.

'I was word perfect for all the things I knew; I only had to learn the things I hadn't done. And Anthony and I work with such an ease together that if we have to re *en* set something it's not difficult. When I came back for the first *Cinderella* after I retired, we didn't actually touch each other till the dress rehearsal. That first performance of *Manon* couldn't have happened if we hadn't had this relationship. It couldn't possibly have worked for any of us, for Kenneth, for me, for anybody.

'I reckon you never get into a new ballet till after ten performances. There's no way you can know a new ballet till you've done ten performances because however much you rehearse—which I hadn't done for this—it's only when you get on stage with an audience there that it starts to live. Anybody will say the same. So had I been there for all those months I don't know how much further I would have got, except I would have created those other numbers. Because certainly with *Manon*, as with any other ballet, it took that many performances to get on the right road.'

Beriosova leans forward, eyes wide, eager to explain. 'There's a great big feedback. You can hear it. You can hear it in the silence more than anywhere else. If you've got a completely silent house when the music stops, and then the applause starts, you know straightaway that you've got through to them.

'You need the audience; they're certainly part of the entire performance. They're an extension of the stage, actually. Many people think the stage is the world: it isn't. If you're in a ballroom, you can't think that the ballroom just has three walls, the right side, the left side, the backdrop. It extends, right through to the back of the amphitheatre—that's where the fourth wall is. They're part of whatever's happening on stage, and you include them in your world. Sometimes you see people look right stage, look left stage, look upstage. They don't bother to look for whatever it is they're seeking out front. Whereas if you feel that's an extension of the lakeside or the ballroom or the woodland or the room, then it draws them in.'

Sibley is leaning forward too now, intent, concentrating: 'I knew exactly what I wanted to do with Manon. I didn't see her as a schemer at all. I saw her as a young girl who'd just come out of a convent and who adored her brother. She was frightfully beautiful and sexy, and she knew it and she loved it and she loved the attention everyone was giving her and she loved jewels and she loved money and she loved anything beautiful, and he opened this treasure box of goodies, and she adored him. From my point of view, she allowed it all to happen to her. She then fell in love, but it didn't bother her too much because she thought she could cope with both. But then she found she couldn't cope with both because des Grieux wasn't going to have that; that's when things did get a bit difficult and she did have to make decisions. But *I'm* not one ever to make decisions until I'm really forced to, so that's how I figured it happened to her. She wasn't going to say no to all those jewels—my God, she loved them as much as she loved her love, and she wasn't going to give up either one if she could help it.

'She leaves des Grieux for preferred riches, but she thinks she'll get him back. He adores her—she's not stupid, she knows that—and she thinks there's going to be a way . . . like when she starts cheating at the gambling and she does get him back. But she still shows off the jewels to him, she still thinks she's going to have them as well. I don't think she's a schemer. Her brother, yes. Her brother's the one that gets it

Symphonic Variations

Top: Enigma Variations with Derek Rencher

Below: Rehearsing *The Nutcracker* with Rudolf Nureyev and Anthony Dowell

Top: The Nutcracker
with Anthony
Dowell

Below: Rehearsing
Jazz Calendar with
Rudolf Nureyev

Dances at a Gathering with Anthony Dowell

OPPOSITE
Top: Giselle

Below: The Sleeping Beauty with Donald MacLeary

Cinderella

OPPOSITE
Daphnis and Chloe and (*inset*) rehearsing *Daphnis and Chloe*
with Frederick Ashton

Scènes de Ballet

Displaying the CBE at the gates of Buckingham Palace, November 1973

With Rudolf Nureyev in Monte Carlo

*A Month in the
Country* with
Mikhail
Baryshnikov

Firebird with David
Wall

Manon

<u>*Top:*</u> Rehearsing,
Derek Rencher in
foreground

<u>*Below:*</u> With Anthony
Dowell as des Grieux

Manon

<u>*Top:*</u> With David Wall as Lescaut

<u>*Below:*</u> Opening night of *Manon*. Kenneth MacMillan is beside the Queen Mother

With her husband, Panton Corbett

Above: Modelling for charity, May 1977

Below: With Sheila Bloom

Isambard and Eloise Corbett

all going, but not her, she doesn't know about anything. And she's sensual but she's never had any sex; she's just come from a convent. I just think she's on a high—she thinks it's all terrific.

'She obviously has quite a few upsets, her biggest trauma being when her brother gets shot. That's when her life starts to crumble, but up till then things have worked very smoothly for her, one thing by one thing by one thing. And then of course comes the nitty-gritty at the end and she meets her doom. That's how I saw her and that's how I did it. Of course, I don't do it at all like that now!

'*Manon, Lilac Garden, Romeo and Juliet*, you're dealing with a real person, a real situation. As the roles come up, they're not all fairy tales, and of course they're all real to you while they're happening. *Giselle*'s no fairy tale; Giselle can be a true person, although the second act is a myth. I absolutely believe in all the roles when I take them over, but I do remember the thrill when Kenneth put the *Manon* book on my place, the thrill thinking, "How wonderful. This is a person as opposed to a fairy tale." '

'*Manon* brought another side out of her altogether,' declares de Valois. 'She'd never been much of a dramatic dancer and that did bring something out in her. We all said that at once. Someone said, "I didn't realize it was Sibley in that first scene." It was so different, and it was very good for her, frankly. She'd been typecast at the beginning, you know, quick, young, pretty, strong and you get all those quick, young, pretty, strong things flung at you, naturally.'

'I just thought she was the natural one to do it,' MacMillan says mildly. 'I can't tell you why. Her body was beautiful—she could do anything, *anything*. And I always thought Antoinette had great allure and glamour on stage, and allure's not the sort of word the Royal Ballet particularly would like to use about someone. Manon as a character does have allure. She attracted men all the time, all through her life.

'Antoinette was lovely, beautiful, in it, but I can tell you what I think her best role ever was. It was *Dances at a Gathering* by Jerome Robbins, because . . . It has something to do with the training of the Royal Ballet, which in essence is lyrical, but which somehow puts too many constraints on a dancer.

.I think Jerry freed Antoinette in that, really for the first time. She was ravishing in it, and I wish we still had it in the repertoire for her to appear in. Suddenly there was Antoinette without reins; she was like a beast that had been let loose—I'm talking about physically. In *Manon* she's constrained by the story. She has to move in a certain way and behave in a certain way because of the character. In *Dances at a Gathering*, which is an abstract ballet, it's all body, the body speaking, and for me that was magical.'

Robbins selected Sibley for the first Royal Ballet cast of *Dances at a Gathering* in 1970, of *Afternoon of a Faun* in 1971 and of *In the Night* in 1973. At his invitation she appeared several times in Spoleto at the Festival of Two Worlds. If you ask him about her today, he is content to call her 'one of the great artists of our time' and leave it at that. If you ask her about him, however, her face lights up and the words tumble over each other: 'The first thing that he did here was *Dances at a Gathering*, and talk about Pisces: out of his cast of ten, five of us are Pisces and one's on the cusp. There's Rudolf, Lynn, me, David Wall and Ann Jenner, and Anthony's Aquarius on the cusp of Pisces. Doesn't that strike you as odd? When I say a cast, I think there were quite a few people around in the very early days, and we all learned nearly every number. The only thing we did know from early on, because Jerry said that was more or less decided, was that Anthony and I would do our first mazurka, the one that Patty McBride did with the lovely lift at the end [Op. 33, No. 3]. And that just clicked immediately.

'I'd never met him, but we had all heard these rumours about rehearsal scenes and we didn't know what to expect, because really everything's quite quiet at Barons Court. You couldn't in any way say Fred was a noisy individual, or Kenneth; they're both most retiring in their rehearsal manner. We were told about the chair-throwing but we didn't meet it on *Dances at a Gathering*, that's all I can tell you. He was ill in the middle of it and for quite a long time while we were rehearsing it. Luckily we'd already learned our various dances and Sally Leland then rehearsed us.

'I did my number with Rudolf [Etude, Op. 25, No. 5] and it was wonderful—it was a very spontaneous thing with us. But we also covered the 'giggle dance' [Waltz, Op. 42], and whenever Monica [Mason] and Mick [Coleman] did it, he was up there, pulling me up, "Come on, we must do this." I had such a time in that ballet—I never really stopped—and I didn't much fancy doing the "giggle dance" as well, but Rudolf longed to do it.

'Jerry wanted us to be just natural—no turning out, no standing in positions, natural—and we all understood this very quickly. And he didn't mind that we put more character-ization in than New York City Ballet, who had created it quite recently. We did it so differently, but he never stopped any of that, never told us to cut down. It was one of the most magical ballets ever to have done, and I really think our cast, I say it myself, was fantastic. It's the one thing I had hoped would come back when I came back, because nearly all the cast was still there; only Ann and Laura [Connor] had gone. Lynn, David, Rudolf, Monica, MacLeary, Mick and Anthony were still around—isn't that an amazing list?—but now already so many of them have gone too.

'*Faun* was absolutely wonderful too, and this comes back to *Giselle* and to *The Ropes of Time*, the Rudi van Dantzig ballet which he was doing for Rudolf and myself and Monica early in 1970. I loved working with Rudi van Dantzig and with Rudolf, but I just could not work with the music. It sounded to me as if glasses were being thrown against a mirror and I couldn't bear it all the time, it made me very nervous. So I had to explain to Rudi van Dantzig that it was nothing to do with the ballet or him, but I just couldn't take it. In fact I got in such a state that I went away, to Madeira.

'However, when I was there, Anthony phoned from London to say that Merle was off and would I do *Giselle* with him. Which was kind of him, but I said, "No, as I haven't yet done *Giselle* with the company, I must have proper time to prepare it. It's wonderful of you to ask me, but I'm going to wait till I'm given my own performance, with time to get it right." So I did get my own performance—*not* with time enough to get it right because it happened in New York where you never have time enough because you're on every night—and I did it in fact with Donald, and Albrecht was one of his best roles. I had worked with him a lot before this, always happily because he was a thoughtful and natural partner—only he and Somes had that totally natural gift.

179

And, incidentally, Donald has been such a help and so encouraging since my return.

'So my first *Giselle* ever with Anthony was back at the Opera House for Peter Wright's new version a year later, and it was a huge success. They'd never seen me do *Giselle* in London, it was with Anthony, and the production was so successful. It was one of those nights with flowers everywhere and the house lights up for our calls.

'Jerry came to see it, and the next day he came round with congratulations and he said, "Don't cut your hair in the holidays." And I said, "Why?" and he said, "I'm going to put on *Afternoon of a Faun* and I don't want you to cut your hair. In fact I want you to grow it even more." Absolute bliss! I went off on holiday in August with that knowledge, and I was staying with Nora [Kaye] and Herbie [Ross] in Los Angeles—it was the between-my-marriages time. I said to Nora, "How did Tanny LeClercq do it?" and I came back with all these preconceived ideas, but Jerry said, "No, no. I want you to do it your way."

'Right up to the last rehearsal, I never knew what was going to happen in that moment at the end, whether Anthony was going to kiss me on the cheek or where he was going to kiss me or whether he was just going to touch me. Jerry told him to do something different every time, so it really was a complete surprise. So whatever he did I reacted to, whether it was on the hand or here or whatever, but then I think we kept to one thing in performance. We adored doing *Faun*. It's slightly enigmatic, very much us.

'I rang Jerry not so long ago because I have nothing to do at a gala if I'm on my own. I don't do *The Dying Swan*. Lynn has her Isadora, Merle has in fact *her* Isadora, Anthony has a solo Fred created for him, but I have nothing. If I haven't got Anthony or somebody, I can't do anything. For Dolin's gala, Nadia [Nerina] didn't want any *pas de deux*, she wanted solos, and I said, "I don't have a solo." The only solo that I adore—and I have performed here—is the one from *Dances* that Violette [Verdy] did originally and Monica did with us [Etude, Op. 25, No. 4]. So I rang Jerry and I said, "I know you don't let any of *Dances at a Gathering* go out of context, but it's for Dolin and I would really love to do it," and he said yes. In the end I couldn't actually do the gala after all.

There were so many principals injured in our company at that time that I had extra *Raymonda*s and extra *Scènes de Ballet*s to do and I got so exhausted that I caught flu. But I was pleased that he was going to let me do it. I find him a very special person.

'Also, talking about *Dances at a Gathering*, I have a great affinity for the earth. One of the books I've always liked best is *The Good Earth* by Pearl Buck, and I've always felt close to nature because of being brought up in the country and always having a cottage there. I seem to get renewed by going to the country; if ever I'm ill or tired, I immediately escape to the grass, the green. In the same way that I have to have a life outside the theatre, feeling part of the earth is what keeps me sane, and that's why I think that particular ballet meant such a lot to me. It was all about that: we weren't dancers *per se* . . . well, we were dancers, but natural dancers.

'I get completely neurotic if I'm stuck with the ballet all the time. I never went to performances when I wasn't on, which I should have, should have watched other people, but if ever I spend my time at a theatre it's at the opera. I liked to be part of the outside world, which is why I chose to be in a flat with people outside the ballet world. It appealed to me greatly—it was getting an out. From the moment I started dancing seriously, Sheila was my friend outside, the thing that kept me sane—nothing to do with the ballet, didn't know about it, didn't give a damn about it. Always I've had to have this other side of my life.

'Anthony and I hardly ever mention ballet when we're together—we really don't, even when we're sitting there in a rehearsal. He's similar to me in this way and we've always had that in common. Whereas with Rudolf one talks about ballet, about the theatre . . . But I'm not like Rudolf. I can't dance every night, I can't have it part of all my life. It's wonderful for me to have the two children and my husband and my friends, and to have nothing to do with the ballet until I just walk in there. That's why Panton was the ideal thing and the only thing for me when we met. I had to get out of the ballet world.

'Although I was with such interesting people between my marriages, eventually I got tired of the search and the trying and the effort and everything involved. At the same time a good friend of mine found herself in the same situation; she was also between marriages. We decided that each one of us would give a dinner party so we could be introduced to each other's friends, so we'd at least meet some new faces. This was January 1973; I know exactly when it was.

'The story is different when Panton tells it, but my story goes like this. Karen Armitage had this dinner party, and it was on and off whether I'd go anyway because I'd had this terrible stomach complaint and I couldn't eat a thing. But because she had gone to such trouble for me, I went, ill as I was, and I had to take this awful consommé and rice with me. She invited two friends she thought I would like. One couldn't turn up—he was stuck in Brazil—so I was told that Panton was taking his place.

'Panton has a completely different version of all this; none of it tallies. But anyway, he sat beside me and I honestly didn't get a chance to speak to the other man at all. You know, you talk to your right and you talk to your left—well, none of that happened because Panton completely took me over and he didn't allow it to happen. And then he got on the subject of art and he said that he hated anything after the eighteenth century. Of course I disagreed vehemently because the Impressionists are my favourite period. He was saying all these provocative things; he kept dismissing anything after the eighteenth century as if it had never happened, and I got very cross. When your emotions are stirred at least you find conversations and feeling running deeper than with the normal, polite, dinner-party chitchat.

'Then he invited me to the opera, which is my favourite thing as you know. But by that time I had to go into the London Clinic because my tummy condition had worsened. So I got in touch with Panton and told him that I wouldn't be able to come to the opera, and that was it.

'My main form of treatment in the clinic was complete rest. Nobody was allowed to visit me. They might have rung me—maybe Sheila did, or Iris [Law], who's been such a good friend all my life—but I wasn't supposed to use the phone much. The whole point was absolute rest.

'I was lying in my bed, ill, and suddenly Panton walked in one Saturday night, laden with flowers. Well, for a start I looked ghastly because my face was covered with spots and I had no makeup on—that was my first thought. As I wasn't expecting him there—I'd only met him once—I wasn't all dollied up or anything. I said, "How did you get in?" and he said, "Oh, I bought some flowers for the sister and I chatted everyone up." He probably said he was my father or my brother, goodness knows what he said. But anyway there he sat on my bed, and all I could think was "God, I look so dreadful." He was so determined; I mean, it had *Do Not Disturb* on the door, on the phone, on the switchboard, everything. So I thought that showed a lot of cheek, which of course he has, a lot of cheek, a lot of spunk.

'And it developed, obviously, from there on. Joy came into my life with the arrival of Panton, utter joy. Joy and humour. He has this amazing sense of humour which I just can't resist in a man. It's a turn of phrase, a way of illustrating a point, it just keels me over—Anthony has it too. It's wonderful for my temperament; I'm a worrier by nature and it's such a refreshing way of facing life.

'He'd always loved the ballet, but he was one of those people who went like every Tuesday. He didn't go for any artist; he saw whatever was on on Tuesday, opera or ballet. He certainly knew who I was . . . but he did completely bring me down to earth one day. I heard him booking tickets in the stalls, and I said, "You really can't see the ballet from the stalls. You've got to be a bit higher; you don't see the patterns at that level." He said, "Oh no, that's the best place, because you can't see the legs so well from anywhere else." I said, "The legs??" And he said, "Well, that's why everyone goes to the ballet." I was absolutely nonplussed. This had been art, art, art all my life, and here we were like the Folies Bergères. It was such a comedown. He obviously said this tongue-in-cheek, but there was a grain of truth to it. He loves beautiful legs, and you suddenly see how lots of men must look at the ballet, not as high art but as beautiful bodies. I'd never thought of it like that!

'You can't say why, but you just do hit it off with somebody. It's something that's in your blood and in their blood, and the vibes; everything just fits in and it just feels right. I don't think either of our divorces had come through when we met, but we were both separated. I'd always wanted to marry again, but I enjoyed my roaming around until it became tiresome. I didn't feel I had to make an effort with Panton. And he did admire me tremendously and respect me as a person, and accept me for being slightly mad, and that was lovely. And he's very proud of me.

"73 was actually my wonderful year, but it was a very hard year. I was dancing with Rudolf all the time and then I had this stomach complaint, but I very soon got better. We discovered it was just absolute exhaustion, it wasn't anything serious, and it just needed rest. Soon after that we went off to Brazil for that very successful tour, with Anthony and me doing all those big opening nights and then that horrendous Brasilia *Bayadère* business. And Panton rang all the time and wrote all the time—we were in constant communication. Then back straight to the Coliseum where we were on every night and I had such hard programmes. When I think of it now I don't know how I did it; I had three ballets a night, like *The Dream* and then two others. And then straight into the autumn which again was hectic. We had started *Manon*, I opened with *Swan Lake* here at the Opera House, then the next morning we went to Brussels for the Common Market gala.

'We continued *Manon* after Brussels, and then it was straight off to the *Giselle*s and the *Cinderella*s in Australia, straight back, and only after all *that* did I start to crumble. I'd been doing all this since the beginning of the season, plus having to do the weight-lifting for the knee. It was an enormous amount of work, so no wonder the knee collapsed under the strain when the rest of *Manon* was being done. In the end I couldn't cope any more and went off to Monte Carlo.

'I was back in March, for *Manon*. Then we went off to New York, with *Manon*, and then to Washington; I know we were at Watergate. Did I tell you about the caviar? The ambassador from Iran, Mr Zahedi, a great friend of Panton's, had come to the first night of *Manon*, not knowing anything about Panton and me, and he had sent all these roses and all this caviar. I was sharing a room with Monica, and Anthony and Monica and I were all in the room—none of us having been on that night—lapping up this whacking huge amount of Beluga caviar. We had never seen so many sturgeon roes. And apparently when we had finished and were sitting back licking our lips, I said, "Shall we order the rest of our meal from room service now?" I suppose I thought of caviar as a starter, although we'd had really enough for a week. They looked at me in total astonishment as I ordered a steak and roast potato and apple tart and ice cream. And ate it too!

'So that was Watergate—oh, and there was a fire in the hotel that same night. Then we came back and then we went off to Plymouth . . . no, then I got married and we put *Manon* on. I know that after my marriage, the next morning we had a stage call of *Manon*. That's literally how it happened. We looked for a day to get married and we didn't really have any time, because Panton was going to Iran all the time for business and I had been in New York and now I was due to go off to Plymouth. We found there was only one time we could do it—that was 11 July—and I think we had three days to let our friends know, and there was some sort of postal strike so we couldn't even get the letters posted. We went round London one Sunday night literally putting the notes in everybody's box.

'Panton rang his father because he thought he better tell him about this impending marriage before he read about it. His father was on his way up to Scotland and first of all he said, "Who is it?" and Panton said, "It's Panton." And he said, "Panton who?"—I mean, Panton's such an unusual name, there must only be one in England. Panton said, "You know, Panton, your son. I thought I'd let you know I'm getting married in three days time." "Oh, to that opera singer, I suppose,"—he *had* seen me dance, the father. So Panton went, "Something like that. She actually is a ballerina. I thought I'd just let you know." "Oh, I'll deal with that when I get home," his father said. So Panton said, "I think I'll have it in hand myself by then."

'So we had a wonderful wedding. We were married in Caxton Hall with all the close friends, Sheebee and Anthony. We then went home to receive two hundred friends who came and went during the afternoon, people from the ballet world like [Lord] Drogheda and Sir Fred and all the dancers, and important people and Panton's friends from the business world. Then we went out with our close friends for a meal, and the next day at the crack of dawn I was at dress rehearsal for *Manon*.

185

'Of course one changes. One goes through so many stages in one's life that what's right for one at one time isn't right for another time. It was absolutely right when I was with Michael, but I always needed escape routes out of the ballet life, always. It stops me feeling blinkered. Panton's quite a different personality from mine, and he was such a stabilizing influence for me, a total anchorage. With him I *almost* felt whole—this was the nearest I'd been to whole. When I really became whole was when I had my children. I then had total fulfilment. I then felt complete, a complete person.'

Six

'I'm sure if everyone knew how physically cruel dancing really is, nobody would watch—only those people who enjoy bullfights.' *Margot Fonteyn*

'The first time I ever knew I had a bad knee was when I was first preparing to do Bluebird, so that must have been '57 or '58. I was downstairs in the tiny little room which used to be a rehearsal room, off the canteen at Covent Garden, going through the Bluebird with Babs Phillips. I finished my variation, and I finish on my right knee, and I couldn't get up. It didn't hurt—I just couldn't get up. And I was petrified in that if something happens without pain, then of course you never know when it's going to happen again. If you've got pain, at least you know something's wrong.

'That's what always happened to me thereafter. There wasn't any pain: it would give way on me. I couldn't be 100 per cent sure of that left leg. After the South Africa tour was the time it really let me down because I had to say no, I couldn't do the next tour. At least with the Bluebird it recovered in time to dance the actual performance, but after South Africa and from then on it got worse and worse, and each time it took longer to recover.

'Up to my first operation I was trying all sorts of treatment on that knee. Resting it: that didn't work. Having injections: that didn't work, or maybe one injection would so I'd think, "Ah, this is the thing for the future," and have lots more. I tried everything because this was the time that I was being given my chances, and the wretched knee was letting me down all the time and making me very nervous because I never knew when it would hold me up and when it wouldn't.

'Anyway, it got so bad that I simply couldn't straighten it properly. The company went abroad, to Berlin and the Eastern Bloc. It was a lovely tour, but I couldn't go. That's when I had my first knee operation, it was '66. I had the operation here and they didn't know, when I went in for it, whether it was the cartilage or what. Mr Aston, who was the surgeon, found that there was a hernia of the joint lining, i.e. the joint lining was split and a bit of fat had come through.'

Sheila Bloom mimes the grim diagnosis with her hands: 'He explained that there's a sheath, like a muscle sheath, that crosses the cartilage, and the sheath had split, worn from the wear and tear. What was actually happening was that when the leg was bent, this split would open and the flesh underneath would push through. Then when she'd straighten the leg, it would close again and grip the flesh, and then gradually the flesh would pull away from the grip. And then she'd do the same again. So he said there would have to be an operation but the cartilage wouldn't be touched, only the sheath would be sewn, and that was the operation she had.'

Sibley doesn't linger over the graphic details: 'So that was that, but I'm sure that the cartilage was already going. Because when it did eventually come out, it was in ribbons, it was shredded and it had lumps on it. And as Dr Tomasson pointed out, that is cumulative; it doesn't happen overnight. It must have taken at least fifteen or twenty years to get like that. So I am sure that if Aston had gone further down and looked at my cartilage, he would have found already that it was in bad shape. Not that you can go back on life, but I've often wondered, if he had looked at that point and taken the cartilage out then, when I was that much younger and pain-free in the knee, would my career have gone faster? Where would it have taken me? How do you ever know?

'I know I took the operation frightfully badly. Because they hadn't known whether it was cartilage or not, because I'd been under this nervous strain with the glandular fever and because I couldn't go on the tour, I was generally in a very low state when I entered that hospital. At that point a cartilage operation on a ballerina was a bad thing, and I didn't know until I came out of the anaesthetic whether it was cartilage or it wasn't. The anaesthetic didn't agree with me either. Nowadays I only have a certain kind, I'm allergic to the normal one, but we didn't know that then. It poisoned my system and I was frightfully ill, and I did have a kind of breakdown. Michael came flying back from the tour to see me, and I was in a really bad mental state, mental almost worse than physical. I couldn't cope any more.

'Although I knew it wasn't cartilage and I should have been all full of hope and energy, I collapsed. This knee had been a long drawn-out thing, really bad from '60, so imagine, six years at that time in your life, when all the work is being offered to you and you can't manage it. And having had the glandular fever in the meantime and still not having got over it properly . . . Bobby Helpmann always said that he didn't get over his for ten years, and he was right. Because what would happen, really for ten years, in decreasing doses, was if I did anything too much I'd be completely knocked out and I'd have to take the next day off. As a dancer you always have to push yourself through that pain barrier anyway; when you're exhausted you have to do that much more than your body's telling you to do. You're used to this, because it's the only way you build up the stamina. But this is the trouble with glandular fever: you can't push yourself. When you're feeling tired you can't do that little bit extra because the next day you'd be in bed all day, unable to lift a brush. So I was fighting this and never knowing if the knee was going to hold me up, so it really was very bad.

'But at that time I had no alternative. I was married to somebody in the dancing world—my world was dancing, 100 per cent. I had nothing else. I'd done everything for the ballet, and right now everything was coming my way. It was always the frustration of what my mind wanted to do and my body couldn't, the frustration of always having to say no, always being let down. I got glandular fever, I got every cold that ever came near me because I was always so low. And later, all the times Rudolf asked me to go places, Vienna, Monte Carlo, I always had the flu or my knee had given up again, something had always happened. I never could fulfil what my mind wanted me to do.'

'She'd have an injury,' Sheila Bloom sighs, 'and she'd do this silly thing of covering. If she was down for a role and the public had booked to see her do a role, and then suddenly she gets the knee, it's a case of "Do I care for the knee and not do the performance and tell the company"—which was always a very bad thing, the company never looked very kindly on it—"or do I struggle through?" There was always this terrible dilemma because she had an immense loyalty, not only to the company but also to the public. She felt responsible to them and it clouded her decisions. And then at the end what she did was fake it: if it was the knee giving way, she'd do it in a different way so the pressure wouldn't be on that knee. But if you do that your balance is wrong and her balance was often wrong, and then she'd create another injury trying to compensate.

'But I don't think she ever consciously thought of giving up. She never said it to me. One time I think she was close to saying it, she was coming out of an injury and she was just about to go on in *Beauty* and she was dreading it. And Rudolf came over to her in the wings and said, "Do you realize what a privilege it is to be able to go out and be doing what you're doing?" He hadn't known she was uptight; he was just talking. And he said, "My God, every time I go on I realize what a privilege it is for me." He *loves* ballet, and Antoinette said to me, "He absolutely inspired me. It was the best thing that could possibly have been said to me at that time. And I went on and felt, 'Yes, it is, and I must do the best I can.' "

'She's been very unfortunate throughout her career,' Svetlana Beriosova murmurs gently, 'and so brave with it. Every time she was knocked down she'd struggle back in, she'd start again, almost stubbornly I would say. She would *not* say die; she wouldn't throw in that towel, ever. And also, you see, the self-confidence goes. You get a battering psychologically when something like that happens. You think, "Oh, will I ever dance again?" You have nightmares thinking "I won't." And you know who your friends are in times like that. It's good to be able to pick up the telephone and say, "Life is just playing merry hell with me," and be able to talk. But I think she did most of it herself.'

'One lucky thing with me,' Sibley admits, '—one has good things and bad things—is that I love life so much in general. Of course if I'm bed-bound I just read or listen to music, but I don't mind lying in bed. I love lying in bed! The frustration would have been missing the performances—it really would have killed me if I couldn't have made that *Romeo and Juliet* after my glandular fever. But I was always able to amuse myself; I had lots of friends, lots of things always to do.

'And my confidence doesn't go from not dancing. The confidence only goes with the physical: "Am I going to be able to do it again? Is it going to let me down again, or is it in fact going to be mended when I do start?" All the time you were off, you never knew if the injury was healed till you tried it. That's the worry. I didn't lose confidence in myself to dance because I have very strong muscles—there are two different kinds. Lynn's muscles, for instance, are very, very soft and pliable, so for her to rely on them she had to be using them all the time. On the contrary, my muscles are rather firm so I had to be careful not to overwork them, and I was always overworking them because I had such a lot of work and it was hard classical work. If I'd had soft muscles it would have taken me ages to get back after an injury, so this was the lucky side for me.

'But I can't remember much about that knee thing because I've had so many ordeals to face, health-wise and injury-wise, that the only way I could deal with it was to put it out of my mind completely the minute I was back. If I'd dwelled on the fact that yet again I was off, I think I would have sunken under. I had always to push this sort of thing aside and forget about it the minute I was all right and on again. It was the only way I could keep going, not to let it accumulate.

'Well, the knee got progressively worse. For years I had to give up the *fouettés* in *Swan Lake* because they were on the left leg and therefore impossible. I never knelt in any way, shape or form in any ballet on that leg. I used to begin the Act II *pas de deux* in *Lac* facing the other way so I could kneel on my right leg. I did my *Fille mal gardée*s to the right instead of the left, I didn't jump off that leg, I had to change everything. And the right leg was wonderful, thank goodness. That's why *Sleeping Beauty* was not the problem of a *Swan Lake*: it's a right – leg ballet. And all the ballets I've created are right leg ballets, *The Dream*, *Manon* . . .

'It gradually got so that it was more often bad than not bad. In class I never went on half-pointe, through the foot, on my left leg, ever. I watched people in amazement who were able just to hold onto the barre and *relevé*. I never did it on that leg, I couldn't do it. I used, at some point, to work only on pointe because I could get on pointe.'

'I used to work with her about twenty minutes every day,' Ailne Phillips recalls, 'very slowly—this was before they discovered that she had this cartilage trouble—trying to get the muscles working round the knee. Personally I thought perhaps she'd overdone it a little bit and it was just the strain and the knee needed a little coaxing to come back. I remember taking her very very carefully, and she said, "I can't feel anything. It's no good." And I said, "Antoinette, you've got to have patience and stick it out for a little bit. You can't tell, just by ten minutes a day, what's going to happen." She found that rather difficult.'

Winifred Edwards met Sibley's impatience with her customary common sense: 'I would say to her, "Stop telling me what you can't do—I can see that perfectly well for myself. Try thinking about the things you can do." There's an old Russian proverb I would tell her: Do you like to toboggan? You must like to carry the sleigh up the hill.'

'Injuries are funny,' remarks Ninette de Valois. 'They can be the psychological effect of other things. I think the worst thing that happened to Antoinette was that very bad attack she had with glandular fever, which went on for over a year. After that you do get injuries; the body is lowered in every way.

'You can't do much except encourage them. You can't. You've just got to see what the doctors say, what they feel themselves. Some of them react better than others, and of course reaction is psychological too. I often think, when I talk to them when they're ill, it's not the illness that's worrying them. It's the background—what's happening in the company, who's coming on—which is understandable. I think she suffered from that a bit too.'

As Sibley picks up the story again, her voice rises in anticipation. 'Up to the operation in '76, I never could rely on that leg at all. And then when I got pregnant, the relief, the release, of not having to dance on this knee and worry about my health, not to be wrapped in a cotton wool ball any more, was fantastic. Just to be a normal human being, not to be precious about myself . . . I was getting so precious about my bloody self. I had to be—it wasn't intended. Because everything was wrong all the time, I had to be ultra-careful. And then to have somebody else, a baby, who needed 125 per cent of my time, energy, thoughts, feelings, to be able to push all that onto somebody else, after all these years, was the most wonderful thing.

'And the funny thing . . . The day I actually stopped dancing, Margot said in class, "Oh, Antoinette, I've got all these practice clothes. I'm not going to need them. I'm not going to go on much longer. Take them." I almost knew that that was my last class as my pregnancy was going to be confirmed a couple of hours later, and all I could think of was the baby. At that moment I couldn't think of ever dancing again, and here she was offering me all her own practice clothes. And of course she danced for many years after this.

'Michael had never wanted a family—that was very definite. And I only once did, when I was on a beach in Italy with him and this adorable baby rushed up. For the first time ever in my life I felt broody, and then never again did it enter my head. Babies can drive you absolutely spare; they're time-consuming, they chatter . . . Except for that one incident, which was a romantic ideal of a baby, I hated them. I didn't have time for the baby business.'

Anthony Dowell laughs, remembering Sibley's life-long attitude: 'There were two people in the company who I thought were least likely *ever* to become mothers, and Antoinette was one of them. We both agreed: "Ugh. Kids." She'd say, "Talk about baby-bashing. I'd probably kill it." And *suddenly* it was like an absolute metamorphosis. Total. Total! And they are her life. It's the first time that she's ever had someone who *totally* needs and trusts her.'

'She never wanted children,' Sheila Bloom agrees. 'She used to say, "I can't imagine anything worse." And I think in the back of her mind too was the idea that it would interrupt her career. But I think later on she was starting to think about her future and to think, "Well, one day I'll have to give up," and she met Panton . . . and the most wonderful thing that ever happened to Antoinette Sibley was Panton Corbett. Now she's gone full circle and nothing in the world is greater for her than the children. She's besotted with them, completely.'

Sibley is adamant that 'only the once did I want children,

on that beach in Italy, and then the idea was gone as quickly as it had come. But the more I was with Panton, the more I did think I would like children. He certainly didn't want them; he'd already got a son, Oliver, by his previous marriage and loved the boy. We thought, "In the future." I thought I'd make my life neat; I'd go on a bit longer, then I'd give up before I was forty and have children. Well, of course life isn't neat.'

In 1977, when Eloise was two years old, the *Sunday Telegraph* quoted her mother as saying, 'Thank goodness I didn't have my baby until I reached this position in the ballet, because I don't know how much I could have loved her if I felt she was stopping me getting to the top. I needed that position . . . I wanted to prove myself.' Today Sibley says, 'I stopped performing before Eloise, in '75, because I wasn't going to do one more step from the moment I knew I was pregnant. I said to my doctor, "Is there a risk in dancing?" and he said, "Of course there's a risk, doing any kind of movement like that. Slight, I'm sure." But I knew I wasn't prepared to take any risk. Having never wanted a child in my life, believe me, now I had a child in my tummy and there was no way I would lose that baby. This is the important thing—I'd never put another ballet shoe on, I'd never do a *plié*, a *battement tendu*. Most ballerinas go on. Merle went on until a couple of weeks before the baby, and Natasha [Makarova], and they put their pointe shoes on in the hospital the minute the baby was born. Nothing could have been further from my mind. I used to sit around literally watching the clouds go by and watching the leaves on the tree changing through the seasons. I didn't do anything except let my mind wander, and this amazing thing happening to me completely took me over, and I was doing nothing.

'*I* was doing nothing. It was sheer wonderment from the moment I was pregnant. To be given this joy and not have to work at it? I'd worked so hard all my life; everything I'd ever done had always involved work and dedication and trying hard, thinking about it. This?? For the first time I had a rest in my whole life. And also for the first time, not having to dance, I didn't have the worry of the knee all the time. It didn't have to keep letting me down because I wasn't doing anything to it. So I felt, "Gosh, this is lucky. It's going to have a chance to rest while I'm pregnant." I mean, anything heals in ten days and I was giving it nine months.

'And when she was born, well, I couldn't get over her, I mean, absolute amazement. She looked like an advertisement for the perfect baby. She was plump, with little dimples, and rounded, and she slept and she ate . . . she did all the things she was supposed to do. A perfect baby!

'She was simply wonderful, literally the best thing that's ever happened to me in my life. I am possessed by babies since then, and I love that they're totally dependant on me. I had thirteen nannies in a year, I must have been impossible, because I really wanted that baby all to myself. And the last thing I wanted in the world was to do a *plié*. All I could think of was feeding, changing nappies, bathing and generally caring for the baby. I just didn't feel like dancing, it was completely the opposite, and I was as happy as a cow is in the field munching grass. I've never known such contentment as with my first baby.

'Now I would have thought all this would have been good for the knee. But the great shock for me, after all this wonderment and total fulfilment, was that on working back the knee was worse than ever. All the red flashing signs went up: Danger, Danger, Danger. It didn't hold me up at all. Of course it didn't—the knee was obviously so bad, deep down, that the only reason I'd been able to go on at all was that I had such strong muscles. And now, I hadn't done a step for a year, eleven months. The rest of my body was in wonderful nick, rested, it loved it, but the knee was the worst it's ever been. So then I knew something was very badly wrong, because nothing takes eleven months to heal. I was weight-lifting inside out, I went to all the exercise people, darling Michael Somes came and helped me do knee exercises, I was doing everything and I couldn't believe my knee was just completely impossible.'

Sibley turned to Beriosova for personal encouragement and professional assistance. 'She needed everything,' says Beriosova matter-of-factly. 'At that point she had to work at home and she needed a tape. So we got a pianist and went up to her home, and I set a barre and she taped it. I only worked with her for a few days, I don't think for long, because very soon she went back into open class at the Royal Ballet school. But of course, she did it all herself. It was up to her fundamentally. I think she may have asked me because she knew that I loved her very much, and that breeds confidence in you, to know that you're loved. It makes you reach out and you don't have to be afraid.'

'I didn't know what to do,' says Sibley, frowning with vexation. 'I went again to all the top doctors and they all said it was psychological, that I didn't want to dance. And of course in a way they were right, because with the knee like that I *didn't* want to dance. On the other hand I *did* want to dance. But not with this knee! I wanted it better and it wasn't any better, and if the top specialists in London knew that something was wrong they couldn't tell me what it was. So it obviously couldn't be anything serious in that they would *know* if it was serious.

'So I was in a really frightful position. I was signed up for my *Romeo and Juliet*s and my *Thaïs*es, I'd given myself five or six months to get back—a long time, but I'd been off virtually for a year—and then I'd signed on for *The Turning Point*. I had so much coming up and now I had such happiness, such security, a feeling I'd never had in my life of contentment and being able to give everything I'd got to something else. And I wanted to express all this and yet I couldn't, because of the same flaming knee. The same thing again: held back at gunpoint when I was ready to give it everything. I was well, I was healthy, I was strong, I'd had proper rest for the first time in my life, and now I was ready to go.

'But you see, I also had all sorts of tearing aparts. Leaving my child every single morning nearly killed me. I thought, "My God, I've got this baby, this sheer joy. What am I doing leaving her to go to this class? I've achieved so much. What am I doing?" But I had to go to class because I'd already organized all this work. I had the film, it was all lined up, and I couldn't *not* do class if that's what I was going to do. Now if I'd been able to whoosh ahead and dance, maybe I'd have been able to reason away the nagging feeling of leaving my child. But the fact was that whenever I went in to dance I damn well couldn't do what I wanted to do. It was awful.

'In the end I was really desperate and I could get no help from the doctors. I wanted to make the season, I wanted to make the film, I had Mischa asking me to go to New York,

Los Angeles and Chicago with ABT and dance with him after the film was completed. And I thought I would maybe play my life like that, do a bit here and a bit there and take my child with me and Panton could travel too. I was trying to organize it so I wouldn't just be slogging away all the time as I had been. And I was getting old, and this, that and the other. But I couldn't do any of this; I couldn't do anything properly with this knee. So I was truly demented.

'After a while I decided I must fly over to consult Dr Tomasson in Denmark, to see if he could throw any light on this enigmatic knee. He was my last chance. I had seen him before; in fact, he had made the correct diagnosis on the hernia—I had gone to consult him then too—and since then he had dealt with other injuries. I consider him a genius in his field.

'He had retired already, but nevertheless he saw me. He examined me for about an hour and then he said, "It's quite simple. You can't see any of this on X-rays,"—everyone had taken X-rays and you couldn't see a thing—"but the cartilage is in terrible shape. It's got about four or five bumps on it and it's frayed. I would give you three months before it snaps on you."

'I came back alone, and I'll always remember . . . I came upstairs here to find my nanny had given in her notice. I had no experience—this was the only nanny who'd ever looked after my baby. Read the envelope, got into the bath, nanny's notice beside me, waiting for my husband to come in. And when he came in the door I didn't know which to tell him first, the bad news or the *bad* news. So I told him about the nanny and then I told him about the knee. And he said, "Now, listen. This man is over seventy. He has to have made a mistake somewhere in his life—even geniuses do. He's made a mistake. If six specialists in England tell you nothing's wrong, and he tells you the worst thing that could possibly be wrong with the knee *is* wrong, he has to be wrong." And I agreed with him; that seemed to me rational. I thought, "How could Tomasson be right, that it's so bad he's given me only three months? It's too bad an injury for one of these specialists not to have noticed if that's the case." If he had said, "Well, maybe it's another hernia like you had before," or, "Maybe something's roughed up, wear and tear," or, "It's

become inflamed. It needs to have the water taken out . . . "
Anything! So I thought, "Panton's right. It does seem reason-
able that Tomasson's wrong."

'So that was the choice I made and that's how I played it.
And Tomasson was absolutely right except for two weeks. It
snapped just two weeks short of the time he'd said. I'd have
finished the film if I'd had the full three months before it
snapped.

'I got through the *Romeo and Juliet*s at the Opera House,
but when I started to try and do *Giselle* for that film, I couldn't
even walk. And the ironic thing was that I was able to go on
at that point, but Mischa couldn't. His knee was so bad that
we had to stop filming for a week, and I went over to his flat
to share his ultra-sound machine. But when Panton came over
for a weekend in New York before I was due to start the
Giselle, I couldn't walk along the road. When you actually
physically can't walk, it's pretty hard to know how the hell
you're going to dance something like *Giselle*, particularly when
you've been off for nearly a year. When I look at that film I
don't know how I did it.

'It seemed clear to me that it was just a matter of how long
the knee would last. So in my mind I thought, "Well, that's
it. I'll do the film, then I give up. I'm not going to take this
any longer." I'd got my daughter, I'd got my husband, I was
very happy not dancing. There's no joy in dancing like this,
none at all. In fact, not only none at all, it's frustrating, it's
upsetting, it's everything bad in life.

'I did the *Giselle* in absolute agony and I then went out to
L.A. I was by myself except for that nine-month-old baby
and a nanny. My little Eloise was the only one with me
throughout these ordeals on the film. The cameras were
rolling one day for the class sequence, we were balancing in
attitude, I had just let go of the barre, and the whole thing
snapped on me. It was like—I'll never forget—it was just like
a ladder going up a stocking. And I just crumpled. I thought
I'd torn my calf; I didn't even think of my knee, because it
went from here at the ankle right the way up the back of my
calf. I took a week off. I wouldn't go to any specialists there
because sometimes they tend to dramatize and I was hoping
that every day I'd be better, but of course it was swollen out
to here. And I had yet the *Romeo and Juliet* to do and the

198

Sleeping Beauty, the Aurora *pas de deux* and solos and coda and all of that. After a week they couldn't hold up the shooting any more: they'd done all the bits they could do without me, and it was too late to take me out and put somebody else in because I had a role and I'd already done all the speaking parts. So I decided to just try and go ahead—the only person who would come off badly was me.

'The first thing I did was the *Romeo and Juliet*, and I never know to this day how I did it because I couldn't possibly run and the first thing you do at the start of the balcony scene is that run in. I can't watch it because even now, when I think about it, I can remember my shoulders going up, my neck tensing, and the most extraordinary pain searing right through my body.

'So we did that and then came the Aurora *pas de deux*, and by then Panton had come out because I knew this was really, really bad news and I was desperate. And it was simply awful; we had the knee tightly bandaged to hold it in, but every time we stopped the shooting it would swell up and we had to just keep pumping the water out throughout the whole *pas de deux*. I couldn't do the solo, there was no way at all I could do the *relevés*, we had to cut that. And it's unfortunate because I think that and the *Giselle* first-act solo were always my very best solos in any classical ballet. But anyway, it was agreed that I would just do the *pas de deux*, but then I found the fish dives completely impossible. Mischa didn't know what to do, he tried every way to help, but I couldn't push off that leg to get on the other. The pain by now was absolutely unreal. I don't know yet how we did it. I haven't seen it, I won't look, I *can't* look, the whole thing was an absolute nightmare and I completely wrote it off.

'I came back home, and I decided never to dance again. I could not go through the agony and torture I'd been through all these nineteen years, and particularly the last years since the baby, wanting to forge ahead and always being stopped. In my mind, the dancing was completely finished—I had my baby, my husband and that was it.

'I was willing to stay exactly as I was, I didn't even want to have the cartilage removed—no more pain!—but Panton persuaded me to have the operation. And then of course, typical, the moment that I'd had the operation my knee was amazing. I didn't get the fluid all up on the knee like most people do. I was up walking on the crutches very early on. I was bending the knee like I'd never been able to bend it before. Mr Strachan did the most wonderful operation on it, in '76. It was a frightfully painful operation, they say the most painful other than having a child, but it healed beautifully and easily. The healing process was so very quick in my case and I was able to do things that I hadn't been able to do for so many years that I felt, "This is wonderful. Maybe I could dance again." '

Sheila Bloom shakes her head in amazement: 'I personally didn't think she'd come back after she did *Turning Point*. She had the cartilage torn in so many places, it was an almost impossible thing to come back. Besides which she had the child, and one thought that was the end of it. But she does have this way of fooling you. Just when you think she can't do it, she's better than she ever was.'

Sibley draws a deep breath and plunges on. 'So I start going back to the classes again and doing the weight-lifting, and it all goes pretty well, but not well enough. I can do more than I'd been able to do for a long time, but it still lets me down very badly on anything coming through the foot—that I can't control. By now it must be two years since I've done a classical ballet, like *Sleeping Beauty* or *Swan Lake*, it's a long time. I worked for a hell of a long time trying to come back, and the one thing I was trying to get back for was *The Dream*. Sir Fred said I could do it and that's what I was aiming for, as my first performance back. It was something for me to really look forward to—it was one of my most favourite things and it would be with Anthony. But I couldn't do those hops on pointe, I couldn't. The knee wouldn't hold me up.

'So I decided, after lots of agony and thought, that it's best to call it a day here and now. Although the knee was better than it had been when I came back after the child, and in fact better than it had been for ages, Mr Tomasson said it was still loose in the joint. And it wasn't good enough, in my mind, to get back to what I thought I had been, to do the classics well and my *Scènes de Ballet* and *The Dream*, obviously. So I made a decision that that was the end of that chapter. It had all been wonderful, and I'd done everything that I had ever wanted. There was only one unfulfilled ambition:

Anthony and I had been invited to dance as guest artists with the Kirov in Russia, but unfortunately the very evening I was discussing it with [Natalia] Dudinskaya, Makarova defected, so naturally that was the end of that. But that was the only thing. So that's when I retired and then I just got on with my life.'

'It's very hard to know when anyone wants to stop,' de Valois points out. 'I stopped as a result of infantile paralysis—nobody'd known that I had it as a child—but I was so full of all these other things I wanted to do and I was in so much pain when I danced, right through my body, all my life. I thought it was natural to have it. When they examined me finally, there were dead tissues down the whole of this left side, so the right side was taking all the strain. And then the back went, very nasty slipped discs. I had to stop, but I didn't mind because suddenly I couldn't get any further because of it. And the dancer who knows she can't do it will stop. They're quite sensible, you see.

'We left it to Antoinette to make her mind up. And when she had that last knee operation, definitely she'd made her mind up that it wasn't good enough, the knee wasn't right and she wasn't going on. And I don't think she was sorry to stop then.'

'What a wonderful life,' Sibley crows. 'I had my little daughter, my baby, who I'd more or less looked after single-handed, because all this time trying to get back I was only doing classes and exercises all day. Also, I know I started learning to drive the day after I retired, to get my mind onto something that was extremely difficult and, well, life and death to other people. I took my test that October.

'I was very happy. I did everything other than ballet. I went to all the races, I went to the Grand National, I saw Red Rum . . . Three times that horse came first in the Grand National and twice he came second—it's never been done before—and I saw the last time that he won, the fifth consecutive race that he'd come first or second. I've never known such excitement; the whole stadium stood up as he came rushing around and took over. He wasn't at all beautiful to look at in the paddock, he was a strange horse but amazing.

'I did all the things I had never had time to do. I went to Ascot and Wimbledon and Lords, I went down a mine, I went to the opera a lot, I travelled to Israel and countries I had never visited before. We were able to go to dinner parties and give them, and I could catch up on my friends, either for a private lunch or for tea parties with them and their children. I love life. I lapped it all up. I was able to get through some of the books and articles piled up beside my bed. And of course I was able to let the nanny go because now I could bring my little one up myself.

'I didn't miss it, not at all, except for certain bits of music that I couldn't hear played because they would upset me. I could not hear *Dances at a Gathering*, I couldn't hear *The Dream*. Other things I could listen to, funnily enough; bits from *The Sleeping Beauty* I listened to quite happily. I can't exactly say why.

'I saw a lot of Sir Fred because I was so fond of him and I wasn't going to lose touch with him or Anthony or Svetlana through stopping dancing, and indeed I didn't. My friendship with Anthony was in no way dimmed; we saw each other as much as we could, often ringing up or going out to lunch. Our friendship wasn't just the dancing—of course not, he's Eloise's godfather. He was in New York when I finally hung my shoes up and he wrote me the most marvellous letter from the Met, which was such a special place for us.'

'It was rather a cold shock,' Dowell confesses, 'because it was seeing it in the printed word. Someone just sent me a cutting from the *Telegraph*, and I read it in my dressing room at the Met while I was at ABT. Having spent so much of our working life together and exchanged so many of our private thoughts, it was very odd, strange, that such an important thing was to be seen in a newspaper. It hadn't really come up before I left. She had a lot of trouble with her knee, had her first child and then worked back. We did just one *Romeo* and a *Thaïs* together, and then the holidays came and off she went to make the movie, and then it got really bad again and then another operation. I didn't think that that would be the end in any way until I saw that cutting.'

The years between Sibley's operation and her official retirement, in May 1979, have all run together in her mind. 'I did the film in October '76, I had the operation in October '76 and I started to work back in January. It couldn't have been '79 I retired. Must have been '78. The performance I was trying to get back for was, I think, in April, so it would have been '77 or '78—yes, definitely '78. If it was '79 I retired, I must have just gone on working—I would only have been working towards *The Dream*. That had to be the first thing. What else could I get back in? After all this, it had to be something I was really at home in. But it must have been ever so slow. I can't imagine going in and doing class for two solid years without going round the twist. What could you do in class for all that time when you're used to performing? I don't understand this time lapse.'

The press didn't understand her unexplained absence either. In November 1978, the *Stage* remarked that 'the Royal Ballet has ceased to list Antoinette Sibley as one of its principals this season. Indeed, although listed last year, she gave not one single performance either. What an unceremonious disappearance from the ranks for such a *prima ballerina assoluta* on the international scene.'

Once she'd retired, Sibley quickly turned her attention from professional matters to more urgent, domestic ones. 'I was able to persuade my husband to have another child, and that was the biggest thing I've ever had to do in my life. He really didn't need another child; he already had his son by his first marriage and his daughter, the love of his life. But from the moment she was born I really couldn't think sanely about anything other than another child. Itching, I was. It isn't anything to do with being rational or anything that you can control. It's an animal instinct in one, and I was being completely taken over by it. Anyway my husband finally said yes, and my goodness, look what I have!

'Isambard was two months premature, but again being pregnant was so magical for me. I'm really happiest when I'm out to here, walking around leaning over backwards. Well, I never got to that stage with him because I only had one month with the baby even starting to show—I was flat till I was six months pregnant.

'Of course I was overjoyed about it all and felt so well, after the usual first three months of feeling sick, that I was moving bookshelves ... We have no absolute proof of why he was so early, but I would imagine that's probably it. I had the bookshelf in the middle of the room and I just couldn't get it over to the other side. Of course all the books were still in it! Then we went to Shropshire and we were climbing the Welsh hills, and I felt probably the healthiest and wellest and happiest that I've ever felt in my entire life, which is the oddness. It was past midnight when we went to bed and I remember saying to Panton, "I've never felt so well." And two hours later I woke up with such a severe haemorrhage that *my* life could have been in danger, apart from the baby's.

'The ambulance came, and I remember lying there, holding my unborn baby in my tummy while the purple light flashed around and the siren blared out as we rushed through the little Shropshire lanes to the hospital. They told us then that if I could keep the baby back for twenty-four hours we had a fifty per cent chance of his survival. Of course we couldn't keep him back—after twelve hours the baby started coming. And I couldn't take any epidural or gas or anything, because his chances were so slight that I couldn't weigh against them any more. So I had all the pain. And although the baby's so small at that age and one would think it would be much easier, they don't have the muscle to help you. My muscles weren't ready at that time because they're not developed two months early, and the baby isn't ready to help. So it was a nightmare . . . well, of course it was much more than a nightmare—it was really life and death.

'In the end I couldn't take the agony any longer; I didn't know how many more hours I would be in labour and they couldn't tell me. I couldn't cope with it, which meant I would *have* to have an epidural, which meant it would be even worse for the baby. I told Panton that he would have to make that decision because it was either me or the baby at this point, and he naturally said, "It must be you."

'And then the baby was born, and to all our amazement not only was he healthy and well but he was 5½ pounds. They had an incubator ready for him and everything was on alert, but they never used it. He was very strong; there was no flesh on him at all, thin like you see the poor, undernourished children in Africa, but he had an ear-splitting yell on him. Now he's wiry and thin, such a charmer, and everybody's always loved him to death. He was born in July of 1980—he was supposed to be born in September.

'Sir Fred was very cross with me when I retired, and whenever I saw him he *always* started up this same conversation of how I should be dancing. He never stopped at Panton and me to stop having these children and for Christ's sake get back onto the stage. I said the reason was I couldn't make the classics any more because this knee just wasn't strong enough, and he said, "Then just come back and do my ballets." Of course I didn't feel I could at that time, but it's more or less what I'm doing now except for a few *Bayadère*s and *Raymonda*s, and latterly *Manon*.'

'Well, my goodness,' Ashton exclaims, 'I thought it was such an absurd waste. She said, "The doctor said if I go on I can only work for two years." And I said, "Well, work for the two years and *then* see. Don't withdraw, as you're doing." I used to go on at Panton too; I used to say, "Get her on the stage." Maybe she had had enough, but she was a loss and I was determined to make her come back, and I did.'

Looking down at her hands, Sibley says, 'Johnny Gilpin also wrote to me continuously to start again. I was very much intertwined with his life, both personally and professionally, right up to his death. I'd known of John Gilpin since I was about five years old, because when I first went to the Arts Educational School I was sitting there with one of the Cones when this little boy went past. They pointed him out and they said, "He's going to be a film star one day." I think he was starting in films then—he was older than me. He then married my best friend from my early school days, Sally Judd, and I danced *Les Sylphides* with him and also *The Sleeping Beauty*. And he helped me such a lot, with Dolin, on Dolin's staging of the *Pas de Quatre*, that I danced in Hamburg recently. I was supposed to do Taglioni and I found I couldn't manage it, so I asked if I could do Grisi which I thought was much more me, the arm-y one. I was with them a lot rehearsing and they'd come to lunch afterwards. This was just a month or two before Johnny died.

'So he wove in and out through my life from a very early age, and I was talking with him at the ballet the night he had his fatal heart attack. And in all his bouts in and out of hospital he would always write and send a poem or something that he had found to get through difficult situations, and continued to say that I must start to dance again. And yet I treated him badly with it. He went on and on, and I'd closed that chapter. Whereas with Fred I might joke about it, with Johnny I wouldn't. I was upset that he kept on at me.'

Understandably, Sibley speaks of her retirement as if it lasted five years, from her last Opera House performances and the filming of *The Turning Point* in 1976 until her return to Covent Garden in the Royal Ballet's fiftieth anniversary celebrations in 1981. 'Well, it does seem that way,' she protests, 'because in fact the last time I danced properly—classical dancing, dancing as a ballerina—was in February '75 before I was first pregnant.' While she certainly wasn't performing for most of that time, only eighteen months passed between the official announcement of her retirement and her next stage appearance, in November 1980, at a gala in aid of the Friends of One-Parent Families which Anthony Dowell had organized.

'Before I was even pregnant with Isambard, Anthony had asked me if I would appear at this gala, which is the start of all the getting back. He asked me to go out for lunch at Tante Claire, and I never drink at lunch, and I certainly don't drink wine because I don't like wine. But I *did* drink wine, which I'm sure is the reason I said Yes, I'd appear at his gala. But I said, "As I can't dance, I'll have to read poetry," and he said, "Fine, then we'll do something with poetry." So that's how we left it. Then I found out I was pregnant and I rang him to tell him, and the first thing he said was, "What about my gala?" *not*, "Congratulations." I said as the baby was due in September I would have had the baby, but I'd still be quite plump from the feeding so I'd read the poetry in a tent dress. So we giggled about that.

'And then the little man was born in July. I think I fed him for three months and then I went away with Panton; we hadn't had a holiday that year with all these dramas and worries, so he took me for a week to Morocco to recover. And while I was in Morocco I started doing a barre because I thought, "All these dancers are going to look so gorgeous and I'm going to look so funny, standing there reading my poetry, unable to walk gracefully on or off the stage."

'Then I came back to Barons Court—I had five weeks now 'til the gala—and Anthony came back from America and it was amazing what I could do. I've never enjoyed doing class, the body certainly hasn't, but in all honesty it really did love it at this point. And when my calves started getting a bit stiff I merely got up on pointe. I was supposed to be in Edwardian high-heeled shoes for *Soupirs*—I had booties made for the gala with all the little buttons up the side—but I was on the pointes after my five weeks of barres. It took us all by complete surprise. When I came to rehearse, Anthony said to Fred, "She's on pointe!" so he said, "How wonderful. We'll do it all on pointe." But we always kept the Edwardian shoes in case the balloon should burst. Of course while we were working on it, it seemed quite difficult, but I was aware that it would be difficult. But funnily enough, coming back to it now after doing all these other things, it actually *is* hard, quite tricky.

'I hadn't thought of *dancing* again. Fred and Anthony thought, they all thought, that Anthony and I must appear together, so maybe we'd do a poetry reading. Fred obviously thought, "She can move around a bit," so we'd do a walk here or a sit-down there. And then suddenly, when it became more and more clear that I could dance, it became, "Well, let's do a real *pas de deux*." But it was just for this occasion: it was for Anthony, my friend, my partner, and for Sir Fred. The funny thing is that when we came into the studio to do our first rehearsal, Fred looked up—he was sitting there smoking his cigarette—and he went, "Oh, it's just like thirty years ago." And Anthony and I, in a breath, the same breath, said, "*Twenty* years ago!"

'Isn't it extraordinary? All chance, total chance. This was the end of November and the company had a programme coming up sometime in the New Year, in '81, for the fiftieth anniversary season, and Helpmann was restaging *Hamlet* for the occasion. And they suggested, as I'd been there doing *Soupirs* on the pointe, surely I could do Ophelia on the half-pointe. So the company approached me and said, "It would be lovely for the fiftieth anniversary if you could just appear," and of course I was thrilled to do that. I'd done the role when Bobby last put it on—seventeen years before!—and it was on half-pointe, so it was an ideal thing for me.

'And then that went to New York, and Jane Hermann at the Met wanted me to do it because she thought the New York public would like me to be in New York. Having left America in such a sad, unfinished way, it was wonderful for me to go back at least like this. Again, no more thoughts or aspirations or anything—it was just lovely to end up doing the *Hamlet* and the fiftieth anniversary with the company.

'And then of course we got on to *The Dream*, and I certainly wouldn't be where I am now if it hadn't been for the *Dream pas de deux*. There was no way Anthony and I were about to do that *pas de deux* for the anniversary gala. Anthony had an injury and I certainly wasn't up to doing it—it's really difficult. But Michael, with Fred, thought it should be in the programme, even if we didn't do it, and they know we're both perfectionists and wouldn't want to go on under par. On the other hand, they thought the occasion was a bit different from a regular performance, that the audience would like to see the ghost of it because the gala was a remembrance of things past. So to see us both actually there on the stage, in the costumes, with the music, even if we were marking sections of it, they thought that would be just the thing. Well, Anthony and I weren't about to do that and we had decided between ourselves that we weren't going to do it.

'We only had three rehearsals, and when we first tried we couldn't do big sections of it. After the first rehearsal we thought, "Well, we've tried, we can't do it, that's it. There's no point at this stage to go on and do something that was so important to us"—and in everybody else's mind, the *Dream pas de deux* is associated with us— "it's a nonsense mucking it up." But Michael played the whole situation wonderfully. I give him 100 out of 100. It was only him, and him saying, "Fred would really be most upset," and, "Let's make changes. Fred wouldn't mind," that made it possible for us to perform. And because he also knew that we weren't about to do it if we didn't do it properly, he knew that somehow we'd *get* ourselves to do it, which we did. It was an extraordinary trust that could only come with him knowing us so well, and us knowing him so well that we allowed ourselves even to get into that position. That was the cleverness of Michael.

'If it hadn't been for that, there's no way I would now be doing anything at all. That was the bridge; when I realized I could do that *pas de deux* the doors then opened for me. Up till then I was merely doing one thing as an off-chance for Anthony and for working with Fred again, and the *Hamlet* literally for the anniversary season and the company. But *The*

Dream was something I'd never . . . That was dancing again, proper dancing, the hard stuff. By the time I got to the third performance and found I could do this hard *pas de deux*—which was the one thing I couldn't do when I was trying to come back—then the whole thing changed for me.

'So then Sir Fred naturally, and Michael, were saying, "Surely if you can do that, maybe there are some other things that you can do." That's when I thought, "Oh, how lovely, just an odd thing here or there," and that's how it really happened. By chance.'

Although she never came 'out of retirement' formally, Sibley has been listed as a Guest Artist of the Royal Ballet since May 1981. To date she has returned to the roles she created in *The Dream, Manon, Enigma Variations, Jazz Calendar*, and *Thaïs* and to the ballerina roles in *Scènes de Ballet, Cinderella, La Bayadère* and *Raymonda Act III*. Since that date she has also created roles in five new works, most notably Ashton's *Varii Capricii*, and made her debut in *A Month in the Country, Birthday Offering, Konservatoriet*, and in the Tango in *Façade*.

'Dolin's *Pas de Quatre* was a debut too, and I've danced as a guest in Spoleto, Palm Beach, Hamburg, Monte Carlo and on two or three galas in New York. And I've worked with Nureyev, Baryshnikov, Schaufuss, Bujones, and of course Anthony, and there's this television thing coming up . . . I've been quite busy.'

'Certainly it's wonderful to see her do *Dream* now,' Frederick Ashton declares. 'Artists develop—they should. They develop an intensity, an expressiveness, they develop as artists. She does *Birthday Offering* very nicely, she brings her personality to it. She was on and on and on about *Month in the Country* and she got her fans to come up and say to me, "We'd love to see Sibley in it." Oh, I'm utterly aware of all that carry-on. But I said to her, "I've got four people now, and there are only a limited number of performances when they come. I can't throw out somebody just to put you in. You'll have to take your place in line." What could I do?'

'Of course it was hard after all this time *not* dancing,' Sibley concedes, 'but on the other hand I didn't have the knee problem that I'd had for twenty years. The great worry was when *Cinderella* came up because how did I know, until I did it, that I could get through three acts? How did I know? It was five years since I'd done a three-act ballet. Rudolf took me through my solo, and both Michael and Donald helped and encouraged me in rehearsals.

'Peter Schaufuss's mother, Mona Vangsaa, was so encouraging on *Konservatoriet*, too. I took that on not knowing if I could do it at all—and I said that to Rudolf—because it is an absolute monster, so technical and so difficult. But it was with Rudolf and Merle and they were so helpful, and because it was so hard it pushed me forward a lot. I never would have attempted to do something like that if it hadn't been for the people I was doing it with and just to see if I could.'

Anthony Dowell seems to be thinking out loud when he says, 'What is so strange in life . . . I was, OK, not much, but a bit younger than her and not plagued so much from injuries all the time. I suppose if you're fit and you've never experienced anything, you can sympathize so far but then it stops, you just get on with what you're doing. It's totally selfish in a way, but all dancers are, because to get yourself on the stage you just think I, I, I.

'So I didn't realize how bad her knee was all those years. I knew there was trouble, but when she said, "I never could do this because of the knee," I was amazed. This is why I think her comeback has taken over. She came back just as a joke thing, because I asked her to, but slowly she's found she's working without this being as bad as when she was doing *Beauty* and *Lac*.'

'Antoinette is the last of her time,' de Valois proclaims. 'She and Merle Park are the last of their period. We all remember them at their absolute peak, which we carry on with them now in our minds. They may not be dancing as strongly—why should they?—as they were ten years ago, but the peak is there, once you've reached it. The peak is like breeding, good breeding. Once you've reached your peak, you've been at the height of your good breeding and even if you get weaker, you don't lose that.

'She's dancing beautifully at the moment, very, very well. She's a bit more mature, and of course now she dances what she knows she can dance, which is reassuring and helpful. She's not being put under the strain she was when she was younger, or any of the younger ones are under her, who have to do everything just as she had to fifteen or twenty years ago. I think she enjoys it thoroughly now.'

'She's lost that thing I was talking about,' Kenneth MacMillan says shyly, 'where she didn't know what her identity was. I feel she now knows who she is, and it's a very satisfying thing to see it happen to her. It was always very worrying to me that she had this crisis going on. I saw her do *Month in the Country* recently and I was astounded, because it was one of the most original interpretations I've seen of the role. She has enough confidence to do it.'

'I never know about that sort of thing,' Ashton shrugs, 'because I don't see that any artist is always confident. When I do a new ballet I'm not confident about it at all. You can't be. It would be rather dreadful if you were. And a dancer can be miserably unhappy and still be wonderful on stage, whether her life is a mess or not. It shouldn't matter. An artist should overcome all that. You don't drag your private miseries onto the stage for all the public to see: you get on and you do a performance, and you must enter into whatever character you're doing whatever you're feeling like. After all, a lot of suffering can help you as an artist. Suffering can increase your sensitivity just as much as happiness can.

'She's not dancing awfully differently. Perhaps there's a little loss of technique. You have to watch her a bit now and point out when things aren't right technically. She's inclined not to point her feet, or one foot, all the time, and you have to watch.

'I like her in all the things she's done. I love her in *Dream;* I think nobody is as good as she is in *Dream*. And she's glorious in Dorabella too, she does that beautifully. She has a very sophisticated air onstage and so, for instance, I never thought that she was right for *Fille*, to play a peasant girl, because she was too sophisticated in a way. Dorabella is a sophisticated character really; although she's young and simple, she wasn't at all a dear, sweet little girl.

'I think she was also very good in the *Beauty*, in a sense better in the *Beauty* than in *Lac* because in *Lac* . . . I don't know . . . I figure the ballerina needs a little more length. It needs another three or four inches for the kind of movement in it, but she was good in it as well. But then I've seen so many swan queens and everybody brings something to it.'

'I remember the actual dance quality in *Lac* and *Beauty* very clearly,' Dowell comments. 'Those ballets were very special. It's an incredible face, the way it carries on stage, tremendous glamour. It's just the structure of it—it reads. Every time I go out front now and watch, it just reads.

'After a long gap of not seeing her, suddenly now when you see her perform you realize what you've perhaps missed in other people's performances that's so unique in hers. You can not really put your finger on what it is. It's just that no one else has got that personality.'

'Antoinette has special qualities that are all her own,' Michael Somes agrees, 'but that doesn't make her unique. They are unique *to her* and no one can ever fulfil those things quite as she did.'

'I'll gradually have to come out of the hard things,' Sibley grants, with a rueful grin, 'but I'm still so amazed that I've done what I've done. And I think in a lot of respects I probably do things better than I did before. I don't mean technically, although some things funnily enough I do, and of course I don't have the same stamina. But maybe by and large, with the more rounded life, I've got more to give. I know I can't go on working as hard as I am at the moment. But before a performance I always go, "This is certainly the last time I do this," and that's the only way I can *ever* get on with the very hard ballets.

'It's absolutely true to say that everything is going well now, except that I compromise on every single level. I don't do all the dancing I either should or probably could and I don't go to all the places I'm asked—for instance, I was asked to dance in Japan and South Africa recently—because I never go away from the children longer than two weeks. And I suppose I'm not the most wonderful mother in that I'm not here 100 per cent. I mean, I'm dancing half the time, and I do get upset and cross when I get nervous for a performance. What I'm trying to say is that I probably do everything to a lesser extent than if I did only one thing. As the wife, I'm the same. All the things I could be doing with Panton, I suddenly say, "I can't go out. I'm exhausted." So I do everything sort of cut down or half-cock.

'One thing is certain though: I couldn't do the dancing now unless I had all these other things. Although I get furious with the children, I could bloody kill them half the time, but equally, they've made me. I used to feel a ballerina. As I walked along the road I could feel my muscles, I felt like a trained racehorse. I certainly don't feel like that now. I feel like a woman, and I feel I have a lot in common with the women I see around me in the streets and the shops. It's just what I needed. I couldn't dance without that now.

'I'm not all lovely and wonderful and delight. I have a terrible temper and I am grotesque more or less for two weeks up to a performance, to anybody—my children, my husband, Sheebee, Anthony—everybody catches it. But this is the way it affects me. It's the digging deep inside myself that hurts and the pressures I'm under to deliver the goods.

'I remember a long time ago Christopher Gable and people saying, "One has to have an image." I remember this question of images coming up very much when I was in Hollywood—I used to go over there on my holidays, during my 'interim' period—and thinking, "No, I don't think I have an image to work on. What sort of image should I make for myself?" I thought for instance about clothes. Should I dress like Margot—I love the way she looks—or Violetta—I love that way too? Each is a part of me, and I did think about all this. But after thinking, I never then put it into practice. I talked to Sheila and Anthony about it and decided, "No, I don't think I have an image, but neither do I have time to think any more about one or work it out. Maybe that's one of the things I'll do later."

'If I've got an image now, it came about not so much by thinking or working at it, but through the circumstances in my life. I've tried, for instance, to be organized, even-tempered, an "early bird catching the worm" type, with unsmudged mascara, but it's proved hopeless. I suppose it's taken all this time evolving to find my own water-level, and I'm content with how I am now and I have confidence in that. I've evolved as a personality, and I don't think of it as a ballerina, I think of it as me. I *am* a ballerina, but as me, as me and what I really love. Now I'm happy with how I am; I can dance and be the mother of my children, and now I feel fulfilled.

'And I don't know . . . the future . . .' Sibley lets her voice trail away and simply smiles. Months earlier she had said,

'The scene that really got me in *Dances at a Gathering* was when we were all standing around at the end. We've all returned to our roots again, having gone through our various relationships and the ups and downs of life. But we're all still there, that's the main thing. We're all still alive, we're all still on the earth, which is the important thing—the earth. And Rudolf just touched it—he did it absolutely magnificently—and all of us breathed this sigh: We're still here. We're living still. We've been through all of this, but we're here.'

Index

217